THE PRESBYTERIAN MISSION ENTERPRISE

The Presbyterian Mission Enterprise

FROM
HEATHEN
TO
PARTNER

MARK J. ENGLUND-KRIEGER

Foreword by Hunter Farrell

WIPF & STOCK · Eugene, Oregon

THE PRESBYTERIAN MISSION ENTERPRISE
From Heathen to Partner

Copyright © 2015 Mark J. Englund-Krieger. All rights reserved. Except for brief quotations in critical publications or reviews, no part of this book may be reproduced in any manner without prior written permission from the publisher. Write: Permissions. Wipf and Stock Publishers, 199 W. 8th Ave., Suite 3, Eugene, OR 97401.

Wipf and Stock
An Imprint of Wipf and Stock Publishers
199 W. 8th Ave., Suite 3
Eugene, OR 97401

www.wipfandstock.com

ISBN 13: 978-1-62564-859-4

Manufactured in the U.S.A. 01/23/2015

Dedicated with gratitude to
PRESBYTERIAN WORLD MISSION,
past, present, and future.

O Thou who wast, and art and art to come, I thank Thee that this Christian way whereon I walk is no untried or uncharted road, but a road beaten hard by the footsteps of saints, apostles, prophets, and martyrs. I thank thee for the finger-posts and danger-signals with which it is marked at every turning and which may be known to me through the study of the Bible, and all history, and of all the great literature of the world. Beyond all I give Thee devout and humble thanks for the great gift of Jesus Christ; the Pioneer of our faith. I praise Thee that Thou hast caused me to be born in an age and in a land which have known His name, and that I am not called upon to face any temptation or trial which He did not first endure. Forbid it, Holy Lord, that I should fail to profit by these great memories of the ages that are gone by; through Jesus Christ my Lord. Amen.

—John Baillie
"Fifth Day: Morning," *Diary of Private Prayer*

Contents

Foreword by Hunter Farrell | ix

Introduction | 1

CHAPTER 1
Francis Makemie | 9

CHAPTER 2
David Brainerd | 22

CHAPTER 3
Ashbel Green | 34

CHAPTER 4
Betsey Stockton | 53

CHAPTER 5
William Carey and Adoniram Judson | 60

CHAPTER 6
Walter Lowrie and John Lowrie | 78

CHAPTER 7
Robert Speer | 100

CHAPTER 8
Robert Speer versus William Hocking | 114

CHAPTER 9
Robert Speer and Pearl Buck | 124

CHAPTER 10
Robert Speer versus Gresham Machen | 129

CHAPTER 11
John Coventry Smith | 134

CHAPTER 12
Clifton Kirkpatrick and Donald McGavran | 153

CHAPTER 13
Hunter Farrell | 175

APPENDIX I
Presbyterians Do Mission in Partnership: 2003 General Assembly Policy Statement | 195

APPENDIX II
Communities of Mission Practice: New Strategic Direction for World Mission: General Assembly Mission Council, February 2010 | 201

Bibliography | 203
Index of Names | 209

Foreword

Rev. Dr. Hunter Farrell
Director of World Mission, Presbyterian Church (U.S.A.)

IN HIS ENCYCLOPEDIC *History of the Expansion of Christianity,* Kenneth Scott Latourette describes the global spread of the Christian movement as the ebb and flow of Christian faith, alternately extending itself to new regions and consolidating and even contracting in subsequent times like the movement of the ocean tide. The component parts of Latourette's analysis are historical "stages" and he examines the growth of the Christian movement in all its ecclesiastical and denominational forms chronologically from the Pentecost to 1914.

In *The Presbyterian Mission Enterprise: From Heathen to Partner*, Mark Englund-Krieger aims a more focused historical analysis on a particular stream of mission history: the part of the Body of Christ known as the Presbyterian Church (U.S.A.) and its predecessor bodies. He helpfully identifies an emblematic leader in ten historical periods to embody and illustrate a key feature of the ebb and flow—the growth and retreat— of Presbyterian mission in that era.

- Thus the pioneering missionary to Native Americans, David Brainerd, is remembered for his extraordinary self-sacrifice and, even though his efforts were not "successful" during his lifetime, his committed response to a sacred calling serves as a model for missional Christians of every age.

- Betsey Stockton— simultaneously the first single woman and the first African American woman to be sent from the United States as a missionary—embodied the profound love for the common people in the society she is called to serve that characterizes so many great Presbyterian missionaries.

- Mid-twentieth century denominational leader Robert Speer is lifted up for his contributions to the mission's growth through his commitment to a moderate approach (frustrating both his fundamentalist and liberal critics) and the more contemporary Clifton Kirkpatrick, in a period of widespread critique of global mission, is noted for his leadership in our church's commitment to engaging in mission in partnership with national Christians around the world.

The result of Englund-Krieger's careful research is a highly readable history of particularly Presbyterian understandings of how the church is called to engage in God's mission in every age. Each chapter identifies a quality of leadership and insight, develops it, and then confronts the modern reader with the question, "How then must we live?" Englund-Krieger's thesis is that the extraordinary mission legacy of the Presbyterian Church serves as an enduring inspiration and guide that can lead our church into the future.

It is noteworthy that Englund-Krieger begins his book by recounting a personal experience of the worldwide church as he enters the pulpit in a Malawian Presbyterian congregation. That experience, as he describes, was the product of a remarkable presbytery partnership between the Pittsburgh Presbytery and the Blantyre Synod of the Church of Central Africa, Presbyterian (CCAP of Malawi). In my humble opinion, that partnership has been one of the most fertile "communities of mission practice," drawing together three groups in a highly collaborative space of mission discernment and action: local Presbyterians from across Pittsburgh Presbytery, leaders and members of Malawi's Blantyre Synod, and Presbyterian Church (U.S.A.) mission workers in Malawi, with some help from Presbyterian World Mission staff. Hundreds of Pennsylvanians and Malawians have been blessed by that enduring partnership and it has transformed not just their understanding of mission, but their fundamental understanding what it means to follow Jesus Christ in our globalized world.

That deeply personal Malawian experience, framed in the context of a larger web of larger and older relationships clearly shaped both Englund-Krieger's open and collaborative understanding of mission and his high value of doing mission in partnership, which he comes to see as an extension of our church's nature as a connectional body:

Foreword

> Certainly, congregation-based mission partnerships are important. There will also be a crucial role for governing bodies...who seek to create opportunities for partnership and shared mission practices across the great barriers of culture and language ... and a revitalized, national agency of Presbyterian World Mission with a team of professional mission personnel... (Introduction, page 7)

For Englund-Krieger, our mission heritage guides our church's future because the Christian Church has always been about reaching out to others with the Good News of Jesus Christ, seeking to be partners. The careful reader of *The Presbyterian Mission Enterprise: From Heathen to Partner* will find many insights that will illuminate the path of the church—not only for Presbyterians but for all Christians—in rapidly changing and often confusing times. I would encourage local Presbyterian mission leaders—mission committee chairpersons, mission network members, presbytery mission advocates, and others— to read this insightful book for both the carefully crafted historical descriptions and their relevance to our churches today.

Introduction

THE MEMORY OF THE moment is powerful in my heart and mind still today. Can such vivid memories which often return, emerging fresh from the depths of our hearts, be a gift from God? It is for me. I was standing in the pulpit of the St. James Presbyterian Church in Blantyre, Malawi.[1] I had been asked to preach at their English-language service. I remember the pulpit being similar to pulpits we might see in any Presbyterian church in the United States. It is elegant carved wood, prominent and sacred. There are one or two steps up and in; it wraps around the preacher. A flat surface was waiting for my Bible. The pulpit is, like many Presbyterian churches, at the front corner of their chancel. The huge communion table of the same gorgeous, dark wood sits in the exact center of the chancel. I remember a comfortable day under a glimmering, blue, sunny African sky; sky with a softer yet more intense blue than our skies at home. From my vantage point in that pulpit, I remember pausing and deliberately looking out for a long moment before any words; the congregation fell silent. Directly in my sight line was the women's choir (we would say dance troupe) with their long, flowing, bright white robes and head scarves, seated tightly in the first pews in the main section of the sanctuary, several steps lower than the chancel. The pastor was seated very close to me in the pulpit chair. The two lines of elders along both sides of the chancel in wooden chairs, packed close, each in formal Sunday clothes, dark suits and white shirts, were all attentive and

---

1. My visit to Malawi was part of the mission partnership between the Presbytery of Pittsburgh and Blantyre Synod, Church of Central Africa Presbyterian in Malawi. This relationship is one of the oldest mission networks in the Presbyterian Church (U.S.A.). The Presbyterian Church in Malawi was actually planted by the Church of Scotland, not North American Presbyterians. Nonetheless, the PC(USA) has had a long and vital mission partnerships in Malawi. Currently the PC(USA) has a solid team of mission co-workers in Malawi. See presbyterianmission.org.

official. Standing in the pulpit, I spun slowly all the way around to catch eye contact with these elders. At my eye contact, bright African smiles erupted back at me from each. The pews in the main section, spreading straight ahead beyond the women's choir, were filled, packed full with worshippers including many, many children. The side sections of the large sanctuary, where all the pews are perpendicular to the main section, were also packed full, and some younger children sat in groups on the floor in the aisles. My eye caught and paused on a strange sight. The side sections of the sanctuary had rows of large, open windows—no glass, no cloth coverings—simply large openings in the high brick walls. These window openings were packed full of people, stuffed, squeezed, close together, looking over and around each other, sitting on the ledge. They were packed in from the outside, all straining, quietly and reverently, to be, at least spiritually, in that sanctuary. I preached. I was blessed. Of course, I could not know at that moment that I would, not many years later, leave the pastoral ministry to take up the mantle of presbytery leadership. I could not know at that moment how crucial the work of Presbyterian World Mission would become in my view of God's providence for our church. I could not know that worship service in Malawi would inspire the research and the writing of this book.

Through the grace of Jesus Christ can such moments be sources of deepest conviction, founts from which a sense of calling springs forth? So it was for me; many experiences before that moment and many, many experiences since then have confirmed one of my deepest convictions. The mission work of the Presbyterian Church is a remarkable and beautiful heritage, and a source which may guide us as a church into God's future. This is my thesis: As Presbyterians, we have received a legacy of world mission work for which we should be tremendously grateful. As Presbyterians, the legacy of our world mission work provides inspiration and motivation for our future.

The Presbyterian Church has been described by its connectional system. This system may be imagined as a series of concentric circles. This description underscores the close, mutual interrelationships between the various councils of the church from the session of the local congregation, the gathering of geographical groups of congregations into presbyteries, the formation of synods as geographical groups of presbyteries, and the General Assembly as the national council of the church. This way of being the church was introduced very early in American Presbyterian history. Francis Makemie (chapter 1) and six colleagues gathered in Philadelphia in

Introduction

1706, an event marked as the formation of the first presbytery in America. There was in these church-planting, frontier, missionary pastors a deep sense of the need to connect together with one another. Their initial desire and calling to be a connectional church which became the first presbytery grew up into what Professor Charles Briggs called a "magnificent system."[2] This calling to be connected is original and foundational. But for many today it is a lost calling. Certainly there are a host of reasons to criticize and correct our traditional connectional system and we have done so repeatedly. The connectional system became a corporate system and too much authority became concentrated. The true sharing of power and decision making has often been interrupted by baser instincts. Most damaging is the dominance recently of what Professor Louis Weeks has named "local church Presbyterians."[3] These are Presbyterians whose interest, knowledge and involvement in the church are confined to their local congregation without any passion or commitment for a larger connectional system. The Presbyterian Church cannot function that way. Thus we need to consider the story of Francis Makemie, his powerful missionary calling to plant churches and to connect them together.

There are people in our history who display with vivid clarity the powerful calling to live outside oneself. David Brainerd (chapter 2) is such an example for Presbyterians and many other Christians. There is this sacred calling to take the church beyond the confines of comfort and ease. There is this deep desire to share the gospel, plant the church, and reach out across stunning barriers of every sort in the name of Jesus Christ. There is the witness of people who have heard a calling and have immersed themselves so deeply in their calling that they lay down their lives. There is mission work that faces such obstacles and barriers that it seems fruitless and impossible but the effort itself, nonetheless, inspires awe. And there are missionaries who have, like David Brainerd, taken on such a calling. There are missionaries whose witness and example often seem to contradict common and powerful themes in the general culture, as Brainerd contradicted white culture's insidious hatred of native culture. David Brainerd was a missionary to the Native Americans in the eastern colonies decades before the American Revolution. He was not, in his day, successful and he ultimately died trying. But his witness has reverberated through the centuries. The story of David Brainerd is inspiring and it is also almost incomprehensible. How can a

---

2. See the full quote in chap. 1.
3. Weeks, *Sustainable Presbyterian Future*, chap. 1.

person have such a powerful sense of call to mission work? What do we learn from this about ourselves, about the church and, most of all, about the work of God?

The American Presbyterians rallied for mission work very early and with careful attention to organizational and administrative concerns. The gifts of organization and administration are also hallmarks of the Presbyterian way. The first meeting of the Presbyterian Board of Foreign Missions in 1837 took place in the midst of a bitter, national church fight, the story of which will be told here.[4] During that first meeting in Baltimore we can also imagine a bit of historical reminiscing took place. The momentous occasion must have inspired many to reflect on the history of their church and their missionary efforts. Thus at that first meeting of the Board of Foreign Missions a resolution was passed asking Ashbel Green (chapter 3), a ferocious patriarch of early Old School Presbyterian theology, to write a brief account of the history of Presbyterian mission work.[5] As an elder statesman in the Presbyterian Church at that time everyone knew that Ashbel Green could write this history from his own personal recollections. A year later, William S. Martien & Company, a popular Philadelphia publisher of Presbyterian authors, brought forth Green's *Historical Sketch or Compendious View of the Domestic and Foreign Missions in the Presbyterian Church of the United States of America*.

The first sentence of the introduction of Green's important historical record offers a truth that needs to be remembered in the church today. We seek now, in part, to rekindle the commitment which seemed so obvious early in our history. Green wrote,

> The propagation of the gospel in North America possessed, essentially, the character of a Missionary enterprise. Its propagators when they fled from persecution in the land of the their fathers, had it in view, not only to be able to worship God according to the dictates of their consciences, free from molestation, but to transmit the gospel in its purity to their descendants, and to other

---

4. The Office of World Mission of the PC(USA) celebrated its 175th anniversary at our General Assembly meeting in 2012. That anniversary is calculated using the first meeting of the Board of Foreign Missions in 1837 as the starting date. That date is an appropriate institutional anniversary. But, as will be discussed here, Presbyterian mission work in the United States is much older.

5. "The Board of Foreign Missions of the Presbyterian Church, at their meeting in Baltimore, in October 1837, passed the following resolution: '*Resolved*, That the Rev. Dr. Green be requested to draw up a history of the Foreign Missionary operations of the Presbyterian church in the United States.'" Green, *Historical Sketch*, 3.

Introduction

emigrants, in all succeeding generations; and they also hoped to impart its blessings to the Pagan tribes, who inhabited the wilderness in which they sought an abode.[6]

What is this missionary enterprise? Who carried it forward and how? How may we participate? And, as we will see was one of Ashbel Green's particular passions, what is the uniquely Presbyterian character of this missionary work? What shall this great enterprise look like in the future?

The story of English Baptist William Carey (chapter 5) is about the seed which grew up to become a movement inspiring churches on both sides of the Atlantic. Reaching back to Jesus' last words in the Gospel of Matthew, popularly considered now the Great Commission, Carey claimed and proclaimed a mandate to carry the gospel to all the world. As an early missionary to India he created a model for mission and preached the church into a powerful foreign mission enterprise. His work in India set a definitive pattern for how missionaries do their work. Presbyterians heard the call and rallied their organization for the effort. The whole Lowrie family was committed, including one son who was an early Protestant martyr in China. Walter Lowrie (chapter 6), an elder statesmen in the US Senate, brought his gifts and skills to Presbyterian foreign mission work. We may take a tour of the world and catch of glimpse of the far-flung places where Presbyterians served via the careful administrative oversight of the Lowries.

How can we measure the status and the influence of a church leader like Robert Speer (chapter 7), a Presbyterian ruling elder who served as secretary of the Board of Foreign Missions for forty-four years? He shepherded the Presbyterian foreign mission enterprise through a remarkable era of growth and expansion for his generation. He was also in the eye of the storm as this mission work was buffeted by criticism from different sides and from very different perspectives. Thus a large piece of Speer's legacy for us is the direction he carefully charted, holding a line directly within the great moderate middle of the church. He did not veer too much toward the Social Gospel end of the spectrum and the rewriting of mission work as only the upbuilding of society without an evangelical message. This was the direction strongly pushed by the Rockefeller-funded Hocking Report (chapter 8) which acquired high-profile support from the glamorous Pearl Buck (chapter 9). On the other side, Speer was able to maintain a middle course despite a withering attack from Gresham Machen (chapter 10) and the vision of a more pure, fundamentalist message as the crux of all mission

6. Ibid., 13.

work. In a denomination where still today the "self-reported theological perspective" of Presbyterians continues to be dominantly "moderate," can we find a way to remain true to Speer's middle course?[7] There has always been a strong moderate middle which has guided the church, preventing it from veering to either extreme. There is a remarkable tenacity in this steadiness. There is within the soul of the Presbyterian Church the biblical virtue of perseverance. This is the witness and example Robert Speer.

Robert Speer was also asking questions in his day about missionary leadership that must be considered today. The questions of mission work are, by definition, questions at the very core of the church's identity. Speer's questions may also be questions for our time and our lives:

> The questions which we are to consider are the questions of the foreign missionary enterprise, but they are also the central questions of the life of the Church at home. What are the secrets of leadership? What are the great aims and methods of the Church's undertaking? How can the Christian Church be made anywhere a living and enlarging power, drawing its nourishment from above and beneath, from God and the people, without weakening support from the side? What is the universal and essential kernel of the gospel, and what the racial and national husk? How much may a human life ask God to do through it and in its own time? These are not questions of a far-away work. They are the living issues of our own land and our own time and our own lives.[8]

The Presbyterian Church has shown a remarkable ability to reform and reorganize. As the world changed, and American culture shifted and quaked, the church responded. After the era of Robert Speer and the great missionary movement, after the destruction of World War II, missionary leaders like John Coventry Smith (chapter 11) enabled the church to make important revisions and reinventions. The day of mission work to the heathen was finished; in its place a bold, new vision of ecumenical relations and mission in partnership was born. A new pressing need to cooperate ecumenically with native, growing churches all around the world was required. The transformation in 1958 from a Board of Foreign Missions to a Commission on Ecumenical Mission and Relations (COEMAR) marks this change. John Coventry Smith was at the center of it. Maybe today we

---

7. See "Trends among Presbyterian Members in Self-Reported Theological Perspective," in Weeks, *Sustainable Presbyterian Future*, chap. 2, n3.

8. Speer, *Studies of Missionary Leadership*, 8.

are in the midst of a similar, traumatic, culture-changing era; how shall the church respond? What can we learn from the ways John Coventry Smith led our mission work through the changes in his era?

Since the 1960s massive demographic changes and cultural disestablishment have made Presbyterians fewer, our administrative structures smaller and our influence in society has waned. We have had debilitating debates around biblical authority and human sexuality. Presbyterians have been limping forward with downsizing and a low morale. Presbyterian leaders like Clifton Kirkpatrick (chapter 12) and Hunter Farrell (chapter 13) have stayed the course. Despite harsh criticism, Kirkpatrick has led us to be involved in a world mission work that must seek true ecumenical relationships through vital, global institutions like the World Council of Church and the new World Communion of Reformed Churches. Farrell understands the signs of the times; everyone wants to be directly involved in mission and the communication and transportation technology today makes that easy.[9] Thus partnership, collaboration and mutuality are the models; each congregation and presbytery has a role. But the revitalized, national Presbyterian World Mission is also crucial. All the constituents need to be in the circle of conversation now conceptualized as a Community of Mission Practice. Now we see patterns of a new growth and the enthusiasm of a new energy. The Presbyterian Church is poised to rally around a vision of world mission based on partnership and a new engagement with a remarkable global Christianity.

The future of the Presbyterian Church (U.S.A.), and all of American mainline Protestantism, will require a greater immersion in the powerful movements of global Christianity. These connections will span the globe gathering brothers and sisters from profoundly different cultures together in the church. When local congregations today see themselves as part of the remarkable movement of Christianity around the world the spark of spiritual vitality and energy will fill hearts and our churches. Certainly, congregation-based mission partnerships are important. There will also be a crucial role for governing bodies and church councils who seek to create opportunities for partnership and shared mission practices across the great barriers of culture and language. And a revitalized, national agency of Presbyterian World Mission with a team of professional mission personnel

---

9. Louis Weeks notes an important sign of the times: "Yet more Presbyterians than ever—perhaps as many as one hundred and fifty thousand of us—took mission trips this past year, many of them to foreign countries." Weeks, *Sustainable Presbyterian Future*, preface.

is evolving into a leading piece of the foreign mission enterprise. Strong connectional systems fostered by church structures, agencies and denominations doing mission across cultures will be vital. But, finally, the future of the church, as it always has been, is about people reaching out in the name of Jesus Christ to other people, seeking to be partners. Our story seeks to encourage those relationships, partnerships and denominational structures that will increasingly bring the church to a new day and new vitality. But we cannot move forward into a new day if we do not know from where we have come. Our heritage will guide our future.

Future directions for discussion, study and prayer:
- What is your experience of global Christianity?
- How has your perception or experience of global Christianity today influenced your understanding of the church?
- This book is organized around individuals in the history of Presbyterian foreign missions. Each chapter focuses on a particular person. In your mind, who is missing? What other influential mission leaders through the ages do you believe should be added to this study?

CHAPTER 1

Francis Makemie

To begin at the beginning we must ponder a small group of rugged, devout and irascible pastors who first gathered in Philadelphia in 1706. Their gathering is considered the first organized meeting of the Presbytery of Philadelphia, the first presbytery in the United States. The pastors were all immigrants from England, Scotland or Ireland. They all understood their task as, to use Ashbel Green's phrase, "a missionary enterprise." Their circumstance was dire. Green described it this way: "They were, with a single exception, almost wholly destitute of property; and the people to whom they ministered, being like themselves in poverty, and struggling for subsistence in a wilderness land, could contribute but a pittance to the support of their pastors."[1] The bold tenacity of these first Presbyterian leaders and their faithful congregations are both remarkable.

With strong ties to the theological, ecclesiastical and ethnic traditions of their native lands these Presbyterians, nonetheless, claimed a new freedom and planted a new church in this land which was uniquely Presbyterian. It was a new thing. Writing his history of Presbyterian mission work in 1837, Ashbel Green expressed a deep amazement and respect for the original American Presbyterian missionaries and asks a discussion question which should echo through the ages since: "It may be questioned whether any missionaries, in more recent time, have made greater exertions to carry the gospel to the destitute, or have endured more hardships in doing it, than were exhibited by these venerable and devoted men."[2]

1. Green, *Historical Sketch*, 14.
2. Ibid., 15.

The Presbyterian Mission Enterprise

In his classic history of the Presbyterians, Lefferts Loetscher praised Francis Makemie.

> With great energy Makemie supported himself by private enterprise and also preached the gospel. From the Carolinas to New York he fulfilled his ministry. Population was scattered, distances were great, horses were scarce, and roads were either nonexistent or hopelessly poor. The traveler was continually in danger from Indians or white robbers. In Maryland, settlements were usually along the rivers, and up these Makemie patiently made his way, bringing Christian exhortation and cheer to many a forgotten cabin. Perhaps as early as 1683 he organized Presbyterian churches at Rehoboth and Snow Hill, Maryland, and later several others nearby... The work for which Francis Makemie is most gratefully remembered was his leadership in organizing the first enduring American presbytery in 1706.[3]

Francis Makemie

Thus the ministry of Francis Makemie may be a moment in history on which we mark the start of Presbyterian mission work. Although a native of Ireland and with reputable Presbyterian instincts, Makemie's ministry was supported by a cooperative effort, expressed in a Plan of Union in 1691, between Congregationalists and Presbyterians in England. Their institutional cooperation in England inspired the London Fund which sponsored

3. Loetscher, *Brief History*, 61.

Makemie as a missionary to America.⁴ In a massive, two volume, early history of Presbyterianism, Ezra Gillett starts with a chapter on Makemie praising his tenacious personality: "Indefatigable in effort, clear-sighted, and sagacious in his views, liberal in sentiment, fearless in the discharge of duty, and shrinking from no burden, his name needs no eulogy beyond the simple record of what he accomplished and endured."⁵

Although the physical travel across the Atlantic Ocean, in the small sailing ships of the day, was arduous the theological convictions and controversies skipped across the sea with ease. The great theological divisions within Protestantism which were now an intimate and centuries old aspect of the history of the England, Scotland and Ireland were all imported to America. Nonetheless the new freedom and the open space in America inspired some attempts at cooperation and compromise. But the ethnic differences and the power of theological convictions became boundary lines and soon also, theological controversies in this new land. Henry Wood, in an early history of the Presbyterians, sees a constant wavering between, on one hand, "jealousies, alienations and strifes" and, on the other hand, "correspondence and union."⁶ Because of their close theological grounding it was the Presbyterians and the Congregationalists who created a sustained historical pattern of weaving together theological systems and thus consequent efforts at church cooperation which all were soon followed by their tearing apart again.

In the first century of the Presbyterian mission enterprise in America we will see a repeated refrain of both harmony with and antagonism between the Congregationalists and Presbyterians. As we know from the elementary folklore of American history, the Congregationalists, often named Puritans, were settled and influential in the New England states. "In 1701 Massachusetts had eighty-six ministers; and in 1713 Connecticut had forty-six churches which had been illumined by about ninety ministers. At that time, therefore, in the history of the American Church, the Congregationalists composed a much larger body than the Presbyterians."⁷ From the first days of the Presbyterian mission enterprise both Presbyterians and Congregationalists were included in the budding structure of Presbyterian

---

4. Wood, *History of the Presbyterian Controversy*, 26.
5. Gillett, *History of the Presbyterian Church*, 6.
6. Wood, *History of the Presbyterian Controversy*, 25.
7. Ibid., 27.

polity which was inspired by its English, Scottish and Irish forbearers but did not simply replicate those patterns.[8]

The first Presbyterian churches were started as haphazard gatherings of frontier folk with church instincts from their motherland who joined in worship under the care of whichever Presbyterian pastor was in the vicinity.[9] The first presbytery meeting included seven ministers representing both Presbyterians and Congregationalist churches, and several churches where that distinction was blurred.[10] Francis Makemie was there under the sponsorship of the London Fund, a group of British Presbyterians sponsoring missionary work in America. The London Fund also sponsored two missionaries to accompany Makemie—John Hampton, an Irishman, and George McNish, a Scotchman. These three missionaries joined Jedidiah Andrews, John Wilson, Nathaniel Taylor and Samuel Davies who were already at work in Pennsylvania and Delaware in the spring of 1706 when the first meeting of a Presbytery in America was called.[11] The Reverend Jedidiah Andrews was the first pastor of the first church of Philadelphia.[12] These seven ministers who gathered voluntarily as the first presbytery are themselves a metaphor for American Presbyterianism which has always been both encouraged and stressed by the mixing together of different flavors of Reformed heritage. In historical reflection on this first gathering, Charles Briggs concluded: "It was a happy union of British Presbyterianism in its several types. It was an interesting combination. Makemie, the Scotch-Irishman; Hampton, the Irishman, and McNish,

---

8. Briggs, *American Presbyterianism*, 129. Briggs concludes, "At the opening of the eighteenth century there was no strife between the Scotch and Irish Presbyterians and the Puritans of England and America, but only the most hearty sympathy and co-operation." Briggs also includes here the text of a "letter of thanks from the Provincial Synod of Glasgow to the Rev. Dr. Mather in New England, dated 1700."

9. Webster, *History of the Presbyterian Church*, 77. Webster describes the first gathering in Philadelphia: "A Presbyterian congregation was slowly formed during the last ten years of the century. It is highly probable that the visit of Francis Makemie to the city in 1692 led to the gathering of the Protestant dissenters for worship at the Barbadoes [sic] store. Jedediah Andrews, from Massachusetts, began to preach statedly [sic] to them in the autumn of 1698." Gillett also describes ministry under Andrews's leadership: "Under the influence and labors of Andrews the heterogeneous mass began to coalesce. In 1705, five adults were baptized; in 1706, four more." Gillett, *History of the Presbyterian Church*, 21.

10. Briggs, *American Presbyterianism*, 127.

11. Ibid., 140.

12. Wood, *History of the Presbyterian Controversy*, 26. Rev. Andrews was a "Congregational Presbyterian. That church was sixty four years without any ruling elders, though under the care of the Presbytery."

the Scotsman, sustained by funds provided by the Presbyterians in London; uniting with Puritan missionaries from new England in organic union in a classical presbytery. We have here in miniature the entire history of American Presbyterianism. It was a broad, generous, tolerant spirit which effected this union."[13]

Statue of Francis Makemie

The purpose of the first presbytery in America was focused and clear. These ministers were motivated to propagate their faith. The commitment to plant new congregations in this new land was their highest priority. Nonetheless, these were ministers who all cut their theological teeth in the great theological divisions and conflicts of Britain, Ireland and Scotland. This same culture of theological divisiveness was, of course, brought to America. Thus theological doctrine and the constant testing and evaluation of theological purity was an important and explicit purpose of the first

13. Briggs, *American Presbyterianism*, 140.

presbytery. Makemie and Andrews emerged as leaders.[14] Makemie's reflections, in a letter after the meeting, of the design of that early presbytery is an important historic record reprinted in Charles Briggs's history of this era:

> Our design is to meet yearly, and oftener if necessary, to consult the most proper measures for advancing religion and propagating Christianity in our various stations, and to maintain such a correspondence as may conduce to the improvement of our ministerial abilities, by prescribing texts to be preached on by two of our number at every meeting, which performance is subject to the censure of our brethren; our subject is Paul's epistle to the Hebrews. I and another began and performed our parts on Verses 1 and 2. The 3rd is presented to Mr. Andrews and another.[15]

The first American presbytery sustained a pattern of meeting annually for the purposes of strengthening the Presbyterian presence in this new land and "censuring" the pastors in their doctrinal convictions. These pastors were church planting missionaries and the new presbytery served as a launching pad for mission. The organization of the first presbytery was a brilliant institutional decision which immediately created a structure by which new pastors could be recruited, examined and sent out. Briggs called the first presbytery a "master stroke of wise policy."[16] The presbytery presented an institutional expression of American Presbyterianism which soon encouraged a more equal tone in the ongoing correspondence and cooperation with Presbyterian bodies in Scotland, Ireland, England and soon also Holland and France. This new American presbytery had a character and design from its British and Scottish forbearers. But it was an American invention. Loestcher noted that "an important feature of this first presbytery was that it was organized 'from the ground up,' not 'from the top down,' as was the Presbyterianism of Scotland which had been adopted by Parliament and implemented by the General Assembly. In America, on the contrary, the higher judicatories were created by the lower, establishing the more democratic nature of American Presbyterianism."[17]

---

14. Gillett, *History of the Presbyterian Church*, 24. "Andrews and Makemie were kindred spirits, and the Presbytery was a result of their cooperative councils. Each was a missionary and felt the burden of care for the Churches."

15. Briggs, *American Presbyterianism*, 142.

16. Ibid., 143.

17. Loetscher, *Brief History*, 61.

The existence of the American Presbytery, despite its small membership and meager resources, served as an important counterweight to the growth of an established Episcopal church in the American colonies. The fledging Episcopal clergy and congregations had all the clout, status and resources of their parent institution, the Church of England, and all the rights and privileges of establishment status under the Crown of England. There quickly developed a clear allegiance between the numerous Congregational churches in New England and the Presbyterian churches in Maryland, New Jersey and eastern Pennsylvania over against the Episcopalians, who were generally in the vicinity of the New York harbor. Quickly Francis Makemie was at the center of the battle between the American Presbytery, and all that it stood for, and an Episcopal vision of an American Bishopric. The lines were drawn between a presbytery and a bishopric. This definitive, theological battle was fought for a century on several fronts, originally in Makemie's fight with New York Episcopalians and later, after the Revolutionary War, in Thomas Jefferson's Virginia where the constitutional commitment to disestablished American Christianity was first codified. Makemie's story is a defining moment in the formation of the wall of separation between church and state. Before Thomas Jefferson and other founding founders conceptualized the disestablishment of the church, Makemie was forcing the practice of this American idea. Makemie's story is immersed in the cooperation of the Puritans and Presbyterians and bitter conflict with the Episcopalians, who were claiming establishment status as an extension of the Church of England.

The story of Puritan-become-Episcopalian pastor William Vesey sets the stage for Makemie's conflict with the crown. A conflict between the churches was centered in the colony of New York where the different denominations were each vying for space and influence. Governor Benjamin Fletcher, colonial governor of New York from 1692 to 1697 representing the royal family and the British government, began to push for the establishment rights of the Church of England despite a long Puritan presence. In 1695 the Puritan leaders in New York selected one of their own as pastor for the several, small, scattered Puritan congregations. Rev. William Vesey had been born in Braintree, Massachusetts, educated at Harvard College and theologically trained under the tutelage of Increase Mather. Thus his Puritan credentials were impeccable. His task was to strengthen and support the Puritan presence in the New York colony. Although this was not the first Puritan clergyman working in New York, this move threatened the leading Episcopalians in the colony. These men, led by a British redcoat Colonel Heathcote, petitioned Governor Fletcher for permission to build a church building in New York; the request that was granted and Trinity Church was soon under construction. Boldly, these Church of England leaders then recruited Puritan pastor Vesey, and held out a significant increase in his stipend, to serve their flock. This was a stunning and unprecedented switch in church allegiance from the dissenting theology of the Puritans to the establishment status of the Church of England. Moreover, they prevailed upon Vesey to return to London and seek ordination in the Church of England in order to serve as the rector of their New York Episcopalian congregation. In 1697 Vesey was ordained by the lord bishop of London and returned to the new world with the rights, privileges and status of a Church of England clergyman, taking up the office as the first Episcopal minister in New York. A letter from the Rev. Alexander Campbell, a staunch Scots Presbyterian in New York, reflects the depth of feeling around perceptions of Vesey's disloyalty: "He was a bigot for the New England Independency before he came over to the Church, and now a bigot for the Church against the Dissenters."[18]

Francis Makemie before Lord Cornbury

18. Briggs, *American Presbyterianism*, 145. Briggs considers that "the conformity of Vesey to the Church of England was the most unfortunate event that could have happened to Presbyterian Puritanism in New York State. It gave the Episcopal Church the primacy in the city, which by rights belonged to the Presbyterian Puritans."

This is the bitter political and ecclesiastical milieu in the colony of New York when Francis Makemie arrived in 1707. Leaving directly from the first meeting of the Presbytery of Philadelphia, Makemie and John Hampton were traveling to New England with the intention of recruiting new pastors from among the Congregationalists. Along their route both pastors sought opportunities to preach. Unfortunately for the energetic young preachers they found themselves in the colony of New York which now was under the British royal authority of Edward Hyde, 3rd Earl of Clarendon, a.k.a. Lord Cornbury. In American history, Lord Cornbury became the example of all that was wrong with the British aristocracy. Briggs repeats an early historical diatribe: "Lord Cornbury who joined the worst form of arrogance to intellectual imbecility."[19] Makemie had an invitation to preach in a Dutch Reformed church but Lord Cornbury immediately intervened to prevent this due to Makemie's lack of a license to preach. Not to be dissuaded, Makemie redirected his efforts and preached in the home of Presbyterian William Jackson. This service was not intended to be hidden or secret; the doors were opened wide to the public and the sermon, as was the custom with a visiting preacher, was printed and available publicly. Hampton received an opportunity to preach at a public meeting house on Long Island. Makemie expected to join Hampton there the next day for a second opportunity to preach in New York. But the long arm of Lord Cornbury arrived first and before the preachers could begin their services at the Long Island meeting house, the sheriff had them arrested under the authority of the governor. Hampton and Makemie were incarcerated in St. Anne's Fort in New York; their repeated appeals for due process were rebuffed by the governor.[20] The issue became a personal vendetta of Lord Cornbury

19. Ibid., 148. See also the *Wikipedia* article on Edward Hyde, 3rd Earl of Clarendon, whose reputation is described: "Cornbury came to be regarded in the historical literature as a moral profligate, sunk in corruption: possibly the worst governor Britain ever imposed on an American colony. The early accounts claim he took bribes and plundered the public treasury. Nineteenth century historian George Bancroft said that Cornbury illustrated the worst form of the English aristocracy's 'arrogance, joined to intellectual imbecility.' Later historians characterize him as a 'degenerate and pervert who is said to have spent half of his time dressed in women's clothes,' a 'fop and a wastrel.' He is said to have delivered a 'flowery panegyric on his wife's ears' after which he invited every gentleman present to feel precisely how shell-like they were; to have misappropriated £1500 meant for the defense of New York Harbor, and, scandalously, to have dressed in women's clothing and lurked 'behind trees to pounce, shrieking with laughter, on his victims.'"

20. Gillett, *History of the Presbyterian Church*, 13–18. Gillett gives a detailed account of the legal proceedings between Makemie and Lord Cornbury and a general description of the legal prejudice the Presbyterians faced throughout the colonies.

against anyone questioning his authority. After six weeks in prison, the captive Presbyterians were given legal access to the Quarter Sessions, the local expression of the British Courts. The prisoners were immediately granted a writ of *habeas corpus*, allowing their case to be heard by the court. Arguing his own case before the court, Makemie demonstrated a clear and precise understanding of the English laws then in effect concerning the toleration of religion in the colonies, and documented the abusive behavior of the governor. Although found *not guilty* and immediately released from prison, nonetheless Makemie was forced to pay a bill for costs while in prison of more than eighty British Pounds.

The Presbytery of Philadelphia grew quickly, supplied with a steady stream of new pastors. Makemie, Andrews and their colleagues were eager to provide pastors for the promising Presbyterian congregations who were now scattered throughout the eastern seaboard. Makemie's reputation and his tireless itinerant preaching put the Presbyterians on the map; the people responded, seeking the religious freedom which was, in part, the inspiration for their migration in the first place. The institutional status of being organized as a presbytery was an enormous boost in their appeals for support. The presbytery sent emissaries and requests far and wide seeking "good men." They wrote and visited New England, Scotland, Ireland, and the Congregational and Presbyterian Unions of London. Letters were sent to Sir Edmund Harrison, an eminent Dissenter in London, to the Presbytery of Dublin, to the Synod of Glasgow. Responses came fast. The allure and attraction of starting fresh in a new land attracted many newly ordained pastors from Scotland and Ireland and also motivated generous financial support. The more settled Congregational churches in New England considered the colonies of New York, New Jersey and Pennsylvania to be their mission field; they were eager to join with Presbyterians with whom, most of all, they shared a common antipathy of the Church of England. Having a common ecclesiastical adversary, who it seemed had all the resources and all the power, overshadowed nuances of doctrinal and polity differences. Deeper yet was the hunger and spiritual ambition of the missionary calling which has always been planted deep into the soul of the Reformed heritage. Thus already at the second meeting of the Presbytery of Philadelphia, in 1707, a candidate came forth for examination and ordination. From Scotland, John Boyd answered the call of this new presbytery while still a "probationer" for ministry; and immediately began service at

Freehold and Middletown in the colony of New Jersey.[21] By 1715 it was determined that, given the rapid growth, it was not feasible for a number of ministers and congregations to maintain a cordial relationship with a presbytery centered in Philadelphia. Thus plans were laid to establish a second presbytery encompassing the churches in the colony of New York and throughout Long Island.

With the influx of new pastors the first presbytery grew quickly motivated by a missionary passion to plant new churches. The growth and expansion continued and within ten years of the formation of the original presbytery there was sufficient energy, commitment and size to form the Synod of New York and Philadelphia, composed of four presbyteries: Philadelphia, New York, New Castle and Snow Hill.[22] The first meeting of the synod took place in Southampton, New York, on April 17, 1717. At this point these presbyteries were mere gatherings of pastors with a burning desire to plant churches and extend the gospel in its Presbyterian expression. Each pastor brought to this work the convictions and practices of their heritage, either Irish, Scottish or British Puritan. There was not a strong doctrinal foundation in earliest days of the synod. The Presbyterians and the Independents and Congregationalists from New England were cooperating and working together.[23] The four presbyteries which were now organized into the first synod were a new, uniquely American church polity. This was not a simple mimicking of the Presbyterian polity of either the Scottish or

---

21. Ibid., 28. Gillett notes these ministers as being received by the Presbytery of Philadelphia in 1708 Joseph Smith (New England); 1710 John Henry (Presbytery of Dublin), James Anderson, Nathaniel Wade, Joseph Morgan (Scotland); 1712 George Gillespie (Presbytery of Glasgow), Daniel McGill (London); 1713 Howell Powell, Malachi Jones, David Evans (Wales), Robert Witherspoon (Scotland); 1715 John Bradner (Scotland), Hugh Conn (Ireland), Robert Orr (Ireland).

22. Ibid., 35. "Here at the commencement of the existence of the Synod, were the nineteen ministers of whom it was composed, scattered at long distances along the coast from Virginia to the eastern part of Long Island. The demand for new laborers in the field was greater than ever before, and new congregations were in process of formation at various points."

23. Ibid., 31. "Thus, in ten years from the formation of the original Presbytery it had grown to a Synod. The period had been one marked also by general harmony, as well as rapid growth. The ministers of the body were from Ireland, Scotland, London, Wales, and New England, and laying aside all difference of minor importance, they had cheerfully and heartily co-operated on a basis broad enough to accommodate them all. As yet there were no doctrinal diversities. All were Calvinists, and all cheerfully assented to, if they did not prefer, the Presbyterian form of government. The labors in the field stood ready to welcome faithful-laborers from whatever quarter they might come."

Irish Presbyterian Churches, although those antecedents were clearly models and examples. The new American Presbyterian Church was closer to the ground, committed and responsive to the life of its congregations and eager to gather new groups of Presbyterian folks into new congregations. The purpose of the synod was a missionary cause; to plant new congregations, serve and support the existing congregations and recruit new pastors to keep up with the growth.[24] This practical, grassroots, missionary enterprise was focused on the congregations as the driving purpose and task, and this clearly overshadowed distinctions of doctrine and theological emphasis. In his history book, Professor Briggs nicely summarized the ethos of these earliest Presbyterians:

> The American Presbyterian Church began historically at the bottom, and only by degrees did it rise into the magnificent system which we now behold. It was not a reconstruction of the old Papal system into a new Presbyterian system, as in Scotland. It was a free and natural growth in accordance with the preferences of the congregations themselves. American Presbyterianism was born and nurtured and reached its maturity in freedom. It developed naturally in accordance with the circumstances of the country. It was not imposed upon the people by civil or ecclesiastical tribunals.[25]

The early era of theological harmony and missionary purpose is important to remember since it did not last long. The different flavors of doctrine and their ethnic foundations from the mother lands soon sparked dissension and controversy. Soon questions of doctrine and theological orthodoxy were part of the discussion at the synod. The story of the Adopting Act of 1729, the early debates over subscription to the Westminster Confession and, inevitably, the split between the New Light and Old Light Presbyterians are threads which became dominant themes and then conflicts in the telling of American Presbyterian history. The story here wants to reclaim a countervailing, earlier narrative. There was a time, at the very beginning of the Presbyterian story, when harmony and shared purpose defined the culture of the church. That shared purpose was a missionary purpose. By reclaiming a bit of this forgotten narrative we may claim a bit of this shared purpose again today.

24. Ibid., 41. "In the ten years that followed, membership in the Synod was largely increased. At the close of this period seven ministers had been received from New England, five from Scotland or Ireland, three from England and Wales, and several were licensed by the presbyteries in this country."

25. Briggs, *American Presbyterianism*, 131.

Future directions for discussion, study and prayer:

- Francis Makemie clearly had a strong calling as a missionary and church planter. He tirelessly traveled the eastern seaboard in colonial America preaching and planting churches. He also had a strong calling and motivation to organize the first presbytery. Compare and contrast the calling to be a church planter and pastor with the calling to connect congregations together into the first presbytery.

- Today we live in an era in which many Presbyterians live their discipleship without any involvement or passion for any expressions of the church outside their local congregation. Professor Louis Weeks contrasts these "local church Presbyterians" from "governing body Presbyterians." How would Francis Makemie respond to the modern phenomenon of "local church Presbyterians" who have no concern for larger connections?

- Consider your local congregation: In what ways does it express a committed connection to others Christians beyond your local congregation? Do you believe this is important to the members of your congregation? In what ways has this changed in recent years?

- For Francis Makemie and his colleagues the first presbytery was understood to be an essential part of the missionary enterprise of the church. Beyond the local congregation, what do you consider to be the essential purpose of the other councils—presbytery, synod and General Assembly—in the Presbyterian Church today?

- Consider you own personal, discipleship in Christ: Can you identify with Francis Makemie's calling to gather and organize the first presbytery? Do you share any of his concern to connect congregations together and work together? For Makemie this connectional system was part of the Presbyterian way, is this important to you today?

CHAPTER 2

David Brainerd

THE ORDINARY CONNOTATION OF mission work brings to mind an outreach to a different people in a different culture. The first mission work of Presbyterian leaders in the infant colonies of these United States was not cross-cultural in that sense. The first mission work, as discussed in chapter 1, was the hard work of planting and organizing new congregations among the immigrants who had moved and settled here who had an inclination for Presbyterian ways. Given the poverty of the people and the dearth of leadership, simply gathering together, organizing and sustaining congregations and soon the presbyteries and larger governing structure was a vital and truly successful expression of the Presbyterian mission enterprise in America. But the calling to reach out and communicate the gospel of Jesus Christ to people of foreign cultures has always inspired Presbyterians. The earliest Presbyterians settling into churches along the eastern seaboard of the United States only needed to lift their gaze a bit to seeing a teeming foreign culture all around them in the many native people who filled this land. The first foreign mission work of the Presbyterian Church was to the Native Americans.

While the first congregations, the presbyteries and the newly formed Synod of New York and Philadelphia were in their infancy a vision and commitment to reach out beyond themselves to the surrounding native communities was already being pondered. Resources and leadership were lacking and thus a plan was devised to request support from the mother church in Scotland. In 1729, Jonathan Dickinson, on behalf of the synod, sent a letter to the "Society in Scotland for Propagating Christian Knowledge." This charitable society had been instituted in Edinburgh through the bequests of several devout Presbyterians including predominantly the Rev. Daniel Williams of London.[1] Dickinson's letter sought to "inform them that there are two tribes of Aboriginal native Indians adjacent to their settlement whose Princes seem inclined to receive Christian instruction, and it is hoped will approve themselves forward to encourage a mission of the gospel among them."[2] The Society in Scotland responded favorably and agreed to provide funding for three missionaries to the Indian frontier. The new American Church was now inspired to embark on this effort in foreign mission work and sent a follow-up letter back to the Society in Scotland. The synod proposed to "find out a suitable man who will reside among the Indians frequently and catechize and teach them to read and preach among them, and also, shall be obliged to get the Indian tongue with all convenient dispatch that so they may in a little time be able to preach to them in their own language. That a place upon the border of Philadelphia upon the borders of the river Susquehanna seems to afford a large prospect of success."[3] Thus what may be considered the first professional missionaries—those called, supported and sent out by the church into a different culture for the purpose of sharing the gospel—were recruited and sent. John Sargent in 1741, Azariah Horton in 1742, and David Brainerd in 1743 were appointed as missionaries to the Indians. Moreover, the Synod of New York was not satisfied to simply accept the charity of the Church of Scotland but requested all the congregations in the New York and New Jersey to collect a special offering twice a year for the "propagation of the Gospel among the Indians." Professor Briggs considers this action of raising funds and sending missionaries to the Native Americans to be the "beginning of the Foreign Mission Work of American Presbyterians."[4]

In his classic history of Presbyterian mission work published in 1838, the influential theologian and church leader Ashbel Green reflected on the ministry of Azariah Horton among the Indians. This gives us a

---

1. On the Society in Scotland for Propagating Christian Knowledge, see Latourette, *Great Century*, 74. The Reverend Daniel Williams also established by bequest Dr. Williams's Library, which continues today as "the pre-eminent research library of English Protestant nonconformity," located in Gordon Square, London. View their website at www.dwlib.co.uk.

2. Quoted in Briggs, *American Presbyterianism*, 299.

3. Ibid., 301.

4. Ibid., 302.

close view of the Presbyterian understanding of mission in those early days. Azariah Horton's

> success, for a time, was highly encouraging. A general reformation of manners speedily appeared, and several gave satisfactory evidence of a saving conversion; a number were taught to read, and in two or three years, he had baptized forty-five adults, and forty-four children. The introduction of spirituous liquors, the bane of the Indians, had an unhappy influence, in arresting the progress of the Gospel among them. Yet it appears, that so late as 1788, the Indians in those places where Mr. Horton laboured were still religiously disposed, had two preachers among them, both Indians, who were well esteemed; and that a number of individuals were then in the full communion of the church.[5]

This description captures the full theology of mission that was undergirding the work of the church. There was a commitment to "manners" and reading, as well as a formal conversion to Christian faith accompanied by baptism. There was an objective to identify "preachers" from among the people themselves with the ultimate goal of being in "full communion" with the church. The mission work of the Presbyterians among the American Indians was successful to a degree but did not inspire any permanency. There were fruitful and cordial relationships established between several of our Presbyterian missionaries and the tribes. Several missionaries were able to fully immerse themselves into the culture of the Indians, and, given the crucial importance of such things, there were conversions and baptisms among the tribes. But the establishment of permanent Indian churches was not viable because the tribes were not settled. Thus the missionaries, in order to maintain relationship with these people, had to follow along as whole tribes regularly moved.[6]

---

5. Green, *Historical Sketch*, 38.

6. Prof. Briggs concluded: "The missions among the American Indians were successful, but the circumstances of the case prevented the attainment of permanent results. The work of the Brainerds, like that of the Eliots and the Mayhews before them, was a mighty work of God in the conversion and consecration of these poor Indians; but it could not result in the establishment of permanent Indians churches. The missionaries were obliged to follow the tribes as they retreated before the advances of civilization, and rescue as many as possible of the multitudes whom the vices and diseases which civilization brought to them were rapidly carrying away. The Christian Indians who survived the diseases of civilization became absorbed in the settled communities as servants in the households and upon the farms of their conquerors." Briggs, *American Presbyterianism*, 303. See also Longfield, *Presbyterians and American Culture*, location 701–46.

The Presbyterian missionary work among the Native Americans may have transformed some individual lives but was meager and insignificant when viewed in terms of the relationship between the Native American culture and the imported European culture. There were some beautiful, courageous and faithful individuals, whose stories we should remember, serving the church in outreach to the Indians; there were many faithful Presbyterians supporting this work; and there is a small legacy of Christian faithfulness among the American Indians to this day. But the church could never overcome the two massively destructive forces that decimated the native populations in the new United States. First was the sheer power of hate. After the French and Indian War and the destruction of any remnant of the French Empire in North America, the culture of the English-speaking Europeans was unalterably determined to expand west into the wilderness areas of North America.[7] There was no stopping the tidal sweep of Europeans westward. Moreover, the native people were caught up in the maelstrom of war imported to North America from Europe. The native populations, despite the ambiguity of different tribes with different allegiances and a convoluted diplomatic history with both English and French powers, were soon and forever stereotyped as the enemy.[8] Cultural mores and customs are never precise and universal but there is no doubt that as European people increasingly took control of North America their culture was imbued with a visceral Indian-hating conviction. In the face of such hate, the sad history of American Indians is the official sanctioning, through the era of the Civil War, of their physical removal by the US government which ultimately contributed to the almost complete annihilation of these native cultures.[9] Sadly, such hate was not the most destructive force.

The decimating power of imported diseases created unfathomable destruction among the Native Americans. This story is, in part, simple biology. For generation upon generation of human civilization the populations

---

7. Anderson, *War That Made America*, location 76. "In bringing to an end the French empire in North America, the French and Indian war undermined, and ultimately destroyed, the ability of native peoples to resist the expansion of Anglo-American settlement."

8. Ibid., location 191. "In fact, three, not two, powers competed in northeastern North America—French, British and the Iroquois Confederacy."

9. Ibid., location 76. "The widespread Indian-hating that the French and Indian War engendered would be reinforced by the war of Independence and contribute to the formation of American cultural identity, sanctioning the removal and annihilation of native peoples as necessary to the advance of civilization."

of North America and Europe never touched in any way.[10] There was no contact; these cultures were absolutely isolated from one another for many centuries. Biologically there was no exchange either in genome or in pathogens. Diseases and natural immune responses developed and evolved differently. But pathogens and diseases arrived in the new world with the first colonizers. The sharing of these happened at the very first contact between these different people. The result for the native populations of the importation of disease is calamitous beyond description. The Native Americans had no immune response to the European diseases—measles, chicken pox, smallpox, diphtheria, influenza and others—that were generations old in Europe and with which the people of Europe had grown up and, to a degree, grown tolerant. With the very first contact the diseases arrived among a biologically unresponsive and unprepared people and thus catapulted to epidemic proportions immediately. Historian Fred Anderson emphasizes the importance of biology in his history of this era. His summary of the statistics begins to capture the horror of this devastation: "The effects of the resulting 'virgin soil' epidemics beggar description. Ultimately they destroyed as much as 90 percent of the native population of North America. One estimate holds that an indigenous population east of the Mississippi numbering more than 2 million in 1600 shrank to less than a quarter-million by 1750 . . . As much as half the population of any given village or band died within days or weeks of an epidemic's appearance."[11]

The formal mission work from the Presbyterian Church to the Native Americans was insignificant from any kind of long term view. But this work had a very different impact and lasting influence which was unintended at

10. Ibid., location 227. "Contact with the strangers from beyond the seas had altered native life in almost unfathomable ways. For perhaps a hundred centuries before regular transatlantic contact began at the end of the fifteenth century, the human populations of the New World and the Old had been isolated from each other, and hence unable to exchange pathogens; as a result, infectious microbes in the Americas had evolved along different paths from those in Eurasia and Africa. When native peoples in the Americas confronted the epidemic diseases that arrived from Europe along with the colonists, therefore, they lacked the immune defenses of colonizers who had been exposed in childhood to viral epidemic diseases like measles that operate on adult victims with calamitous intensity. The establishment of permanent settlement beachheads at Jamestown (1607), Quebec (1608), Plymouth (1620), and Fort Orange (on the site of modern Albany, 1624) brought close, continuous contact between native and European populations that permitted not only measles, but also chicken pox, smallpox, diphtheria, influenza, and other infections to enter the neighboring Indian communities and then to spread along lines of trade among local native groups, into the surrounding regions."

11. Ibid., location 227.

the time, only visible with the luxury of hindsight. This powerful, lasting influence was not on the native peoples but was on the church itself. Specifically the career and Christian witness of David Brainerd has had a lasting and continuing influence on the church in the United States reaching through the ages and crossing over many different denominational boundaries. Describing Brainerd, Latourette wrote, "Extraordinarily sensitive, a mystic, deeply devoted, although he died young he exercised a profound influence. His diary was widely read and helped to inspire many to become missionaries, not only in America, but also in other parts of the world."[12] This influence was not Brainerd's intention, and it was not a purpose he sought or encouraged. In fact, the lasting power of this influence is magnified by the circumstances of his early death. Moreover this lasting influence was not primarily created by Brainerd himself but is the result of the book written about Brainerd by one of the most influential American theologians of all time, Jonathan Edwards. This book, *The Life and Diary of David Brainerd*, is the best-selling of all of Edwards's many books.[13] To this day this book has been an influential spiritual guide and devotional inspiration for countless Christians.

David Brainerd

12. Latourette, *Centuries of Advance*, 220.

13. *The Life and Diary of David Brainerd* continues to be in print to this day, and moreover is now available in electronic format.

The life and Christian witness of David Brainerd with its incredible courage and perseverance is a remarkable example of Christian biography which has inspired and encouraged faithful Christians through the ages, most especially those called to foreign missionary service in the heyday of missions in the 1800s. Edwards's words in his preface convey the spiritual benefit which Brainerd's witness has had through the ages: "I am persuaded every pious and judicious reader will acknowledge, that what is here set before him is indeed a remarkable instance of true and eminent Christian piety in heart and practice—tending greatly to confirm the reality of vital religion, and the power of godliness—that it is most worthy of imitation, and many ways calculated to promote the spiritual benefit of the careful observer."[14]

Like missionary Azariah Horton before him, David Brainerd initially received financial support from the Church of Scotland through the Society for Propagating Christian Knowledge, which had been instituted in Edinburgh in 1709 and which created a Board of Correspondence in New York in 1741. The support of the society was a principle connection between the Church of Scotland and the new Presbyterian General Assembly and thus funds from Scotland were the primary means of financial support for the earliest American missionary work. David Brainerd, an early beneficiary of the Scottish support, was first commissioned to preach by the association of congregational pastors who officially gathered at Danbury, Connecticut, on July 29, 1742, to examine Brainerd for ordination. His initial licentiate to preach inspired him to evangelize the Native American community then named Kaunamumeek, west of Albany, New York. With this experience as licensed preacher, Brainerd was ordained as a missionary to the Indians by the Presbytery of New York, meeting in Newark, New Jersey, on June 12, 1744. Thus was launched a remarkable but very brief missionary career to the Native Americans inspired by a deep perseverance and piety and cut short by disease, probably tuberculosis, at the young age of 29 on October 9, 1747. Brainerd's daily work among the Indians, and more importantly his profound theological and spiritual reflection often with emotional anguish, was carefully recorded in a diary. The diary itself was kept, edited and expanded with a parallel commentary by Jonathan Edwards.

Despite the handicap of his illness, which repeatedly debilitated him, Brainerd reached out with a missionary fervor to Native Americans in three different locations, which were not proximate with one another. One was in

---

14. Edwards, *Life and Diary of David Brainerd*, preface.

the colony of New Jersey, south of New Brunswick. The colony by the native name was called Crossweeksung, and by the British name, Crossweeks. Brainerd also initiated two missionary posts in the colony of Pennsylvania, one near the forks of the Delaware River, north of Philadelphia, and the other further west in a village established next to the Susquehanna River. Of these three missionary fields, Brainerd's only significant success was within the village of Crossweeksung. He reflected on his work there in a diary entry on June 19, 1746:

> This day makes up a complete year, from the first time of my preaching to these Indians in New Jersey. What amazing things has God wrought, in this space of time, for this people! What a surprising change appears in their tempers and behaviour! How are morose and savage pagans, in this short period, transformed into agreeable, affectionate, and humble Christians! And their drunken and pagan howlings turned into devout and fervent praises to God! They "who were sometimes in darkness are now become light in the Lord." May they "walk as children of the light and of the day!" And now, to Him that is of power to establish them, according to the Gospel and the preaching of Christ, to God only wise, by glory, through Jesus Christ, forever and ever. Amen.[15]

---

15. Green, *Historical Sketch*, 41.

> AN
>
> ACCOUNT of the LIFE
>
> Of the late REVEREND
>
> Mr *David Brainerd,*
>
> Minister of the Gospel,
>
> Missionary to the Indians, from the Honourable Society in Scotland, for the Propagation of Christian Knowledge, and Pastor of a Church of *Christian Indians* in New-Jersey.
>
> Who died at Northampton in New-England, October 9. 1747, in the 30th Year of his Age.
>
> Chiefly taken from his own *Diary*, and other private Writings, written for his own Use; and now published,
>
> By JONATHAN EDWARDS, A. M.
> Then Minister of the Gospel at Northampton, afterwards President of the College of New-Jersey.
>
> To which is annexed,
>
> I. Mr Brainerd's JOURNAL while among the Indians.
> II. Mr Pemberton's Sermon at his ORDINATION. With an APPENDIX relative to the Indian Affairs.
>
> EDINBURGH:
> Printed by JOHN GRAY and GAVIN ALSTON.
> For WILLIAM GRAY in the Front of the Exchange.
> MDCCLXV.

The cover page of Jonathan Edwards's famous biography including the journal of David Brainerd.

Because of the constant encroachment of the English settlers and the unfavorable conditions for any farming, Brainerd encouraged the Indian villagers at Crossweekung to move their village further west, onto land they still considered their own, but which was more hospitable for farming. Here, at a new settlement named Cranberry, the small Indian village under Brainerd's gentle leadership thrived. Of the almost 150 people that moved to the new village, about forty became communicant members of the new church, about thirty of the children attended a new school which Brainerd established and for which he recruited a head master. David Brainerd, almost unable to move because of the agony of his illness, retired to the care of Jonathan Dickinson in Elizabethtown, New Jersey, where he convalesced for four months. He recovered enough strength to return to his beloved village in February 1747, for what became his final farewell. In October 1747, at the age of 29, David Brainerd died. The witness of his faithfulness, his spiritual journey as intimately recorded in his diary, his relentless Christian compassion and love for his Indian friends, and his early death sealed his reputation as a blessed Christian example within American Christian history.

David's beloved brother John carried on the ministry at Cranberry. John visited his dying brother while David lay on his death bed in Jonathan Dickinson's home; it must have been an emotional farewell and a touching passing of the torch from one brother to the other. Under John's leadership the ministry continued and thrived. John was a member of the Presbytery of New York, and recruited the Rev. William Tennant to join him in support of the mission. Finally, as the Revolutionary War roiled the American colonies, and consistent with the unethical treatment of native groups throughout the early colonies, the Brainerds' small village at Cranberry was forced to move to a new location, first to New Stockbridge, Massachusetts, and ultimately, in the 1830s, to the Lenape reservation in Wisconsin. After the death of John Brainerd in 1780 and without a constant pastoral presence, the Christian faith of the Native Indians which the Brainerd brothers had so dearly nurtured dissipated.[16]

The inspiring and persevering faith of David Brainerd has touched countless Christians, many whom themselves were immersed in lives of missionary service. Brainerd, especially in the light of the vision of evangelizing the world, was an archetype. Indeed, Jonathan Edwards, saw in Brainerd an example of the kind of converted, passionate ministry which Edwards himself so energetically was calling for in the churches of his era.

16. See Latourette, *Great Century*, 299–300. Latourette wrote: "In the Indians of the United States Christianity faced an extraordinarily difficult problem . . . In many a tribe a mission was initiated and progress was made in gathering congregations and conducting schools, only to have the enterprise disrupted by the forcible removal of the tribe to another habitat. The wars which frequently punctuated these removals temporarily made the work of the missionary all but impossible."

A glimpse of Brainerd's inspiring faith is evident in this excerpt from his journal as it was included in Edwards' biography:

> Wednesday Jan. 8. In the evening my heart was drawn out after God in secret: my soul was refreshed and quickened; and, I trust, faith was in exercise. I had great hopes of the ingathering of precious souls to Christ; not only among my own people, but others also. I was sweetly resigned and composed under my bodily weakness; and was willing to live or die, and desirous to labour for God to the utmost of my strength.[17]

After the Revolutionary War and throughout the first half of the nineteenth century, the destructive policies of the US government resettled the vast majority of the eastern Native American tribes to new reserved lands in the West. These policies were replete with broken promises, unfulfilled commitments, and in total, mark a great, systematic injustice. Nonetheless, the Presbyterian Board of Foreign Missions, after its formation in 1837, kept up a relentless effort to reach the native people with our mission work. The effort was commendable but the native cultures, now resettled in the western United States, were not a fertile ground for the planting of the European gospel and the church did not take root. In fact, the missionary work of the church could never overcome the profound injustice inflicted on these people by the United States government or the deep hatred of these people by the vast majority of the Europeans.

In his influential history of the Presbyterian mission enterprise, published in 1838, Ashbel Green still held onto a bright hope for this work. But the "solemn guarantee" which Green refers to here was in fact rescinded and revised over and over again in the face of the European conquest of the land. Nonetheless, Green's vision and hope give hint of the passion which motivated the Presbyterian mission enterprise, although in this case a passion that would never bear fruit:

> Beyond the limits of the respective states and east of the Rocky Mountains, are 40 tribes of various sizes, containing a population of near 200,000. Ten other tribes, or parts of tribes, east of the Mississippi River, with a population of 50,000, are under treaty stipulations to move west of the river; thus making an aggregate of 250,000, all more or less accessible to the labors of the missionary ... Here are no interferences with the jurisdictions or rights of any

---

17. Edwards, *Life and Diary of David Brainerd*, part 7, "From His Beginning to Preach to the Indians at Crossweeksung..."

of the states: and the whole Indian territory will be held by them, under the solemn guarantee of the Government of the United States. In every treaty, the most ample provision has been made for the support of schools, and for teaching agriculture and the most simple mechanic arts. It is a most important question, will this experiment of government, in thus providing a permanent home, save the remnants of this noble race, from the melancholy destiny of those who have perished before the advance of the white man? Is it practicable to elevate the mass of this population, so that in time they may be safely entrusted with all the rights of citizens, and brought into the Union, on an equal footing with the original states? It would not be difficult to prove, that if proper means are used, both of these questions may be safely answered in the affirmative . . . This experiment will fail most certainly, unless the Indians are made acquainted with the Gospel of Jesus Christ. How important then is the agency the church has to perform; and how great will be her guilt, if from apathy the part assigned to her is left undone, and thereby all the other efforts fail![18]

Future directions of discussion, study and prayer:

- David Brainerd was motivated by a powerful calling to reach out to the Native Americans in his era. In what ways is his story inspiring for you? Are there ways you identify with David Brainerd's story?

- What do we learn about the challenges of mission work from the relationship between European culture and native culture in colonial America?

- If world mission is to grow as a core identity and purpose for the church today, do we need personal role models like David Brainerd? How has the importance of individuals as examples and role models changed? Are there any Christian role models today in our culture? For you personally?

---

18. Green, *Historical Sketch*, 165–66.

CHAPTER 3

Ashbel Green

THE CONVENTION OF OLD School delegates that met in Pittsburgh in May 1835 forwarded a resolution to the General Assembly asking for a renewed commitment to mission:

> That the Presbyterian Church owes it as a sacred duty to her glorified Head, to yield a far more exemplary obedience, (And that in her distinctive character as a church,) to the command which he gave at his ascension into heaven: "Go ye into all the world, and preach the Gospel to every creature." It is believed to be among the causes of the frowns of the great head of the church, which are now resting on our beloved Zion, in the declension of vital piety and the disorders and divisions that distract us, that we have done so little—comparatively nothing—in our distinctive character as a Church of Christ, to send the Gospel to the heathen.[1]

The phrase twice used in this resolution, "distinctive character," are fighting words. This phrase captures an idea which transformed the Presbyterian Church theologically and organizationally. The distinctive character of the Presbyterian Church refers to those features, doctrines and convictions that are uniquely Presbyterian. The distinctive character of Presbyterianism took time to emerge and coalesce. From the earliest days in the colonies the Congregationalists who were generally settled in New England and the Presbyterians who were generally settled in the middle and southern colonies enjoyed cooperation and harmony. In reflecting on this early

---

1. Green, *Historical Sketch*, 170–71.

history of the Presbyterian Church, Henry Wood describes the relationship between these different Reformed bodies this way:

> Presbyterians and Congregationalists flying from intolerance and persecution in the Old World, would find little difficulty in uniting, when sharing in the toils and privations of a settlement in the wilds of America. The Presbyterians, who settled in New England States, generally united with the Congregationalists; and the Congregationalists, who settled in the middle and Southern states, united with Presbyterians . . . It was not to be expected that Scotch Presbyterians, Huguenots, Independents, &c. coming from so many different countries—England, Scotland, Wales, Ireland, France, Germany, &c.—could unite in any rigid system. The result was a modified Congregationalism in New England, and a modified system of Presbyterianism south and west of New England.[2]

Nonetheless, in the earliest days of American Presbyterian history, prior to the Revolutionary War, this spirit of compromise and cooperation could not hold. The Presbyterian Church split apart in 1741 driven by what Dr. Woods calls the "liberal party" and the "rigid party." The liberal party, in Woods's assessment, was generally English Presbyterians comfortable with cooperation with the New England Congregationalists and encouraging of the Great Awakening that was sweeping the colonies with the powerful preaching of people like Jonathan Edwards and George Whitefield. The rigid party was Scots Irish Presbyterians, committed to a strict subscription to the Westminster Confession and a highly qualified, educated clergy.[3] Organizationally, this division forced the creation of separate Presbyterian synods. The first synod, the Synod of Philadelphia, represented the rigid Scots Irish party. The opposing party gathered themselves officially as the Synod of New York, and represented the liberal party. This original and first splitting of the Presbyterian Church in America lasted for seventeen years, until a full reunion was achieved in 1758. The reunited Presbyterian Church organized under one synod now named the Synod of New York and Philadelphia.

A generation of Presbyterian leaders including Ashbel Green, whom we will highlight here, hardened their theological convictions in the furnace of the American Revolution. They were convinced of the contribution which the Presbyterian doctrine and way of life had made to the successful

---

2. Woods, *History of the Presbyterian Controversy*, 26.
3. Ibid., 33.

separation of the colonies from their mother land, and hence of the birth of the United States. They were proud of the contributions Presbyterianism made to the formative ideas of the United States' government. The experience of this Revolutionary War generation of Presbyterian leaders bolstered a pride and vision in the rightness of Presbyterianism and the tremendous influence this way of life would have on the infant United States. It was a fertile time for the church and the new nation; both were growing quickly.

Ashbel Green

Obviously the context is significantly different in the post-Revolutionary War era. The creation of the federal government of the United States and the writing and approval of the United States Constitution all occurred at the same time and in the same cultural milieu as the growth and development of the Presbyterian Church. In May of 1785 the Synod of New York and Philadelphia established a special committee "to prepare the form of a constitution" for the Presbyterian Church. The first constitution of the Presbyterian Church was ratified and adopted by the synod on

May 16, 1788.[4] With the constitution of the church established, the first General Assembly was convened in 1789 with renowned Dr. Witherspoon preaching at the opening worship service and presiding until the assembly elected Dr. John Rodgers as the first moderator. It is interesting to note, given the separations he would help force several decades hence, that in his autobiography Ashbel Green carefully highlights his own contribution at the second General Assembly in 1790: "I made a motion that the intercourse between us and the New England churches should, with their approbation, be renewed."[5] Toward that end, Ashbel Green had traveled throughout New England nurturing a network of relationships throughout the Congregational Churches of the region and serving as a delegate from the Presbyterian General Assembly to the General Association of Connecticut in 1806.[6]

By the early 1800s, the idea of the distinctive character of the Presbyterian Church drove a wedge of conflict and division. The General Assembly claimed a unique, denominational identity. In this first generation as an independent United States the nation grew and stretched out. The population generally, and church membership, grew exponentially. There was a pervasive feeling of excited expansion, unprecedented growth, and institutional vitality. The Presbyterians, given their presence in this new nation from the earliest days and their sacrificial commitment to the war, now stood with a proud vigor. The powerful demand for the full institutional expression of the distinctive character of Presbyterianism played out in three interlocking but distinct arenas. First, this push to express the distinctiveness of Presbyterianism forced a split from the Congregational Churches of

4. The Synod of 1787, "after reading and considering the draught of the committee of the preceding year, and availing itself of the written suggestions of the Presbyteries, issued another pamphlet, containing a more complete system than the former one, and ordered a thousand copies to be distributed to the several Presbyteries. The system contained in this latter pamphlet, formed the basis of the deliberations of the Synod of 1788, which issues in the formation and publication of the 'The Constitution of the Presbyterian Church in the United States of America: containing the Confession of Faith, the Catechisms, the Government and Discipline, and the Directory for the worship of God—ratified and adopted by the Synod of New York and Philadelphia May the 16th, 1788.'" Green, *Life of Ashbel Green*, 181.

5. Ibid., 197. In this chapter reminiscing about the creation of the Constitution of the Presbyterian Church and the early meetings of the General Assembly, Green muses "that for a considerable time past I have been the only surviving member of the Synod that adopted the constitution of the Church to which I belong; and in which I have ministered for something more than fifty-five years" (ibid., 185).

6. Ibid., 305.

New England. This involved a repudiation of the numerous plans of union which had been carefully negotiated between the Presbyterians and various associations of Congregationalists. The emphasis on the distinctive character of the Presbyterian Church motivated the massive Old School and New School schism. Through a host of antecedent denominations this story has come down through the generations and is expressed in the difference today between the Presbyterian Church (U.S.A.) and the United Church of Christ. Second, Presbyterian distinctiveness was expressed in the area of domestic mission work which included the planting and support of new congregations in the western frontier. The call for a distinctive Presbyterian expression of domestic mission work exacted a complete break with the American Home Missionary Society and a general disdain for Presbyterian involvement in voluntary societies. Third, and specifically relevant to the focus of this study, the call for and commitment to the unique, distinctive character of Presbyterian foreign mission work required a break from the cooperative efforts of the American Board of Commissioners for Foreign Missions (ABCFM). In place of the cooperative foreign mission work of the American Board, the Presbyterian Church formed the uniquely Presbyterian Board of Foreign Missions in 1837. Possibly more than anyone, the person who worked tirelessly in each of these different areas to fully express the distinctive character of the Presbyterian Church was Ashbel Green

Born into an "eminently pious" Presbyterian family, it was a natural course of life for Ashbel Green (1762–1848) to become a leading Presbyterian theologian, scholar and advocate for foreign missions. Green's maternal grandfather, the Rev. John Pierson, was the long-serving pastor of the congregation in Woodbridge, New Jersey. Ashbel's father, the Rev. Jacob Green, served as the pastor of the Presbyterian Church in Hanover, New Jersey, for forty-five years. A strict observance of the Sabbath day, enforced by both his mother and father, as well as comprehensive theological education starting at a young age were features of his childhood which he forever cherished. At the age of eighty-two, Ashbel began writing his autobiography. At the start of that work the image of his father's leading the Sabbath-day exercises with the family at home after his morning church services is a touching memory:

> I see him sitting in his arm chair, asking in regular order every question in the Westminster Shorter catechism, helping or correcting those who could not repeat it perfectly; and sometimes making remarks on particular answers, or on the whole catechism

after it had been repeated. When this part of the exercise was finished, the children of the family, of whom there were five or six, were questioned on five chapters previously prescribed, the questioner still neither using nor needing a book. To this succeeded an inquiry in regard to the text or texts he had preached on; and what we could recollect of the sermons we had heard. This was followed by asking the elder children what other books they had read besides the Bible, and by the repetition of short sentences of devotional poetry which any of us could remember. The whole was concluded sometimes with a short address from my father, and always by an impressive prayer.[7]

A small, idiosyncratic detail from the early life of Ashbel Green, as he reflected back on it while writing his autobiography, may have had a significant influence on the course of the complicated relationships between the Presbyterian and Congregationalist Churches. After an intense childhood education under the tutelage of his father, Green was prepared to attend college in the spring of 1782. His choice was confined to the college at New Haven and that at Princeton. Both of these schools had suspended operations during the Revolutionary War and were just beginning their reorganization when Green was searching. At this point the Presbyterians and the Congregationalists had cordial relationships which allowed both the pastors and the congregations to blur the distinctions of polity. Nonetheless, the college at New Haven was the theological home of the New England theology and the Congregationalists. Princeton was the flagship institution for the Presbyterians. Green had formed a friendship with an alumnus of New Haven who was serving as one to the tutors helping with the reorganization of the student body. Green sent his friend a long letter inquiring about matriculation at New Haven. In his autobiography Green writes what may be considered an influential quirk in Presbyterian Church history:

> I waited for an answer to my letter till I ceased to expect it, and then a friend, who was afterwards my class mate and room mate, took a ride to Nassau Hall. His report decided us to go there. We went accordingly, and about a fortnight after we were matriculated, I received my long expected letter from Yale, which had been lying, for probably six weeks, in a post office within seven miles of my father's residence. Had I received it seasonably, (and I never

---

7. Green, *Life of Ashbel Green*, 20.

could tell why I did not,) I should certainly have gone to Yale, and not to Nassau Hall.[8]

Of course, given his theological perspective Green saw the "overruling providence of God" in this little quirk. Nonetheless, Green's connection with Princeton was powerful and long lasting. His history tells of interactions and relationships with many leaders of the Presbyterian Church where Princeton served as the connecting link. This connection comes to full fruition when Ashbel Green was chosen as the eighth president of Princeton, serving from 1812 to 1822. The influential career of Ashbel Green, the strict tone of Old School Presbyterianism, the place of Princeton as a locus of those great debates, and the distinctive character of Presbyterian foreign mission work may all have played out differently if a letter did not get lost in a local post office and Green had thus attended New Haven. Such is the poetry of history. As his pastoral career developed over many years, Ashbel Green became a forceful advocate for the Old School and the distinctive character of Presbyterianism. Green was instrumental in the repudiation of the plans of union, the separation from the Congregationalists and other New School Presbyterians, and the creation of domestic and foreign mission boards within the General Assembly.

Following the Revolutionary War, both the Presbyterian Church and the Congregational Churches of New England were vigorously pushing west.[9] The thrust into the frontier lands of western New York and into the wilderness of the Ohio territory created opportunities for Presbyterians and Congregationalists to work side by side. The remoteness of this mission work from the eastern seaboard and the challenge of finding qualified clergy to serve these areas sparked a cooperative spirit within the Presbyterian General Assembly. A practical working out of the details of this cooperation was articulated in the "Plan of Union of 1801" between the General Assembly of the Presbyterian Church and the General Association of the State of Connecticut. These regulations were intended "to prevent alienation and promote union and harmony in those new settlements

---

8. Green, *Life of Ashbel Green*, 130.

9. "In the first fifty years after the Constitution went into effect in 1789, the population of the United States ballooned at a greater rate than it has ever since. During that period, the population grew more than fourfold, from 3,929,214 in 1790, the year of the first census, to 17,069,453 in 1840." See "Growth of U.S. Population, 1790–1840," http://www.granburyisd.org/cms/lib/TX01000552/Centricity/Domain/287/Fact_Sheet_U5_Growth_in_Population.pdf.

which are composed of inhabitants from these bodies."[10] This was the first and the model for a series of cooperative agreements between Presbyterians and Congregationalists which included the Plan of Union and Correspondence between the General Assembly and the Convention of Vermont in 1803; the Plan of Union between the Synod of Albany and the Middle Association in the Western District of the State of New York in 1808, the Plan of Union and Correspondence between the General Assembly and the General Association of Massachusetts in 1811 and the Plan of Union between the General Assembly and the Associate Reformed Synod, commonly known as the Seceders, in 1821. Given the blurring together of these two Reformed traditions it was often difficult to distinguish them. The New England Associations of Congregational Churches achieved a cohesion that often resembled presbyteries. Within the Presbyterian Church there were presbyteries that included Congregational pastors and also individual congregations that did not elect ruling elders. The various plans of union often included provision for the denominations to grant representation from the other, including the rights of voice and vote, at their large annual gatherings. For example, Ashbel Green was a delegate to the meeting of the General Association of Connecticut in 1806.

These cooperative efforts reached their fullest expression in the planting of new churches in the western frontier, particularly in New York. The Plan of Union allowed congregations founded by one tradition to call a pastor from the other. There was provision to establish a special council made up of both Congregational members and Presbyterians in the event of a disagreement or conflict within the congregation. Importantly, the Plan of Union encouraged the formation of union churches with both Congregationalist and Presbyterian members which would maintain relationships with both traditions. Clearly this cooperative effort was intended to support the effort to plant new churches and spread the gospel into the growing western regions of the United States. Soon this cooperative spirit moved into full institutional merger. With the 1808 Plan of Accommodation, the Synod of Albany proposed to make a whole association of Congregational churches within its bounds a full member of the synod. Essentially, the synod was absorbing an Association of Congregational Churches as one of its

---

10. "It is strictly enjoined on all their missionaries to the new settlements, to endeavor, by all proper means, to promote mutual forbearance and accommodation, between those inhabitants of the new settlements who hold Presbyterian and those who hold Congregational form of church government." Plan of Union of 1801 is quoted from the General Assembly's Digest in Woods, *History of the Presbyterian Controversy*, 41.

own presbyteries while it maintained Congregational practices and affiliations. This created a model which was replicated in more western regions of New York and into the Western Reserve of Ohio, the initial precedent of the Presbytery of Western Reserve. In this way hundreds of congregations were absorbed in mass into the Presbyterian Church.[11]

This institutional sharing was expressed in practical ways in the life of congregations, their associations and their presbyteries. This cooperation also had a common theological source expressed powerfully in the Westminster Confession. This systematic and precise theological system informed the theological ethos of both the Congregationalist and Presbyterian traditions in America from the beginning. Professor James Moorhead offers a succinct and clear summary of this foundational, covenant theology:

> This theology envisioned the human condition in terms of two covenants. In the first, God made a covenant of works with Adam who stood as the representative for all humanity. By this covenant, Adam's transgression was imputed or assigned to his posterity who, as a result, were born into a state of sin and were utterly incapable of doing God's will. Salvation came only through the covenant of grace made between God the Father and Christ. By his suffering on the cross, Christ vicariously paid the penalty for sin on behalf of the elect. His righteousness was counted as theirs and only in this fashion could the elect be saved.[12]

New School and Old School Theology

But soon cracks started to appear in the strong theological foundation of covenant theology which had been the bedrock of both traditions. Some softening of the harsh edges of this theological system began to show up in the work New England Congregationalist theologians centered at Yale Divinity School. Soon named the "New Divinity," these theological modifications of the Westminster bastion morphed into the "New School." Soon small theological modifications became large chasms and ultimately a brutal theological rending into separate institutions: the New School and Old School division. The context of a growing, expanding, vast, new United States significantly influenced these theological stirrings and debates. The

---

11. See Moorhead, "Restless Spirit of Radicalism," 21.
12. Ibid., 22.

Westminster theology had been transplanted from a stodgy, old, crowded and small context in England and Scotland to a huge, wide open, new land. The theologians of the New Divinity were looking for a compelling and evangelistic expression of the gospel to answer the call to plant churches in an expanding new land. The theologians of the Old School tried mightily to hold onto a sacred, historic expression of their faith while everything in their culture and environment was changing quickly.

Theologians of the New Divinity, following in the footsteps of their master and mentor, Jonathan Edwards, began exploring some nuance and modification in their Reformed theological heritage. Key among these theologians were Samuel Hopkins (1721–1803), Joseph Bellamy (1719–1790) and Samuel Emmons (1745–1840). Soon the New Divinity's theological ponderings were offering a different tone and interpretation of the doctrines of original sin, the atonement, and the question of human free will. The New Divinity backed down from the austere doctrine of original sin, although not rejecting it, and sought an understanding of sin based in one's own behavior and thus a more immediate culpability for one's actions. Christian theology through the ages has always reached for language to explain the meaning of Christ's crucifixion. Following in a long tradition of theology, the Westminster formulation used the image of debt and debtor. Jesus' death on the cross paid the debt of a sinful humanity. The New Divinity

> replaced the debtor-creditor image with a governmental metaphor. Sin was not a debt owed God; it was a crime committed against the divine government. Punishment was necessary to uphold God's government, lest the law be flouted and sinners feel free to sin with impunity. The atonement, then, was not Christ's payment of the debt owed by the sinner, for a sin was crime not a debt. Instead the atonement was Christ's bearing of the punishment due for the breaking of the law and expression of God's aversion to sin.[13]

In similar fashion, the New Divinity teased out a deeper affirmation of human free will. The lack of free will, which is the tone of the classic Westminster theology, was for the new theologians softened as they reached for more individual and personal responsibility. "Since no external, mechanical law compelled an individual to sin, he or she possessed a natural freedom to avoid sin. However, since the dispositions and habits of the unregenerate were wicked, they would inevitably use that freedom to choose sin. In a

---

13. Ibid.

word, men and women possessed a natural ability to refrain from sin, but not a moral ability since their souls were warped."[14] For the Old School Presbyterians, geographically centered around Philadelphia, the New Divinity was out of bounds. For example, in 1811, Old School theologian Ezra Stiles Ely railed against the New Divinity considering it a complete abandonment of the classic Reformed understanding of sin and the nature of Christ's redeeming work on the cross. "Encouraging sinners to think that they might contribute something toward their own redemption, it tended toward the ancient heresy of Pelagianism."[15] All of these issues can be contained within the question of the interpretation of the Westminster Confession. Indeed, the authority of Westminster is the heart of the matter. Since the earliest days, going back to the first organization of the synod, the Presbyterians debated whether "subscription to the Westminster Confession" should be required of all pastors. The New School and Old School may itself be seen as another flaring up of this old debate.

By the 1830s a potpourri of events and attitudes mixed with enough energy to push things over the edge; a formal schism was initiated. In academic circles, the work of theologian Nathaniel William Taylor at Yale pushed the controversial edges of the New Divinity provoking some sharp written responses from Princeton theologians. These exchanges continued the nuanced debates and interpretations of the imputation of Adam's sin, Christ's atonement, and the nature of repentance, regeneration, salvation and sanctification.[16] Closer to the day-to-day life of ordinary church folks, the Old School's heresy trials against Albert Barnes in Philadelphia were an important precipitating factor. His case was appealed several times, in 1831 and 1836, to the General Assembly of the Presbyterian Church and played out in many public forums. In the wake of the Barnes trials, formal disciplinary action for similar theological innovation was taken against Lyman Beecher in Ohio, George Duffield in Pennsylvania, and James Wheelock in Indiana. There was a larger dynamic also at work around questions of proper church order and decorum provoked by the influential evangelistic campaigns of Charles G. Finney. His success as an evangelist, mimicking the earlier success of Methodist revivalists, was inspired by his vigorous preaching which used the common parlance of the lower class, working people who crowded his revivals. Finney shouted out and condemned spe-

---

14. Ibid., 23.
15. Ibid.
16. Ibid., 24.

cific sinful behavior thus demanding immediate change. Moreover, Finney was one of the first large scale itinerant preachers who started explicitly naming slavery as a sin. This introduced a new dividing line which soon allowed an alignment of the Presbyterians of the southern states with the Old School of the north over against the New School. Finney also pushed another divisive issue by welcoming and encouraging women to speak and preach at his gatherings. Finney was a Congregational minister and later a professor at the young Oberlin College in Ohio, thus he was outside the reach of formal Presbyterian disciplinary action.

In addition to the trauma and division within the realm of church life there were deeper and more subtle social changes taking place. Moorhead nicely summarized these:

> Beneath these specific changes was a transformation of consciousness that some historians have called a "democratization of mind," a new outlook in which ordinary people vaunted their right to take charge of their own lives without the help of traditional authority and without deference to their "betters." Evidences of that determination appeared in the popular assault against professional elites in medicine and law and in the extension of suffrage to the vast majority of white males. With the electorate vastly widening, politics was increasingly converted into a form of popular mobilization and entertainment as the so-called second party system of the United Stated coalesced in the 1830s.[17]

As part of these deeper changes, the Presbyterian Church split into what may be viewed as a two-party system, the Old School and the New School. By the meeting of the Presbyterian General Assembly in 1837 the Old School advocates, bolstered by the support of all of southern Presbyterianism, had the upper hand. Any tone of negotiation and compromise was cast aside; the Old School controlled the General Assembly and invoked radical action. The Plan of Union from 1801 was repudiated; all four synods—throughout New York and Ohio—which had been created on the basis of cooperation with the Congregationalists were cast out of the Presbyterian Church. And, as we will see, all cooperative arrangements, through voluntary associations, in the realms of domestic and foreign missions were repudiated. Presbyterian institutions were established within the Old School General Assembly to carry on this work with the distinctive character of Presbyterianism. The Old School and the New School Presbyterian

---

17. Ibid., 27.

Churches each lurched forward as separate and distinct denominations for a generation.

When the Congregational Churches themselves cast aside the old plans of union in 1852, the New School Presbyterian Church started veering back toward their older heritage. In the 1850s an influential and moderate Presbyterian theologian, Henry Boynton Smith, working at Union Seminary in New York, a New School institution, articulated a Reformed Theology around which Old School and New School Presbyterians could gather.[18] There was movement toward healing. Of course, with the Civil War the Old School Presbyterian Church split along north-south lines. Thus a much diminished Old School Presbyterian Church, now without its southern churches, had more incentive to heal the breach with the New School. The New School and Old School Presbyterians, now all located in the north, shared a commitment to the Union through the Civil War which overshadowed all their differences. The Old School and New School Presbyterian Churches were reunited in 1870 to the form the Presbyterian Church in the United States of America.

Voluntary Societies

Consideration of the Old School and New School conflict in Presbyterian history typically emphasizes the significant theological differences which we reviewed here and which could not be reconciled. This division brought to light permanent theological differences in American Presbyterianism which has functioned as a two party system. These divisions have been a dominant feature of Presbyterianism perennially. Although taking different forms, these fault lines have repeatedly quaked into divisions, schisms and bitter debate throughout our history, down to the present day. But in the 1830s these important theological factors may not have driven the situation to full institutional separation if not for the compounding issue of the many voluntary societies, particularly missionary societies.

---

18. In 1864, "at the opening of the New School Assembly at Dayton, Ohio, a sermon was preached by the retiring moderator, the Rev. Henry B. Smith, D.D., which presented the whole subject of a Reunited Church with a singular felicity and power. These documents were widely circulated and freely discussed throughout the country; signs multiplied in every direction of an ever-increasing disposition and purpose to unite the two branches of the Presbyterian Church in the United States." *Presbyterian Re-Union Memorial Volume, 1837–1871*, 251.

As we have seen, at the dawn of the nineteenth century there was an abiding commitment to Protestant cooperation motivated by a spirit of growth and expansion. For Presbyterians the cooperation and collaboration with the Congregationalists, as expressed in formal ways like the Plan of Union in 1801, was a leading example of the larger Protestant effort. This drive toward cooperation brought with it the era of the Protestant voluntary societies in which Presbyterians were very involved. Undergirding this work was a vision of Christian America. The Protestant churches and the Protestant ethos were strong, domineering and controlling. In response to a growing population which was quickly spreading out in the western lands the mainline Protestants organized and supported a vast array of new organizations which all together were intended to promote the Christianization of the nation. Virtue, citizenship and Christian faith were blurred together into the ideal of the devout Christian individual not only engaged in the work of their own congregation but also joining with other like-minded Christians in the support of this new army of voluntary societies that pushed the Christian vision into every aspect of social life. Devout and faithful Christians joined together in voluntary organizations bolstered by a vision of a Christian nation. This created a cohesive Christian social strategy, the American benevolent empire. This deep cooperative spirit among Protestants inspired the creation of numerous voluntary associations generally distinguished between those focused on domestic missions and foreign missions.[19]

Professor Dana Robert highlighted the power and the influence of the voluntary missionary societies: "The pieces all fell into place in the late eighteenth century with the rise of the 'voluntary society,' the idea that ordinary church members would donate money on a regular basis to send people like themselves to distant parts of the world, with the purpose of translating the Bible, founding churches and schools, improving people's lives through western medicine and agriculture, and convincing them that their eternal salvation would be secured by following Jesus."[20]

---

19. Longfield discussed the importance of voluntary societies in this era and their theological foundation and quotes a sermon by Lyman Beecher in which Beecher envisioned voluntary societies as "a sort of disciplined moral militia, prepared to act upon every emergency, and repel every encroachment upon the liberties and morals of the State." Longfield includes a list of voluntary societies which emerged in this era including the New York Missionary Society, the American Bible Society, the American Sunday School Union and the American Colonization Society. Longfield, *Presbyterians and American Culture*, chap. 3, "Christian America: Awakenings and Reform."

20. Robert, *Christian Mission*, chap. 2.

From the start there were questions raised in Presbyterian circles about this wholesale cooperation with the other Protestant denominations. Ashbel Green, with his acute sensitivity to anything that would dilute the distinctive character of Presbyterianism, started articulating a complaint against this wholesale Protestant, institutional cooperation. In his autobiography he summarized the zeal that was inspiring the formation of voluntary missionary societies and his own feelings:

> In 1796, the New York Missionary Society was organized, consisting principally of members of the Presbyterian Church. It owed it origin to the missionary zeal excited by the accounts then recently received in this country of the institution, animated exertions, and flattering prospects of the London Missionary Society. The present writer can state, from a distinct recollection of his feelings and language at the period now referred to, that although he highly approved the zeal of the founders of this society, and was perfectly willing that they should prosecute their own views of duty, yet for himself, he saw no need of any new organization for missionary operations in the Presbyterian Church. He thought the zeal now awakened should be cherished and carried into the General Assembly of our Church; that in this body we had already an organization, than which none could be devised better adapted to the prosecution of foreign as well and domestic mission.[21]

Ashbel Green's perception here names a fracture that will widen and shatter the Presbyterian Church. Coupled with the significant theological differences, this concern for a unique Presbyterian mission work institutionalized within the General Assembly is a key contribution to the New School and Old School division, and a lasting divide in Presbyterianism. It is here that the long influence of the Old School and New School division within the Presbyterian Church has also transformed Presbyterian mission work down to the present day.

In the realm of domestic mission work the American Home Missionary Society is an important piece of this story.[22] This robust national voluntary society was formed out of the merger of a several smaller, local domestic missionary efforts, reflecting a commitment to support new

---

21. Green, *Life of Ashbel Green*, 322–23.

22. This history of the American Home Missionary Society is borrowed extensively from David G. Horvath. See the "Biographical Note" at the American Home Missionary Society records, 1816–1907, http://www.amistadresearchcenter.org/archon/?p=accessions/accession&id=22.

congregations toward self-sufficiency on the American frontier. Initially, the Young Men's Missionary Society of New York was formed in 1815 and likewise the New York Evangelical Missionary Society in 1816. These efforts were small and local; thus they could not rally the resources to provide missionaries to the expanding western frontier. Realizing these limitations, these groups along with several other local societies, merged in 1822 to form the United Domestic Missionary Society with a goal of a national missionary outreach to plant and support new churches. This society was primarily supported by Presbyterians and created an effective mission soon sending 125 missionaries to the far western states including Ohio, Indiana, Missouri, Michigan, and also Florida. There was an upswelling of support, money and leadership for these efforts and an intuitive desire to cooperate. The different pieces of this work from within the Protestant churches continued to attract one another and coalesce. By 1826 Presbyterian, Congregationalist, Dutch Reformed, and the Associate Reformed Church members from thirteen different states gathered for a convention in New York City and created the American Home Missionary Society.[23] During the same convention the United Domestic Missionary Society voted to join also. This missionary effort was now truly national in scope with a centralized organization and the potential for aggressive fundraising through the direct connections with congregations from a long list of Protestant denominations. Most important in this effort were the Presbyterians and the Congregationalists; and the Plan of Union of 1801 was a vital administrative bulwark for the society. Because of the Plan of Union, the American Home Missionary Board had a church polity structure in place to share services, church buildings and hire both Presbyterian and Congregationalist ministers as missionaries and, of course, to solicit Presbyterians and Congregationalists for funds.

For the first decade of the 1800s the American Home Missionary Society served as a voluntary, ecumenical mission agency recruiting pastors and supporting the growth of congregations all along the western frontier of the growing United States. This effort was, in fact, in direct competition with the work of the Standing Committee for Mission of the General Assembly. The Presbyterian Standing Committee had been formed in 1802 with Ashbel Green serving as it first chairman.[24] Green energetically served as the

---

23. Green, *Historical Sketch*, 27.

24. "In one year of its existence, the Committee recommended, and the Assembly sanctioned, fifty-one missionary appointments." Green, *Historical Sketch*, 20.

leader of the Presbyterian domestic mission effort until he was recruited to serve as the president of Princeton in 1812. When Green returned to Philadelphia in 1822 to take up again his service to the General Assembly he found, as he related in his autobiography, "the Board of Missions of our Church reduced in funds exceedingly, by the rival exertions of other missionary societies . . . so that it seemed to be on the point of extinction in everything but in name."[25] Green rallied support for a uniquely Presbyterian home mission board within the General Assembly, and the General Assembly responded enthusiastically as Green related: "The old Board was re-organized, with a distinct specification of powers to appoint an executive committee, to choose a corresponding secretary, and to prosecute missions both domestic and foreign, to pay the missionaries, and with no other restriction than making of an annual report to the General Assembly."[26]

The contours of a conflict are now defined. On one hand the American Home Missionary Society is thriving as a voluntary agency with support from across the spectrum of Protestantism in an effort to shore up new congregations on the frontier. On the other hand, at the same time, the Presbyterians are working the same field, doing the same work, raising support in an effort to plant and support Presbyterian congregations served by Presbyterian pastors on the frontier. This competition of the voluntary society versus the denomination's mission board becomes bitter and hostile, and soon a driving wedge between Old and New School Presbyterians. A sense of the depth of feeling and the vitriol which emerged around this question of the relationship of the church to voluntary societies is expressed, for example, in an attacking pamphlet written by Rev. J. L. Wilson, the pastor of the First Presbyterian Church in Cincinnati:

> The Presbyterian Church, in the United States of America, under the care of the General Assembly, has been, for several years, much disquieted by the claims and importunities of a voluntary society called, "The American Home Missionary Society" . . . when, without affording any security for orthodoxy or piety, in her members

---

25. Green, *Life of Ashbel Green*, 323.

26. Green, *Life of Ashbel Green*, 324. Green also included these details of the working the domestic mission board: "I was elected both as president of the Board and the chairman of the executive committee. The meetings of the committee were held for a considerable time in my study, but subsequently a room was hired for our meeting; and ultimately a house was rented for the accommodation of our Board, and the Education Board." From May 1833, Rev. John McDowell was chairman of the executive committee although Green continued as president of the board.

> or officers, she claims the patronage of the Presbyterian Church, interferes with her plans, distracts her counsels, divides her members, draws off her resources and weakens her strength, by enticing Churches, Presbyteries, and Synods, from their constitutional obligations and plighted faith; it becomes as clear as the mid-day sun, that if there be any thing in the doctrines, discipline, and Missionary operations of the Presbyterian Church worth preserving, the claims and importunities of the A.H.M. Society must be firmly and boldly resisted.[27]

Thus the General Assembly of the Presbyterian Church in 1837 made some momentous decisions. In addition to exscinding the four synods of the New School, which included twenty-eight presbyteries, out of the Presbyterian Church a resolution was passed breaking all relationships and cooperation with many voluntary societies of the day:

> Resolved, That while we desire that no body of Christian men of other denominations, should be prevented from choosing their own plans of doing good; and while we claim no right to complain, should they exceed us in energy and zeal—we believe that facts too familiar to need repetition here, warrant us in affirming, that the organization and operations of the so called American Home Missionary Society, and American Education Society, and its branches of whatever name, are exceedingly injurious to the peace and purity of the Presbyterian church. We recommend, accordingly, that they should cease to operate within our Churches.[28]

Thus the General Assembly of the Presbyterian Church in the year 1837 must be remembered as a crucial event with lasting consequences. Of course, the split of the church between its Old School and New School factions is the most obvious and devastating result. The theological differences beneath this separation are lasting and continue to exist as fault lines in the church. The New School and Old School Presbyterian Churches struggled forward as separate denominations with separate church bureaucracies and separate General Assemblies. In small towns and cities across Pennsylvania

---

27. Wilson (pastor of the First Presbyterian Church, Cincinnati), *Four Propositions*, 3. Ashbel Green has the same tone in his attack on the American Home Missionary Society: "It refused, although kindly invited, to co-operate in missionary concerns with the Assembly's Board, but came forth against it in open hostility, and laboured for some years, to thwart its operations and destroy its influence." Green, *Historical Sketch*, 28.

28. Green, *Historical Sketch*, 29. Green adds a long footnote in his book, at this page, explaining the theological rationale for this resolution.

and New York this split often resulted in the presence of different Presbyterian congregations, one Old School and one New School, across the street or down the block from one another. It was not until the Civil War shifted the whole cultural and religious landscape of America that these factions were finally able to reunite in 1870. More relevant to our story is that, in 1837, there was a wholesale effort to disconnect mission work from any cooperative, ecumenical voluntary societies and embed it fully within the administrative structure of the General Assembly. With a focus on domestic mission we reviewed the strain between the American Home Missionary Society, a successful, robust voluntary society, and the General Assembly's Standing Board of Mission. The story of this same stress and strain but in regard to the work of foreign mission work is vital to our whole story and requires its own chapter. But first we consider the beautiful story of Betsey Stockton, the slave who became a missionary.

Directions for future discussion, study and prayer:

- What is your experience of division and schism within the Presbyterian Church? How do you explain the history of schism in American Presbyterianism?

- Do you believe that the Presbyterian Church has a "distinctive character" today? How would you describe it?

CHAPTER 4

Betsey Stockton

As a friend of missionaries, Ashbel Green was repeatedly raising support and encouraging their work. In the earliest days of the mission effort of the American Board of Commissioners for Foreign Missions and at the first fledging, distinctive Presbyterian efforts Green served as an important spiritual and financial base for numerous missionaries from his early home in Philadelphia and later also from Princeton. He reflected in his autobiography, "In several other instances I had opportunity of helping forward the early missionaries of that Board to their destined fields, and always was glad of the opportunity of rendering them any aid."[1]

Betsey Stockton

1. Green, *Life of Ashbel Green*, 326.

Betsey Stockton, who was first encouraged and sent out with Green's support, is a unique and special story. In his autobiography Ashbel Green included only these several sentences about her:

> When Mr. Stewart and his wife went to the Sandwich Islands, a coloured girl by the name of Betsey Stockton, (who had been given as a slave to my first wife, and with her concurrence was freed by myself,) and who at the time was on wages in my family at Princeton, was invited to go in the character of a missionary, and as an assistant to Mrs. Stewart in the concerns of the family. Betsey had become hopefully pious, and by the instruction received in my family, principally from my son James, had made laudable improvements in knowledge. She had saved her wages, by which, with some small assistance from myself, she was able to prepare her outfit for the mission.[2]

The remarkable story of Betsey Stockton is told with care by Eileen F. Moffet in her *International Bulletin of Missionary Research* article, "Betsey Stockton: Pioneer American Missionary."[3] Betsey had been born and raised as a slave. As such the details of her early life, and the precise identity of her parents, are all lost to history. Nonetheless, the life of Betsey Stockton is historically significant as she was the first single woman missionary sent out from North America. This fact is particularly stunning given that she was also an African American woman and a former slave. There is no record of Betsey's father at all; Betsey's mother was owned by Robert Stockton, a leading family in Princeton. This, obviously, is the source of Betsey's family name. The Stockton clan is one of the original pioneer families on the eastern seaboard and became wealthy landowners in New Jersey. The patriarch Richard Stockton was one of the signers of the Declaration of Independence. When Betsey was a small child, Robert Stockton gave her to his oldest daughter Elizabeth, and thus Betsey was raised as a domestic slave. Elizabeth Stockton married Ashbel Green; and Betsey served the Green family.

Ashbel Green was a prominent leader of Old School Presbyterianism and a strong anti-slavery advocate, as was his father before him, also a Presbyterian minister. But Betsey was owned by Ashbel's wife Elizabeth and as such was raised as a domestic slave within the Green home. Betsey developed a very close personal and supportive relationship within the Green

---

2. Ibid.
3. This chapter is fully indebted to Moffet's careful research and article.

household. She was educated in their home through the private tutoring of the Green's son, Jacob. Apparently, growing up, Betsey, like the Green children, had ready access to Ashbel Green's extensive library which she took advantage of; moreover, she was included in the family's devotions, Bible study and catechism lessons. In significant ways, Betsey functioned on a day to day basis as part of the Green family. Moffett concludes from the bits and pieces that she gathered from the historical record that Betsey "was systematically tutored in the academic and spiritual disciplines given their own children."[4] This begs the question of her baptism. Although the Green's took responsibility for Betsey's Christian nurture and education within their home, they did not sponsor her for baptism. There were, at this time, significant ambiguity and regional differences within the Presbyterian Church on the practice of masters and mistresses sponsoring the slave children under their care for baptism.

Betsey stayed on with the Green family after the death of Elizabeth Stockton Green in 1807. Ashbel Green was serving as the president of the College of Princeton when, during the 1814–1815 school year, a powerful "revival of religion" broke out on campus. The spiritual power of this revival soon touched Betsey also. Moffat writes,

> When the revival broke out in early 1815, the atmosphere of community life among the students was greatly affected for good, and this eventually spilled over into Betsey's life. She attributes here conversion, though, to the ministry of a seminary student, Eliphalet Wheeler Gilbert, over a year later, in the summer of 1816, while sitting in the gallery of Princeton's First Presbyterian (now Nassau) Church. The session minutes of that congregation record that on September 20, 1816, "Betsey Stockton, a coloured woman living in the family of Rev. Dr. Green, applied for admission to the Lord's table." The session was satisfied as to the evidence of what they called her "experimental acquaintance with religion" and her good conduct and agreed to receive her into full communicant membership. She was publicly baptized at that time and admitted to the Lord's table.[5]

Soon thereafter, within the Green family, there was a very significant transformation in the life of Betsey. Betsey was manumitted from slavery but continued within the Green household as a paid, domestic servant. The

---

4. Moffett, "Betsey Stockton," 71.
5. Ibid., 72.

concept and practice of manumission in colonial America was complex and varied from region to region, and later from state to state. We do not have any glimpse of the discussion that may have taken place within the Green household around these questions. We do not know if Ashbel Green made a direct or theological connection between his decision to manumit Betsey and her baptism and membership in the Presbyterian Church. Also at this time Betsey organized a small academy for several black children from the Princeton area. Here her gifts and skills as a teacher were first expressed.

Given her close association with Ashbel Green, his family and the larger Princeton community Betsey was immersed in the strong evangelical theology of the day which was inspiring the great missionary movement. Within these circles there was a spiritual calling and deep sense of obligation toward the "lost" or "heathen" populations of the world that had not been introduced to Jesus Christ as their Savior and Lord. News of mission work from around the world and reports from missionaries acquainted with Ashbel Green or connected with Princeton were constantly before her. This missionary sense of call was growing in Betsey, as she was increasingly aware of various missionaries who came within Ashbel Green's influence. Initially a desire to do mission work in Africa began to form in Betsey's heart; she waited and studied, devoting herself to her teaching opportunities with the children in the Princeton community.

One particular seminary student, Charles Stewart, was a regular visitor in the Green household. He fostered a relationship with Ashbel Green during his studies and was discerning a call to missionary service.[6] There is no record of their first meeting or initial conversation, but Betsey was soon pondering whether there was any possible means by which she could join Charles Stewart and his fiancée, Harriet, as they began concrete preparations for missionary service. We do not know what role Ashbel Green may have played in encouraging Betsey's sense of call and the details of her potential missionary service with the Stewarts. But we do know that on September 11, 1821, Ashbel Green wrote influential letters of recommendation for both the Stewarts and Betsey Stockton to the American Board of Commissioners for Foreign Missions preparing the way for their service to the Sandwich Islands.[7] Betsey's appointment was carefully worded in

---

6. See the biography of Rev. and Mrs. Charles Samuel Stewart at http://www.phcmontreat.org/bios/Bio-index-overall.htm.

7. The Sandwich Islands are now named Hawaii. These islands were discovered by Captain James Cook in 1778 and named after the Earl of Sandwich, who had invented one of the most enduring fast foods in the western world.

the American Board's official documentation: "She was to be regarded and treated, neither as an equal nor as a servant, but as a humble Christian friend."[8] Through the era of the missionary movement there were twelve companies of missionaries from the American Board of Commissioners sent to Hawaii.[9]

Charles Stewart graduated from Princeton in 1821 and was married to Harriet in June, 1822. On November 19, 1822, the Stewarts with Betsey set sail from New Haven, Connecticut, for the Sandwich Islands to reinforce the missionary team that had gone there three years earlier. Aboard the sailing ship, the Thames, this was a treacherous, five-month voyage across the Atlantic ocean, around the horn of Africa, across the Indian Ocean and eastward across the Pacific Ocean to the islands. Writing in her journal, Betsey noted an almost "deathlike sickness" while sailing through ferocious storms. Later on a calm day she wrote, "If it were in my power I would like to describe the phosphorescence of the sea. But to do so would require the pen of a Milton: and he, I think, would fail, were he to attempt it."[10]

The missionaries arrived safely in Honolulu Bay on April 23, 1823, only to be immediately shocked at the site of the native islanders, large groups of whom paddled out in their primitive canoes to greet the arriving schooner. Betsey described her feelings upon that first glimpse of the people to whom she was called to serve. "They were most naked except for a narrow strip of tapa around their loins. When they first came on board, the ladies retired to the cabin and burst into tears; and some of the gentlemen turned pale . . . my own soul sickened within me, and every nerve trembled. Are these, thought I, the beings with whom I must spend the remainder of my life? They are men and have souls—was the reply which conscience made . . . We informed them that we were missionaries, come to live with them and do them good. At which an old man exclaimed in his native dialect, 'That is very good. By and by know God.' In a short time our unpleasant feelings were much dissipated."[11] Soon, though, the missionaries were warmed and welcomed by the generous hospitality of the islanders.

Harriet Stewart had started the strenuous ocean voyage leaving New Haven knowing that she was pregnant. She gave birth on board only weeks before they reached their destination. When they arrived on the islands,

8. Moffett, "Betsey Stockton," 73.
9. *Wikipedia*, s.v. "List of Missionaries to Hawaii."
10. Moffett, "Betsey Stockton," 73.
11. Ibid.

Betsey assumed responsibility for their baby girl and Harriet, who was quite sick for weeks after childbirth. Despite all the effort of caring for the new baby and Harriet, the Stewarts along with Betsey set out to start a new mission at Lahaina on the island of Maui. Immediately, in addition to her domestic responsibilities caring for the baby, Betsey organized a small school for the common people in the area. Although earlier missionaries had started schools for the upper classes and the royalty, Betsey's school was the first for the common people. Her pride in this work was reflected in her note back to Ashbel Green, "I have now a fine school of the lower classes of people, the first, I believe, that has ever been established."[12]

Thus Betsey Stockton is remembered as the first single woman and the first African American woman sent out into the mission field as part of the great missionary movement. Her transformation from a child born into slavery to a literate, skilled missionary schoolteacher is one of the remarkable stories of the missionary era. But her missionary service was short-lived. In 1825, Harriet Stewart was so dangerously ill that Charles decided to return to the States. Betsey returned with them. Betsey remained a close friend, and formally a paid domestic servant, with the Stewarts. Harriet died in 1830, Betsey continued on essentially raising the Stewart's now three children. Charles Stewart had taken a position with the Navy which required long stretches as sea. Eventually Charles remarried and Betsey returned to Princeton. She lived there the remainder of her life, receiving support from Ashbel Green's son, Jacob, a successful attorney. Betsey immersed herself in teaching classes for the poorest African American children in the community and also Sunday school. In the 1830s the racial tension of the era entered also into the life of the First Presbyterian Church in Princeton. This had always been the Green's home church and Betsey's. But now the black members of the congregation withdrew to form a new congregation called the First Presbyterian Church of Colour, which is now Witherspoon Street Presbyterian Church. Betsey was a founding member of this church, and started their Sabbath school. She taught in the Church school there for thirty years.

In her beautiful essay Eileen Moffett concludes, "Aunt Betsey grew to be one of Princeton's most admired and beloved figures, though unassuming and gentle in spirit. She had a quiet steady Christian influence,

---

12. Ibid., 74.

particularly on young people, with whom she was always surrounded in week-day school and in Sunday school."[13]

Betsey Stockton died in 1865, only months after the assassination of Abraham Lincoln. There was a distinguished memorial service conducted by the faculty of Princeton Seminary, including President John Maclean and Professors Duffield and Hodge.

Directions for future study, discussion and prayer:
- Betsey Stockton's transformation from a slave to a missionary is remarkable and beautiful. What causes such a powerful change? Have you ever experienced any such power in your life?

13. Ibid.

CHAPTER 5

William Carey and Adoniram Judson

WITH LOTS OF HOOPLA the Mission Agency of the Presbyterian Church (U.S.A.) commemorated the 175th anniversary of Presbyterian World Mission at its General Assembly in Pittsburgh in 2012. This anniversary marks a remarkable legacy of global mission work by one of the classic, mainline Protestant denominations. The signification of the 175th year of this work is tied to the meeting of the General Assembly of the Presbyterian Church in the United States of America in 1837. As was common in the early days of American Presbyterianism, the General Assembly in 1837 met in Philadelphia and the action which we commemorate took place on June 7. This official resolution marks the start date which we now celebrate: it was resolved "that the General Assembly will superintend and conduct, by its own proper authority, the work of Foreign Missions of the Presbyterian Church, by a Board appointed for that purpose, and directly amenable to said Assembly."[1]

Behind this resolution there is a huge trail of conflict and monumental theological controversy. There is a full, long train of events which finally brought the General Assembly to this action. For example, there is loaded in the simple phrase, "by its own proper authority," the story of a bitter conflict in the church. Also included in this resolution was the noteworthy action empowering the new board of directors of the new Board of Foreign Missions to bring under the General Assembly's umbrella all the previous, voluntary foreign mission work: "The Board of Directors shall have power,

---

1. *Minutes of the Board of Foreign Missions of the Presbyterian Church, October 31st, 1837* (New York: Carter, 1838), 3.

and they are hereby authorized to receive, a transfer of the Foreign Mission Societies, or either of them, now existing in the Presbyterian Church, with all the Missions and funds under the care of, and belonging to, such Societies."[2] In Baltimore on October 31, 1837, the newly constituted Board of Foreign Missions of the Presbyterian Church in the United States of American officially met for the first time.

Naming this anniversary the 175th year of Presbyterian World Mission is itself not precisely accurate. Historically informed Presbyterians in Pittsburgh will be quick to note that what is being commemorated is only the General Assembly's official creation of a national Board of Foreign Missions for the Presbyterian Church. But Presbyterians in Pittsburgh intentionally started a foreign mission program six years earlier, precisely because the General Assembly had not done so. In their official minutes in 1837, the Synod of Pittsburgh remembers the first movements toward a Presbyterian foreign mission effort. "Six years ago, when no movement in behalf of this object existed in any part of our church, trusting in the aid and blessing of the glorified Redeemer, this Synod ventured to establish a Board of Foreign Missions, intended to secure the action of its own churches in behalf of the heathen, and to unite and combine in the effort all who were willing to cooperate with them in thus attempting to spread the everlasting Gospel of Jesus Christ." In 1831 the Synod of Pittsburgh created the Presbyterian Foreign Mission society, which served as the avenue through which the Presbyterian Church of western Pennsylvania supported a mission work to the world.[3] Six years later, when the General Assembly acted to create the Board of Foreign Missions, the Synod of Pittsburgh was pleased to relinquish full jurisdiction of their mission society to the new board.[4]

---

2. Ibid., 4.

3. *Historical Sketch of the Board of Foreign Missions of the Presbyterian Church, 1837–1888* (New York: Jones, 1888), 3. "In November 1831, the Synod of Pittsburgh, which from its organization in 1802 had exhibited marked missionary zeal, organized the 'Western Foreign Missionary Society' for the purpose of 'conveying the Gospel to whatever parts of the hearthen and anti-Christian world, the Providence of God might enable the Society to extend its evangelical exertions.'"

4. The Synod of Philadelphia, also in time for the first meeting, had taken action to add their support to the General Assembly's new Board of Foreign Missions. The two southern synods were not immediately able to fully support the new board, but agreed with the effort. Both the Synod of Virginia and the Synod of North Carolina had previously cooperated in support of the Central Board of Foreign Missions. Unlike Pittsburgh and Philadelphia, the southern synods could not immediately disengage from these prior efforts in order to join the General Assembly's effort. The minutes of the first meeting of

The creation of the new Board of Foreign Missions by the 1837 General Assembly was not an isolated action. Internally within American Presbyterianism, this action was a piece of a massive internal clash of worldviews which become known in Presbyterian jargon as the split between the New School and the Old School. Outside of and larger than the Presbyterian Church, the creation of the Board of Foreign Missions was part of a huge rising tide of Protestant commitment to evangelize the world. The Board of Foreign Missions was the Presbyterians' effort to join a much larger, global effort. Motivated by the Old School majority at the 1837 General Assembly, the Board of Foreign Missions expressed the "distinctive character" of the Presbyterian Church. The decision was made that a unique and distinctive Presbyterian faith required its own, autonomous Board of Foreign Missions. But the Presbyterian effort was motivated by and an expression of a much larger and older effort at world evangelism. In 1837 the Presbyterians created their distinctive agency for world mission but this was part of a larger commitment to evangelize the world which takes us back to the story of William Carey.

William Carey

---

the Board of Foreign Missions records the correspondence from the southern synods which notes their intention: "Resolved, That the Synod of Virginia cordially concurs with the Synod of North Carolina, in the sentiment that it is expedient and desirable to alter the relation for the Central Board of Foreign Missions, so as to render it auxiliary to the Board of Missions of the General Assembly, as soon as circumstances will fairly permit." See *Minutes of the Board of Foreign Missions, 1837* (New York, 1838), 6. It was not long before all the synods were supporting the General Assembly's new Board of Foreign Missions.

William Carey and Adoniram Judson

In April of 1789 William Carey was called to serve as the pastor of a Baptist congregation in the town of Leicester in the east midlands of England. Carey, as had been his habit, soon gathered with an association of colleagues and church leaders who met regularly for Bible reading, mutual support and theological discussion. At an association gathering in 1791 Carey had been invited to share some reflections. As George Smith reports in his biography, "A most solemn feeling pervaded the assembly. Carey, deeply moved, and hoping that his hour had come, urged his brethren no longer to delay in the matter of the evangelization of the heathen."[5] Carey's own life story is simple and common coming out of the working class. Margaret Applegarth's children's book about Carey is titled *The Career of a Cobbler*, referring to his early profession as a shoemaker. Thus Carey's appeal reached beyond the limits of the professional academics and professors of theology; he incited a movement for world mission which inspired the imagination of lay people. Carey's colleagues asked that his remarks be published; this became the first articulation of his famous pamphlet. At the next annual meeting of the association Carey was asked to preach. He choose Isaiah 54:2 and 3.[6] The different themes of these two verses became the outline of his sermon, and inspired the new motto for the missionary society which was quickly formed: "Expect great things from God; attempt great things for God." On October 2, 1792, this association of ministers gathered for the inaugural meeting of the Baptist Missionary Society. Carey pledged all the proceeds from the publication of his manuscript to the work of the missionary society. Carey initiated a theological revolution in support of missions starting with a fresh reading of the Bible, which was clear, direct and accessible to lay people. This vision transformed and inspired the mainline Protestant churches in England from which the great missionary societies soon emerged. This transformative energy reached across the ocean to the expanding Protestant mainline churches in America which were forming a strong religious and moral establishment in the growing United States.

---

5. Myers, *William Carey*, 30.

6. "Enlarge the site of your tent, and let the curtains of your habitations be stretched out; do not hold back; lengthen the cords and strengthen your stakes. For you will spread out to the right and to the left, and your descendants will possess the nations and will settle the desolate towns" (NRSV).

Carey's influential theme was published in a little book which considered a straightforward question: Is the Great Commission from Matthew 25 still an obligation for Christians?[7]

> Our Lord Jesus Christ, a little before his departure, commissioned his apostles to *Go, and teach all nations*; or, as another evangelist expresses it, *Go into all the world, and preach the gospel to every creature*. This commission was as extensive as possible, and laid them under obligation to disperse themselves into every country of the habitable globe, and preach to all the inhabitants, without expectation, or limitation. They accordingly went forth in obedience to the command, and the power of God evidently wrought with them. Many attempts of the same kind have been made since their day, and which have been attended with various successes; but the work has not taken up, or prosecuted of late years (except by a few individuals) with that zeal and perseverance with which the primitive Christians went about it.[8]

William Carey's influence was much more than a sermon, a small book and the start of an early mission agency. His long career as a missionary to India is remembered to this day as a stellar witness of a successful and thoughtful missionary life. It started on June 13, 1793, when Carey and Dr. John Thomas, a medical missionary, set out from Dover aboard the Kron Princessa Maria for India. Over a long career in India, Carey had a deep commitment to equipping native Indian leaders in the church since Carey knew that England could not and should not indefinitely provide the leadership for the Indian church. Carey's mission work in India also had a foundational commitment to education, without regard to the class or caste of the students. His mission planted several schools. Moreover, Carey was ahead of his time with his commitment to the importance of translating the Bible. Immediately upon arriving in India, Carey began to learn the Bengali language and translate the New Testament into Bengali. Early in his career Carey began formulating themes which would become established missionary practice: the financial self-reliance of missionaries, the training of indigenous people for all manner of church leadership, the value of schools as a vital aspect of mission work,[9] and the importance of translating the

---

7. "I shall enquire, whether the commission given by our Lord to his disciples be not still binding on us . . ." Carey, *Enquiry into the Obligations of Christians*, 6.

8. Ibid., 7, 8, italics in original.

9. Semaphore College and the Agri Horticultural Society of India were both founded by Carey. The William Carey International School, the William Carey Academy in

Bible into the native tongue.[10] Presbyterian mission leader Robert Speer, in his Cole Lecture at Vanderbilt University about William Carey and his colleagues, highlights his "moral superiority of character and the daring and originality of their schemes."[11]

In his *Enquiry into the Obligations of Christians*, Carey called the Protestant churches back to a commitment to world missions. It was a commitment Christians in Europe and America were poised to make. Particularly for the English, the exploits of Captain James Cook sailing throughout and accurately charting the Pacific Ocean were exciting the imaginations of ordinary people and motivating a vision of how accessible the whole world was becoming. Carey coupled that excitement with a deep theological commitment to share the gospel in obedience to the direct command of Jesus Christ. Moreover, Carey began a more careful, thoughtful and scientific approach to this mission work. He created a careful accounting of all the nations of the world, listing their population and known religious affiliations. The many pages of carefully, calculated, lined charts offer an impressive image of the scope and hope of his plea. Carey with evident Christian earnestness and a systematic, scientific presentation advocated that the Christian gospel must be extended to every nation, every culture and every people of the world. This is a clear eyed proposal without a hint of idealistic romanticism. For Carey this is simply, clearly, unquestionably the obligation of the followers of Christ. His summary of this world wide review of nations does not flinch at the sheer magnitude of the task he is advocating. For Carey this obligation to reach the world with the gospel is not unrealistic, insurmountable or unattainable; it is nothing less than the task set before the followers of Jesus.

> The inhabitants of the world according to this calculation, amount to about seven hundred and thirty-one millions, four hundred and twenty millions of whom are still in pagan darkness; an hundred and thirty million the followers of Mahomet; an hundred millions

---

Bangladesh and Carey College in Sri Lanka are named in honor of his important contributions to education.

10. Carey, and a team of missionaries who soon supported this effort, first translated the Bible into Bengali and Sanskrit and began work to translate the sacred literature in Sanskrit into English. Over a lifetime of mission work, Carey translated the Bible into forty-four languages or dialects. A full printing press exported from England to India was part of their mission, an innovation which was soon copied by many mission sites around the world.

11. Speer, *Some Great Leaders*, 57.

catholics; forty-four millions of the greek and Armenian churches, and perhaps seven millions of jews. It must undoubtedly strike every considerate mind, what a vast proportion of the sons of Adam there are, who yet remain in the most deplorable state of heathen darkness, without any means of knowing the true God, except what are afforded them by the works of nature; and utterly destitute of the knowledge of the gospel of Christ, or of any means of obtaining it.[12]

Carey continued in the last section of this treatise to consider the mundane organizational details for the robust effort at world evangelism. He lists specific ways that this work should be organized and funded. He particularly encouraged the participation and support of every Christian person as an obligation to Christ. Despite his commanding vision for reaching the world with the gospel, Carey takes into account, in his organizational scheme, the reality of the animosity between the denominations and their inability to cooperate. This is particularly true of the Old School Presbyterians, but they are not specifically named by Carey. Nonetheless, Carey's vision brushes aside the strident denominationalism of his day:

> I do not mean by this, in any wise to confine it to one denomination of Christians. I wish with all my heart, that everyone who loves our Lord Jesus Christ in sincerity, should in some way or other engage in it. But in the present divided state of Christendom, it would be more likely for good to be done by each denomination engaging separately in the work, than if they were to embark in it conjointly. There is room enough for us all, without interfering with each other; and if no unfriendly interference took place, each denomination would bear good will to the other, and wish, and pray for its success, considering it as upon the whole friendly to the great cause of true religion; but if all were intermingled, it is likely their private discords might throw a damp upon their spirits, and must retard their public usefulness.[13]

As one of the first generation of missionaries, William Carey helped to create the pattern for the great world missionary movement that was to come. His first principle was to learn the language of the people. Carey wrote some advice to his own son when he started as a missionary on one of the Malayan Islands:

12. Carey, *Enquiry into the Obligations of Christians*, 62; all words are rendered here as they appear in the original.
13. Carey, *Enquiry into the Obligations of Christians*, 84.

> Labor incessantly to become a perfect master of the Malay language. In order to do this, associate with the natives, walk out with them, ask the name of everything you see, and note it down; visit their homes, especially when any of them are sick. Every night arrange the words you get in alphabetical order. Try to talk as you get a few words, and be as much as possible one of them. A course of kind and attentive conduct will gain their esteem and confidence and give you an opportunity of doing much good.[14]

Beyond the importance of learning the native languages, Carey devised influential strategies for developing a sustained mission presence. He was committed to encouraging and supporting the newly formed mission agencies in England; his advice and counsel from his real experience in India was heeded. In a letter back to the new Baptist Missionary Society in England he expressed his clear advice:

> I then earnestly entreat the Society to set their faces this way and send out more missionaries. We ought to be given seven or eight families together; and it is absolutely necessary for the wives of the missionaries to be as hearty in their work as their husbands. Our families should be considered nurseries of the mission; and among us should be a person capable of teaching school, so as to educate our children. I recommend all living together, in a number of little straw houses, forming a line or square, and of having nothing of our own, but all general stock. One or two should be elected stewards to preside over all the management, which should, with respect to eating, drinking, worship, learning, preaching, excursions, etc. be reduced to fixed rules.[15]

In 1799 the Baptist Mission Society, the formation of which Carey had initially inspired, sent a team of missionaries to join him in India.[16] Carey choose a mission site in Serampore, where he spent the rest of his life until his death on June 9, 1834. With a comprehensive vision the mission at Serampore thrived. One of their mission team, Hannah Marshman, established the first girls' school. The team also established Serampore College which became the training school for indigenous church leaders in the growing church, and provided education to anyone regardless of class or caste. They founded the Serampore Mission Press which printed Carey's

14. Quoted in Speer, *Some Great Leaders*, 66.
15. Ibid., 68.
16. Initially the Baptist Mission Society sent Joshua and Hannah Marshman and William Ward to join Carey in India.

translation of the New Testament in Bengali, and soon a series of English language and Bengali newspapers, periodicals and books.

The influence of William Carey's mission in Serampore India soon reached across the Atlantic Ocean to the United States. By an interesting turn of events Carey significantly contributed to the development of the great mission agencies in the United States through his relationship with the early American missionary Adoniram Judson. For the mainline Protestant churches the story of William Carey is an important event in the development of the great missionary movement in Britain; the story of Adoniram Judson may be considered a significant starting point on the American side of the Atlantic Ocean. Of course, the British and American mission enterprises were intertwined in many ways with the relationship of Carey and Judson as one, early example.

Adoniram Judson

Adoniram Judson, the son of a Congregationalist pastor, was raised within the pervasive social, educational and religious establishment of the Congregational Churches in New England at the turn of the nineteenth century. Born in Malden, just north of Boston, the Judson family moved less than twenty miles further north to Wenham, Massachusetts, in 1793. In Wenham, Adoniram lived the formative years of his childhood, until the age of twelve, with his parents, his sister, Abigail Brown Judson, who became a lifelong close companion and a younger brother, Elnathan, who went on to a successful career as a surgeon in the US Navy. Another younger sister, Mary, died at six months of age during these years in Wenham. As was common in the culture of Congregational clergy families of the time, Adoniram was immersed in a classical education from a young age, ushered around to various tutors and private schools seeking the optimal educational experiences. Much later his own son, Edward, summarizes in the biography of his father this childhood, "As a boy, he was spirited, self-confident, and exceedingly enthusiastic, very active and energetic, but fonder of his books than of play."[17] In 1804 Judson entered Providence College, which subsequently became Brown University. During his senior year, he started teaching at a small academy in Plymouth, which did not distract him from graduating as the valedictorian of his class.

After the Plymouth Academy closed for the summer and after graduation services at Providence, Adoniram treated himself to a "tour through the Northern States" including a visit to Albany to "see the wonder of the world, the newly-invented Robert Fulton steamer."[18] Adoniram stayed at an inn next door to the room of a young, dying man. This experience proved to be the context for a deep spiritual conversion. "Sounds came from the sick-chamber—sometimes the movements of the watchers, sometimes the groans of the sufferer; but it was not these which disturbed him. He thought of what the landlord had said—the stranger was probably in a dying state; and was he prepared? Alone, and in the dead of the night, he felt a blush of shame steal over him at the question, for it proved the shallowness of his philosophy."[19] Indeed, the stranger in the next room died during that dark night; Adoniram abandoned his travels, returned to Plymouth and immediately enrolled in the Theological Institute at Andover. "On the 2nd of December, 1808, he made a solemn dedication of himself to God;

---

17. Judson, *Life of Adoniram*, 5. Edward Judson's biography of his father was first published in 1883. Given the popularity of this story, *The Life of Adoniram Judson* was revised, significantly shortened and published again in 1894.

18. Robert Fulton is widely credited with inventing the first steamboat. In 1807, his North River Steamboat began regular, passenger service from Albany to New York; it was a commercial success. See *Wikipedia*, s.v. "Robert Fulton."

19. Judson, *Life of Adoniram*, 12.

and on the 28th of May, 1809, at the age of twenty-one, joined the Third Congregational church in Plymouth."[20] By February 1810, he had made a "final resolve to become a missionary to the heathen." He reflected on this decision in a letter to his future wife:

> It was during a solitary walk in the woods behind the college, while meditating and praying on the subject, and feeling half inclined to give it up, that the command of Christ, "Go into all the world and preach the Gospel to every creature," was presented to my mind with such clearness and power, that I came to a full decision, and though great difficulties appeared in my way, resolved to obey the command at all events.[21]

When Samuel Nott Jr. enrolled at the seminary early in 1810, Adoniram and Samuel began an abiding friendship and life long journey together as missionary colleagues. These two inseparable friends delved into the discernment of a missionary calling together. Soon a small group formed around this question of missionary service. Samuel J. Mills Jr., James Richards, Luther Rice, and Gordon Hall all enrolled at Andover after graduating together from Williams College. "At Williamstown, on the spot where now stands the famous Haystack Monument, these young men consecrated themselves to the work of Foreign Missions, and poured out their fervent prayers for the conversion of the world; and this green nook among the Berkshire hills may well be called the birthplace of American Foreign Missions."[22]

The young seminary students at Andover who gathered regularly to ponder and pray about missionary service conceived of a vocation and an organization that did not yet exist in the United States, although already stories of William Carey's work and the new London Missionary Society were being heard among American Protestants. The boys were directed by a faculty advisor to submit a formal proposal to the General Association of Congregational Churches in the State of Massachusetts. In their formal and respectful petition to the Association the young men express the impression they have had "with the duty and importance of personally attempting a mission to the heathen." Their letter continues with a clear outline of the options before them as they discerned a missionary calling:

20. Ibid., 13.
21. Ibid., 17.
22. Ibid., 17–18.

The Haystack Monument

They now offer the following inquiries, on which they solicit the opinion and advice of this Association: Whether, with their present views and feeling, they ought to renounce the object of mission, as either visionary or impracticable; if not, whether they ought to direct their attention to the Eastern or the Western world; whether they may expect patronage and support from a missionary society in this country, or must commit themselves to the direction of a European society; and what preparatory measures they ought to take previous to actual engagement.[23]

In response to their request the American Board of Commissioners for Foreign Missions was officially organized, becoming the voluntary society associated with the Congregational Churches of New England and the institutional starting point for the foreign missions movement.[24] But the

---

23. Ibid., 24.

24. "This society, representing the Congregationalists of this country, may justly claim to be the mother of American missionary bodies." Ibid., 555.

faith journey of Adoniram Judson took a significant spiritual turn while in route to the mission field. Adoniram and his young wife, Anne, with the support of the new American Board, arrived in Calcutta, India, on June 17, 1812. Although raised and educated as a Congregationalist and now supported by the Congregationalist Churches in Massachusetts, Judson veered in a significantly different direction during the long weeks of sailing to India. Prior to setting out Judson had arranged an appointment with William Carey upon their arrival in India. Carey would serve as the host and mentor for the Judsons as they ventured into the mission field. Judson knew that Carey was Baptist. From a practical point of view, Judson was concerned about setting up a Congregational mission within the same purview as Carey's mission work because of this theological difference over the practice of baptism. Judson reasoned that it would be confusing to the native peoples they were trying to reach if two different Christian doctrines both presented themselves within the same vicinity. Thus while sailing to India, Judson focused his personal reflection and study time on baptism. In studying the Bible, Judson soon became convinced that only the practice of believer's baptism was theologically and biblically valid. Thus while he had been commissioned and was being supported by the Congregationalists, this change in a vital theological conviction compromised his connection with the American Board and the Congregationalists. Nonetheless, Judson and his wife were adamant in their new Baptist theological identity. When he arrived in India, the Judsons were warmly greeted by Carey; and soon they were both baptized by immersion. Carey, of course, had by now a lot of experience working with mission agencies. Carey directly intervened in response to the Judson's plight. By letter, Carey rallied American Baptists to take over support for Judson's mission since his theological change led to a break with the Congregationalist American Board. Judson's conversion to Baptist theology and William Carey's effort on his behalf led to the formation in 1814 of the first American Baptist Mission Board, the General Missionary Convention of the Baptist Denomination in the United States of America for Foreign Mission, later commonly known as the Triennial

Convention.[25] Many American Baptist denominations today are directly or indirectly descended from this Convention.[26]

In 1813, now working with grounding in Baptist theology and with support from Baptist congregations in the United States, the Judsons moved to Burma,[27] and served under the missiological tutelage of William Carey. Following Carey's example the Judson's long years of mission work in Burma included a commitment to education and translation. The first printed materials in Burmese were eight hundred copies of Judson's translation of the Gospel of Matthew. Much later, in 1883, the Judson's son Edward published a moving and heartfelt biography of his father. Here, at length, is a beautiful summary of what was accomplished in Burma written with a son's pride and praise:

> Mr. Judson's achievements far transcended the wildest aspirations of his youth. During the early years in Rangoon, when the mighty purpose of evangelizing Burma began to take definite shape in his mind; even before the first convert, Moung Nau, was baptized; when indeed the young missionary was almost forgotten by his fellow Christians at home, or merely pitied as a good-hearted enthusiast—the outermost limit reached by his strong-winged hope was that he might, before he died, build up a church of a hundred converted Burmas and translate the whole Bible into their language. But far more than this was accomplished during the ten years in Rangoon, the two years in Ava, and the twenty-three years in Maulmain. At the time of his death, the native Christians (Burmas and Karens[28] publicly baptized upon the profession of

---

25. The Triennial Convention, so named because it met every three years, was the first national Baptist denomination in the United States. As issues around the north and south divide became increasingly prominent, the Baptist Associations in the southern states withdrew to form the Southern Baptist Convention in 1845. Thus the Triennial Convention was largely northern Baptist churches and renamed itself the Northern Baptist Convention. In 1972, the Northern Baptist Convention reorganized into the American Baptist Churches USA. See *Wikipedia*, s.v. "Triennial Convention."

26. See also, e.g., www.internationalministries.org for the website of International Ministries. This parachurch world mission agency today traces its history to the conversion and mission work of Adoniram Judson. The financial support for International Ministries comes predominantly from Baptist congregations throughout the United States.

27. Burma today is officially the Republic of the Union of Myanmar.

28. The Karen people are a large ethnic minority in Burma generally settled in the southern and southeastern regions and across the border in Thailand. The early mission work in Burma, led by the Judsons, focused on the Karen people. Today about 25 percent of the Karen people identify themselves as Christian, compared with 4 percent in all of Burma. The Karen Baptist Convention exists today and includes the Karen

their faith) numbered over seven thousand. Besides this, hundreds throughout Burma had died rejoicing in the Christian faith. He had not only finished the translation of the Bible, but had accomplished the larger and the more difficult part of the compilation of a Burmese dictionary. At the time of his death there were sixty-three churches established among the Burmans and Karens. These churches were under the oversight of one hundred and sixty-three missionaries, native pastors, and assistants. He had laid the foundation of Christianity deep down in the Burman heart where they could never by washed away.[29]

There is a circuitous, indirect but important link between the mission work of the Adoniram and Ann Judson in Burma and the Board of Foreign Missions of the Presbyterian Church. For the Protestants in both America and Great Britain who were inspired by the vision of world evangelization, the pioneering work of William Carey was transformative. Carey was a practicing missionary with a lifelong successful mission in India, which itself inspired admiration and following. Carey also created a pattern for other missionaries to follow, and clearly articulated this missionary model for the Protestant mission agencies. Carey's work inspired the Baptist Missionary Society in England. Adoniram Judson, and his seminary friends whose inspiration to world mission is remembered at the Haymarket Monument, knew of Carey's important work and of the emergence of the great British mission agencies. Thus it is not *ex nihilo* that the American Board of Commissioners for Foreign Missions emerged from the Congregationalist Churches in New England. This vision of world mission was spreading throughout the mainline Protestant establishment in both England and America. Following the British, in America the first mission agencies were voluntary associations, not affiliated with a specific denomination, but drawing support across the Christian landscape. The American Board was the preeminent and earliest example of this work on the American side of the Atlantic and Adoniram Judson was their first missionary. But Judson's theological conversion embracing believer's baptism complicated this story. The Judson's and their lifelong efforts in Burma are under the purview of Carey's work in India; both Carey's team and Judson's team received

---

Baptist Theological Seminary. The city of Maulmain mentioned here (modern spelling Moulmein) where the Judsons spent twenty-three years is a large port city in the region dominated by the Karen people. See *Wikipedia*, "Karen People."

29. Judson, *Life of Adoniram*, 552.

support from Baptist congregations and Baptist mission agencies on their respective sides of the Atlantic.

The American Board, with growing support from the Congregationalists and the Presbyterians, continued to thrive separated, of course, from these Baptist efforts. The American Board developed as the premier foreign mission agency for the mainline Protestant churches. "By the time of its centenary in 1910, the Board was responsible for 102 mission stations and a missionary staff of 600 in India, Ceylon, West Central Africa, (Angola), South Africa, and Rhodesia, Turkey, China, Japan, Micronesia, Hawaii, the Philippines, North American Native tribes, and the 'Papal Islands' of Mexico and Austria."[30] Today the American Board has a direct descendent, through many changes in denominational affiliation, in the "Global Ministries" of the United Church of Christ and the Christian Churches (Disciples of Christ).

It is easy and common to perceive these deep denominational particularities as expressions of division and difference; indeed, Adoniram Judson did switch allegiances from Congregationalist to the Baptist. And these different traditions have never cooperated on the mission field. But Edward Judson, in his biography of his father, interprets these distinctive theological and ecclesiastical separations with a more gracious vision. He wants to give his father credit for inspiring a missionary conviction in many different theological streams:

> All these vigorous Christian societies sustained by the missionary conviction of the churches in America, with their vast army of missionaries and native communicants now pressing against the systems of heathenism at a thousand points, when they come to tell the story of their origin, do not fail to make mention of the name of Adoniram Judson. His life formed a part of the fountainhead from which flow these beneficent streams which fringe with verdure the wastes of paganism.[31]

Given the early cooperation of the Congregationalists and the Presbyterians in the first decades of the nineteenth century, it is not surprising that Presbyterians quickly became robust supporters of the American Board of Commissioners for Foreign Missions. While the Presbyterians were gathering energy, resources and organizing their own denominational efforts in both domestic and foreign missions, the Congregationalists were

30. See GlobalMinistries.org, the website of the United Church of Christ.
31. Judson, *Life of Adoniram*, 557.

growing support for the American Board. Thus the stalwart Presbyterian leader Ashbel Green, even while he was advocating and supporting the development of distinctive Presbyterian mission work, was, nonetheless, supportive of the Congregationalist efforts. Thus Green writes in his autobiography: "Adhering steadfastly to the opinion that our Church was admirably adapted, from its constitutional organization, both for foreign and domestic missions, and never giving up the hope that at some future day she would awake to her duty in regard to both, I thought that in the mean time I would join in the operations of the American Board of Foreign Missions"[32]

Thus there are multiple starting points, and different sources of inspiration and motivation for the great missionary movement. The vision of carrying the gospel of Jesus Christ to all the world and planting the church in every land lifted all of mainline Protestantism. But this rising tide would not create a single stream or a common vision. Like the churches themselves which were fragmented into denominations, the missionary movement followed the same course. The great missionary movement succeeded in spreading denominationalism around the world. The Presbyterians were particularly distinctive in the formation of the Presbyterian Board of Foreign Missions which made stellar contributions to the spread of global Christianity. We turn now to the uniquely Presbyterian story.

Direction for future discussion, study and prayer:

- What do you consider to be the impact and consequence of the great missionary movement initiated by William Carey?
- Professor Lamin Sanneh, professor of missions and world Christianity and professor of history at Yale University, has written an influential book reevaluating our understanding of the great missionary movement.[33] This book offers a full revision of the typical interpretation of the great missionary movement as primarily an expression of western imperialism. Sanneh argues that the great, and powerfully transformative, contribution of the missionary movement was the gift of the vernacular translation of the Bible to cultures all around the world. "Missionary promotion of the vernacular, therefore, was tantamount to adopting indigenous cultural criteria for the message, a piece of

---

32. Green, *Life of Ashbel Green*, 325.
33. See Sanneh, *Translating the Message*.

radical indigenization far more potent than the standard portrayal of mission as Western cultural imperialism."[34] Lamin Sanneh also praises William Carey as one of the early missionaries who exemplified this commitment to translation as part of the missionary enterprise:

> At Serampore, Carey and his colleagues set up a printing press, and at their suggestions, he took up employment again with the East India Company where he taught Bengali. His developed linguistic research contributed to the renaissance of Bengali prose literature. With his missionary companions at Serampore, Carey took a leading part in establishing Serampore as a major translation center. By 1832 the press there had produced religious material in forty-four languages and dialects . . . As is well known, Carey and his colleagues made few conversion inroads into India. The importance of their work lay less in statistical gains than in their brilliant development of the vernacular, and that notwithstanding their self-avowedly evangelical motives.[35]

- How do you assess Professor Sanneh's thesis that the greatest contribution of the movement was the translation of the Bible?

---

34. Ibid., 3.
35. Ibid., 138–39.

CHAPTER 6

Walter Lowrie and John Lowrie

AN IMPORTANT ADMINISTRATIVE DECISION, behind the scenes, significantly contributed to the long-term success of the Board of Foreign Missions when it was created by the General Assembly of the Presbyterian Church in 1837. The Honorable Walter Lowrie was recruited to serve as the corresponding secretary of the new board; a position he then held for thirty years.[1] After short service on the mission field in India, Walter's son, John, also joined the administrative team at the board. After his father's death, John's leadership at the board continued until 1891. Thus from 1837 to 1891, the Lowrie's presided over the original and burgeoning growth of the Presbyterian Board of Foreign Missions.

Walter Lowrie

---

1. Speer, *Studies of Missionary Leadership*, 23.

The Presbyterian Church has a heritage formed by the immigration of Scots-Irish folks in the eighteenth century. The Lowrie family was an example of this. Walter Lowrie's mother was a Highland Scot; Lowrie's father was a Lowland Scot. This was an unlikely courtship, as Lowrie remembered, "At that time my mother could not speak a word of English, but my father, though a resident of the Lowlands, spoke Gaelic fluently."[2] Walter was born in Edinburgh, Scotland, on December 10, 1784. Later, he described his parents as "poor, respectable and pious"; an accurate description of tens of thousands of Scots-Irish who like the Lowries came to America. Walter was only eight years old when his family settled in the town of Butler in western Pennsylvania, a region that would become a Presbyterian stronghold.

Walter Lowrie excelled at the classical education which his parents scraped together at home and from various tutors, private schools and academies around Butler. As he grew into his teenage years, his parents reached for the support of a neighboring pastor, the Rev. John McPherrin, to teach and train Walter. Lowrie recalled in his memoirs, "By this time I was fully satisfied that with diligence and perseverance I could master these three languages—the Latin, Greek, and Hebrew—without further instruction."[3] Thus after reaching a point of educational proficiency himself, Lowrie opened his own academy near McPherrin's home and was soon teaching forty students the same rudiments of a classical education. While teaching, he also started as the Clerk to the County Commissioners and thus a long and auspicious career in public service.[4] There were other attractions. Without the approval of either set of parents, Lowrie and Rev. McPherrin's daughter, Amelia, eloped. Walter "put his bride on a horse and rode away with her."[5] Maybe he was unconsciously mimicking the unlikely courtship of his own parents in Scotland many years before. In 1811, in the third year of their marriage, he was elected as a Pennsylvania state legislator. He served only one year in the House of Representatives before being elected to a full six-year term in the State Senate.

The United States was quickly pushing westward. Walter Lowrie served as the chairperson of an important interstate commission, including Pennsylvania, Ohio, Kentucky, and Indiana, charged with opening up the Ohio River to navigation and commerce. The commission was responsible

2. Lowrie, *Memoirs*, 2.
3. Ibid., 17.
4. Speer, *Studies of Missionary Leadership*, 26.
5. Ibid.

for surveying, mapping and clearing the Ohio River from Pittsburgh to Louisville, which soon developed into a vital commercial artery.[6] Because of such effective and noticeable government work, Lowrie acquired a reputation as a leader, organizer, and administrator. While still seated as a state senator, he was elected to the United States Senate in 1818. Again, his organizational and administrative skills were noticed. Upon completion of his Senate term he was commended to the position of secretary of the Senate, an office elected internally by the senators themselves. Although volatile politics changed the party affiliation of both the Senate and the presidency during these years, Lowrie's administrative expertise and fair, even-handed style allowed him to hold his position serving the Senate from 1825 to 1836. Walter Lowrie resigned his position as secretary of the United States Senate to accept the position of corresponding secretary of the Presbyterian Board of Foreign Missions in 1837. Poor health required his retirement in 1867.[7] "When he took charge of the missions in 1837 there were three missionaries among the Indians, in India ten and in Siam three, with a view to a future mission in China. The annual income was $44,748. And there were in 1867, at his death, seventy missionaries in nineteen missions, and the income was $218,855."[8]

The family of Walter and Amelia Lowrie included eight children, six sons and two daughters. Three of the children died young before their parents; the second son started a promising career as a lawyer but died when he was only twenty-five years old; the first daughter died when she was only eighteen years old; and the youngest child, a son, died before his first birthday. Three of their sons were called to missionary service. In 1833, their oldest son, John Cameron Lowrie and his wife Louisa (Wilson) were sent as Presbyterian missionaries to India from the Western Foreign Missionary Society, the immediate predecessor of the Board of Foreign Missions. Along with Mr. and Mrs. William Reed, they sailed from Philadelphia and arrived in Calcutta on October 15, 1833. Only weeks later, on November 21, Louisa Lowrie died. Determined to continue the missionary work, John established the first church and the first missionary school in northern India in

---

6. "It was a measure that required skillful and difficult labour and much fatigue, for several months, and considerable expense; but it was one of far-seeing wisdom and great benefit—not only to the five States, but to the other large sections of the country, west, northwest, and southwest . . . Few systems of river navigation combine usefulness and beauty to so great a degree." Lowrie, *Memoirs*, 22.

7. Speer, *Studies of Missionary Leadership*, 27.

8. Ibid., 37.

1837. Broken by poor health and his bereavement, he returned to the United States in 1838. He supported the fledging Board of Foreign Mission, serving as his father's assistant. He continued in administrative work with the board until 1891.[9]

John C. Lowrie

Walter Macon Lowrie, the third son of Walter and Amelia Lowrie, was born in Butler on February 18, 1819. A graduate of Princeton Theological Seminary, he was called to an evangelistic mission in Canton and Ningpo, China, in 1842. Walter made significant contributions to the translation of the New Testament into Chinese. The story of his tragic death is included, by his brother, in the memoirs of their father:

> His proficiency in the study of the language led his brethren to appoint him as their delegate to a conference at Shanghai of the leading missionaries in China, for the revision of a translation of the Scriptures into Chinese; and he was able to take a modest, but appreciated, part in this work . . . On this journey (back to the Ningpo Mission) he met with his death, under the most distressing circumstances. Accompanied by his faithful Ningpo servant, and another Ningpo man in the employment of the Ningpo

---

9. Presbyterian Heritage Center, Biographical Index of Missionaries, "Lowrie, Rev. John Cameron & Mrs. (Louisa A. Wilson)," www.phcmontreat.org.

Mission, they took the inland journey, which required the crossing of Chapoo Bay in a small native craft. A Chinese piratical barque soon bore down on this small boat for purposes of plunder. At first they did not molest the foreigner, who they found on board; but, probably fearing that his presence might endanger their own safety, after a little consultation among themselves, they threw him overboard, and kept him from returning by their spears. His Bible, which he was reading while they were plundering the boat, he threw on deck as he was forced over, and it was secured by his servant. It is still in service by a member of his family. Other incidents were reported by his Chinese servant. Evidently his mind was kept in peace until the end came. That end was surely a blessed one, after sorrowful and great tribulation.[10]

Walter M. Lowrie is remembered as one of the first martyrs of the Protestant missionary movement.

Reuben P. Lowrie, born on November 24, 1827, was inspired by his older brother's martyrdom. With his wife, Amelia (Tuttle), they were commissioned for evangelistic missionary service in Shanghai, China, in 1854. Sickness claimed Reuben who, refusing to return to the United States for medical care, died in 1860. Amelia returned to the United States for the education of their two young children. She returned to China as a missionary to women along with her son, the Rev. J. Walter Lowrie, and her daughter who served in China with her medical missionary husband.

Thus while Walter Lowrie served from the office in New York as the corresponding secretary of the Board of Foreign Missions three of his sons served in the foreign mission field; and two died in China. In his memorial for Lowrie, the Rev. David Wells remembered them well, "Of these two sons it may be said with perfect truth, that they were among the ablest and most consecrated men ever sent by the Church to the Foreign field."[11]

---

10. Lowrie, *Memoirs*, 125.
11. Wells, *Walter Lowrie*, 7.

Under the Lowrie's leadership, the offices of the Board of Foreign Missions were moved to the "Mission House," 23 Centre Street, New York City.[12]

The Lowrie family is a particular example of the energy and commitment that had burst forth in support of foreign missions. Within the Protestant churches of both Europe and the United States there was a huge rallying in support of these mission efforts. The first half of the nineteenth century, prior to the Civil War, was a time when the population of the United States was increasing quickly; the economy was expanding driven by multiple growth factors including technological advances in numerous

---

12. "In the Mission House, besides the Treasurer's and Secretaries' offices, there are apartments for packing and storing goods to be sent to the missions. These occupy the basement story. When several missionary families are about to sail, their trunks, boxes, parcels, articles of furniture, &c., fill up these apartments, often to an uncomfortable degree; and both the economy and the convenience of these rooms become quite apparent... The rooms devoted to the Museum, in the third story, contain a rare variety of idol gods and goddesses, from India, Siam, China, Africa, and other heathen countries, besides numerous other objects of interest... A large room is occupied by the Library... A number of works by Chinese authors occupy a recess in the same room. Lowrie, *Manual of Missions*, 13.

fields; a lucrative system of world trade was developing in an increasingly interconnected world; the United States was expanding wildly westward. The Protestant mainline churches were booming. A spirit of growth, expansion and progress defined the cultural ethos of the nation and the churches. This spirit motivated the churches to evangelize the world.

In 1854 John C. Lowrie, now working as an assistant secretary under his father at the New York offices of the Board of Foreign Missions, wrote a comprehensive *Manual of Missions* which articulates the vision of global evangelism and quantifies the Presbyterian work to that point. His opening paragraph introduces the sense of energy and commitment that was propelling this effort. And a careful reading helps us glimpse the theological and ethical foundations of this mission work. Lowrie's book, *A Manual of Missions*, gives us a sweeping, early perspective on the great Presbyterian effort in foreign missions as it was being carried out by the fledging Board of Foreign Missions:

> The work of Christian Missions has become one of the marked features of this age. The larger bodies of Christians, and many of the smaller, have their missionary stations in various parts of the world. Large sums of money are expended for the support of missionaries, the establishment of schools, and the printing of the Holy Scriptures. Hundreds of men of superior education, and their wives, women of refined manners and cultivated minds, have gone to live among the Indians of our western forests, the Negroes, and the Hottentots of Africa, the Hindus and the Chinese, the Feejeeans [sic] and others in the islands of the sea; they and their families are found living far from their early homes, in unfriendly climes, amongst rude and debased tribes, and patiently laboring year after year to instruct the ignorant, and convert the depraved and degraded people around them. This stands out to public view.[13]

---

13. Ibid., 5.

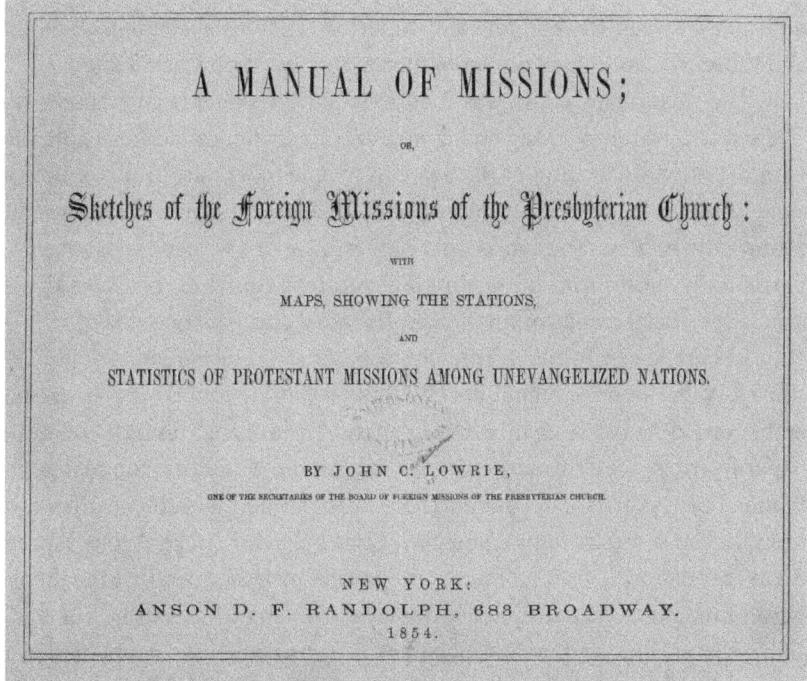

The title page of John Lowrie's *Manual of Missions*.

In this introductory essay of his *Manual of Missions*, Lowrie mentions the strategy of the foreign missions of his day as evangelism, the building of schools and the translation of the Scriptures into the native languages. In addition to these practical strategies, Lowrie hints at the important cultural biases that were being carried forth by the missionaries and the sending churches. The missionaries and their culture were refined and superior; the foreign peoples to whom the missionaries were sent were "rude," "debased," "depraved" and "degraded." This common perception of the moral and social difference between the sending societies and the receiving societies is the foundation of the concept of "heathen" which informed the whole era of the great missionary movement in the nineteenth century. The missionaries, with abundant support from their churches, were going to seek, convert and save the heathen people. The word itself is very common in the early missionary literature. The missionary movement benefited from this clear and clean distinction between those who were living in the light and those still in darkness, between those who had received the gospel and those who had not, between the enlightened, superior missionary-sending societies and those to whom this mission of mercy and salvation was directed.

The missionary effort was a comprehensive intellectual framework. There was certainly a strong eschatological dimension concerned explicitly with the eternal salvation of the heathen people to whom the missionaries were sent. But this primary concern with preaching a saving faith does not capture the fullness of the missionary enterprise. The western missionaries, particularly those from the mainline Protestant churches, considered the moral and social results of mission work a vital consequence as well.

Robert Speer, in his lecture commemorating the missionary leadership of Walter Lowrie, highlights Lowrie's reflections concerning the moral and social dimension of missionary work. Speer cites a long theological paper from 1830, *A Treatise on Divine Revelation*, which was found among Walter Lowrie's personal papers. The treatise argued that the heathen nations lacked a moral foundation for social behavior because they lacked divine revelation. This is an important point; Lowrie argued that the theology of mission did not simply rest on hope of an eternal salvation. The mission effort included a theological commitment to creating a moral and just society. Speaking of the heathen nations, Lowrie reflected, "The Egyptians, Greeks, and Romans were enlightened and civilized nations, but without divine revelation. There we find them grossly ignorant of the most vital and important truths." For Lowrie it was not simplistically that the foreign nations lacked civilization or a social organization. He knew that many of the heathen nations had a sophisticated social structure and organization. But even the most advanced society could not know the truth and could not promote moral living if it did not have the gift of divine revelation in Jesus Christ. "Hence, their morals were corrupt and corresponded with the moral darkness of the mind. It could not be otherwise. Man is a creature actuated by motives. But where was the motive for holiness, for purity of heart and life, when holiness and the worship of the heart were not known. It is remarkable also that the most civilized and barbarous nations were nearly alike in their ignorance of divine things and in their moral depravity of conduct."[14]

Walter's son, John Lowrie, in his *Manual for Mission*, also sought to articulate a full, straightforward theological summary for mission work. Foreign mission work was inspired by God. The work of foreign missions

---

14. Speer, *Studies of Missionary Leadership*, 30.

was "nothing lower nor later than the eternal love and purpose of God." This theological foundation within the eternal purpose of God also defined the purpose of the church. The church was created and formed by God exactly for this purpose; to bring the gospel to all people.

> The invitation is now sent forth, among the Heathen, Mohammedans, Jews, and all others, "Look unto me and be ye saved, all the ends of the earth." He that believeth shall be saved; he that believeth not is condemned already. The Church has been established among men, and her ministers and members have received the means of grace for their own salvation, and as trustees for those who are destitute. Freely they have received, freely they must give. Their agency in this work is contemplated in the divine purpose. Angels might have been employed as missionaries, but this was not the will of God. His purpose to save his people was to be fulfilled by the agency of redeemed sinners.[15]

John Lowrie seeks to arouse the church. For a biblical foundation Lowrie repeats an emphasis on the Great Commission from Matthew chapter 28; this passage was earlier claimed by William Carey as the motivation for all mission work. Lowrie understands the Great Commission as a "permanent obligation" for the church. Thus the "missionary spirit" was an essential characteristic of the primitive church; so it must be today. Of course, the Apostle Paul was the oft-cited example of missionary passion. According to the witness of the New Testament, even though the church itself was "few in numbers, feeble in resources, in the midst of a heathen city" there was, nonetheless, a powerful missionary effort. "She scattered, and yet increased. The faith, and love, and devotedness of her own members were strengthened by their missionary labors." Thus for Lowrie and his generation of missionary leaders, a unique era had arrived, inspired by God, and now the church was poised for great things. A special, providential confluence of events was motivating a powerful new commitment to foreign missions.

> The changes among the nations of the earth within the last twenty years have removed many barriers to the spread of the gospel, and opened doors which had been closed for centuries. The wonderful progress of commerce is tributary to the progress of missions. The steam printing-press, the steam railway-coach, the ocean steam-ship, and the electric telegraph, are all servants of the God

---

15. Lowrie, *Manual of Missions*, 5.

of missions, and tend greatly to promote the interests of the missionary work. Christian and pagan nations are now brought into close relationship.[16]

In 1913 Robert Speer delivered his Smyth Lecture concerning the missionary leadership of Walter Lowrie; Walter Lowrie had retired and died in 1868. Thus Speer's lecture was a historical reflection looking back almost fifty years earlier at the work of the Board of Foreign Missions. In his lecture Speer offered revealing hints at some of the significant strategic shifts in Presbyterian mission work since Lowrie's era of leadership with the Board of Foreign Missions. Speer mentions three particular categories of mission work with which Walter Lowrie was greatly concerned but which had fallen completely out of the purview of the board by 1914. The first was "Indian work" which had "now ceased" as a focus of the board. By 1914, Native Americans were no longer considered a foreign mission field due to the expansion of the United States and the, at times unjust and cruel, assimilation of the native people. Moreover, the Native Americans were generally living in areas surrounded by established, well-defined states since the United States government had aggressively created and enforced the concept of reservations. Native Americans as a foreign nation receiving foreign mission was thus an abandoned strategy. On a more positive note, the mission work with Native Americans was absorbed within the General Assembly's Board of Home Missions and thus not considered a foreign mission concern.

In the time between Walter Lowrie's retirement in 1868 and Speer's reflection on his long career in 1914, the Board of Foreign Missions had abandoned, secondly, an interest in mission work to Roman Catholics in "Papal Europe" and, thirdly, any mission effort directed at Jews. In these shifts there are glimpses of theological revision. The stark duality between those who had received the gospel and those who had not was nuanced a bit with time. The relationship between Protestants and Roman Catholics shifted and developed significantly over the generations since the Protestant Reformation; and these developments always take on a local and provincial character. Clearly, by 1914 Roman Catholics in Europe were no longer considered an appropriate focus for Presbyterian foreign mission work. In similar ways but for different reasons, Jews were no longer considered an appropriate target for mission work and evangelism. These changes, over many years, demonstrate subtle ways that the theological basis for foreign

16. Ibid., 7.

mission work was revised and reformed. These shifting perceptions and attitudes toward Native Americans, Roman Catholics and Jews offer a clear vision of these slow developments and theological reforms.[17]

In 1854, John Lowrie published his *Manual of Missions* as an educational piece for the Church. He sought, first of all, to explain the biblical and theological motivation for foreign mission work. As one of the assistant secretaries in the office of the Board of Missions, Lowrie also offered a statistical summary of all the foreign mission work with which the Presbyterian Church was then engaged, including maps marking the mission stations, statistics on the number and location of the missionaries, and some comparative statistics with other denominations. Published in the middle decade of the nineteenth century and after the Board of Foreign Mission's first twenty years of work as an organized mission agency within the General Assembly, Lowrie's summary is a helpful snapshot of the work of the Presbyterian Church. Lowrie's *Manual of Missions* is an vital resource in our consideration of the earliest days of the Presbyterian mission enterprise.

Missions to West Africa

Lowrie includes a lengthy discussion of "Missions in Western Africa." Of course, in 1854 when Lowrie published his *Manual*, the United States were beginning to roil concerning the question of slavery. The Civil War was only a decade away and the question of slavery as a theological and biblical issue was dividing the churches; lines were being drawn which would become schisms in all of the national, mainline Protestant denominations, including the Presbyterian Church. Lowrie's discussion of foreign missions in Africa necessarily delved into this quagmire about slavery. Lowrie's *Manual for Missions* seems to officially represent the views of the Board of Foreign Missions, which is not surprising given his position on staff and his father's position as corresponding secretary. It is significant that Lowrie included in his summary of the board's work in Africa a decisively antislavery tone. With passionate language Lowrie rejects slavery and

> all the cruelty, oppression, and loss of life which follow in the train of the horrible traffic in slaves, so long characteristic of this part of the world. The marauding excursions, the midnight attacks on sleeping villages, the burning houses, the screams of terror from helpless women and children, the murder of aged and

---

17. Speer, *Studies of Missionary Leadership*, 37.

feeble persons, the breaking up of families, the savage treatment of captives, the hurrying and cruel march to the sea-coast, the heartless foreigners, the horrors of the middle passage—these are scenes better worthy of hell than of earth, and the actors in them should be one the devils themselves. Yet, alas for human nature in its fallen state! these doings of our fellow-men, who have the same passion with ourselves . . . A better day is now dawning on this dark land. Varied and powerful agencies are already at work to restrain existing evils, and to set up the kingdom of righteousness and peace.[18]

Lowrie's emphasis and the work of the Board of Foreign Missions in Africa were focused on western Africa and specifically the nations of Sierra Leone and Liberia. Both of these new nations were carved out of Africa by colonial powers; both were new nations settled with returning slaves. Great Britain set up a colonial government in Sierra Leone; many former slaves who sought refuge with the British troops during the American Revolution were settled in Freetown, Sierra Leone, as early as 1787. The modern history of Sierra Leone is conflicted given the cultural and ethnic differences between the African Americans who emigrated from the United States and the many indigenous tribes. The religious landscape of Sierra Leona today is very diverse. Liberia, the nation due east of Sierra Leone, was colonized by freed slaves from the United States beginning in 1820. With the help of the American Colonization Society, Liberia was created and the new nation established a government modeled on the United States. The capital city of Monrovia was named in honor of James Monroe, the fifth president of the United States and a prominent supporter of the idea of recolonization in Africa. Although devastated by violence in the modern, postcolonial era, Liberia today has a dominant Christian majority.

In his description of these two new nations Lowrie saw great hope:

We look to both these Christian settlements, Sierra Leone and Liberia, with the deepest interest, as well adapted to repress the slave-trade and other evils, to foster legitimate commerce, and to furnish stations for missionary labor among the natives of the country; and our hopes are the more confident, because they are objects of special interest to the two great Protestant nations of our age. It must be for gracious purposes that God has planted these Christian settlements on the borders of this dark continent

---

18. Lowrie, *Manual of Missions*, 28.

and enlisted for their prosperity the sympathies and prayers of so many of his people in Great Britain and our own country.[19]

The mission work in western Africa was brutally difficult due in large part to malaria, the African fever, for which there was not yet an effective medical treatment or prophylactic.[20] The Rev. John B. Pinney, with support from the Board of Foreign Missions, arrived in Monrovia in February 1833 to make the appropriate inquiries and arrangements prior to the establishment of a full mission station. Rev. Pinney returned to the States, itinerated throughout the church raising support, and departed again as a part of a larger, permanent mission team which included Rev. and Mrs. John Laird, Rev. and Mrs. John Cloud and Mr. James Temple, "a colored young man, who was a candidate for the ministry." Tragedy struck; within months Rev. and Mrs. Laird and Rev. Cloud were dead from malaria. The mission continued despite the extraordinary risk of malaria. In 1839 Rev. Oren K. Canfield and Mr. Jonathan P. Alward joined the mission in Monrovia; both were dead within a year.[21] The mission continued.[22]

The Presbyterians, of course, were not the only mission agency. The Protestant mission effort into western Africa was massive: "The English Baptist, Episcopal, and Wesleyan Societies, the Scotch United Presbyterian, the German, the American Baptist, Congregational, Episcopal, Methodist, and Presbyterian bodies are all engaged in missionary work in Western Africa. They support over one hundred ministers of the gospel at various

---

19. Ibid., 29.

20. "The most serious obstacle to missionary labor in this part of the world is the unhealthiness of the country to foreigners." Ibid., 30.

21. Lowrie lists and describes many of the Presbyterian missionaries who served in western Africa including the Rev. and Mrs. Robert Sawyer, the Rev. Thomas Wilson, the Rev. James M. Priest, Mr. Washington McDonough, "a colored teacher," the Rev. James M. Connelly, the Rev. Harrison W. Ellis, "a colored man, formerly a slave, who with his family had been redeemed from bondage by Christian friends in the South," Mr. H. W. Erskine, "a colored teacher and licentiate preacher," and Mr. B. V. R. James, "another colored teacher, who had been for some years under the patronage of a Society of ladies in New York for promoting education in Africa," the Rev. and Mrs. David A. Wilson, the Rev. and Mrs. James L. Mackey, the Rev. and Mrs. George W. Simpson, the Rev. J. Leighton Wilson, the Rev. and Mrs. Edwin T. Williams and the Rev. and Mrs. William Clemens. Lowrie, *Manual of Missions*, 31–33. See also Presbyterian Heritage Center, Biographical Index of Missionaries, www.phcmontreat.org.

22. Churches in western Africa today are prolific. For one example of a successor denomination, see the Evangelical Church of West Africa, recently renamed the Evangelical Church Winning All, at www.ecwa.org.ng.

stations, with a considerable number of assistant missionaries. Over 13,000 communicants, including about 1,000 in Liberia who are most of American birth."[23]

Mission in North India

In his *Manual for Mission*, the chapter on "Missions in North India" was more personal to John Lowie. He and his wife, Louisa, had served there and she died soon after they arrived in 1833. In addition to his summary of the Missions in North India in the *Manual for Missions*, Lowrie also wrote a book-length reflection on his experience, *Two Years in Upper India*. Including the early, prominent and influential work of William Carey, the Protestant mission effort into India was immense and sustained, supported in part by the British colonial administration and a growing and lucrative trade promoted by the British East India Company. The foreign mission work into India was one of the earliest and largest of the Presbyterian Board of Foreign Missions. Before his careful and personal description of the Presbyterian effort, Lowrie summarized the whole British and American Protestant effort in India:

> From carefully-collected statistics published last year in Calcutta, it appeared that there were in India, at the beginning of the year 1852, missionaries connected with twenty-two European and American Societies, to the number of four hundred and forty-three, of who forty-eight were native ministers; nearly seven hundred native catechists; three hundred and thirty-one churches, containing over eighteen thousand native communicants, with over one hundred thousand native Christians, not communicants; upwards of thirteen hundred vernacular schools, in which nearly forty-eight thousand boys; and one hundred and two similar schools, with over twenty-seven hundred native girls; one hundred and twenty-six superior day-schools for education in English, with nearly fifteen thousand boys and young men; and three hundred and forty-seven day-schools for girls, containing nearly twelve thousand scholars—in all making over eighty thousand Hindu children and youth receiving a more or less thorough Christian education.[24]

23. Lowrie, *Manual of Missions*, 30.
24. Lowrie, *Manual of Missions*, 39.

In addition to the emphasis on education, all the missions focused on language study, translation, and printing. Lowrie reported that "twenty-five printing-presses are maintained in India by Missionary Societies; and the Bible has been translated into ten languages, the New Testament into five others, and separate Gospels into four others."[25] This translation work is a remarkable accomplishment.

In his description of "Missions in North India" Lowrie wrote with a typical tone of cultural and religious superiority. This tone defined the understanding of all non-Christian cultures as heathen. He described and dismissed the Hindu religion, including the "pernicious" system of caste. He sought to rally the Presbyterian churches throughout the United States to support this work by defining clearly the profound difference the Christian faith, when planted by our missionaries, will make in the lives of the Indian people.

> Their hope of better circumstances depends on Christianity. This will set them free from idolatry and superstition, which now consume much of their time and property. It will break the yoke of caste and allow scope for enterprise. It will substitute the holy day of rest for numerous festivals, demoralizing and expensive. It will teach them truth, integrity, contentment, domestic happiness, so needful to all men, but especially to the poor. Religion will then be their best support, instead of being, as it surely is now, their greatest burden.[26]

American Presbyterian missions in India started in 1833 when Rev. and Mrs. John C. Lowrie and Rev. and Mrs. William Reed arrived. With advice from British missionaries, they choose the city of Lodiana[27] on the Sutlej River in the remote northwestern part of the country for the site of their mission.[28] Mrs. Lowrie and Rev. Reed died in the first year; Mrs. Reed traveled home. In 1835 the Rev. and Mrs. James Wilson and the Rev. and Mrs. John Newton arrived in Lodiana; in 1836 John Lowrie returned home in grief and poor health. The third company of missionaries reached Calcutta in March 1836. In his description of this mission work, Lowrie writes with an exuberant attitude of growth, progress and development. A church was organized at Lodiana in 1837. Rev. McEwen and his wife established

25. Ibid.
26. Ibid., 35.
27. Today the name of this city is spelled "Ludhiana."
28. Lowrie, *Manual of Missions*, 39–45.

a church in Allahabad in 1838. Two new mission stations were formed, Saharunpur, southeast from Lodiana, and Sabathu, northeast. Presbyterian missionaries supported by the Board of Foreign Missions were arriving in waves every year.[29] In 1841 churches were organized at Saharunpur and Futtehguhr. Of course, Presbyterian missionaries from the United States organized Presbyterian structures in India; in 1842 three presbyteries were organized each named for their central city, Lodiana, Furrukhabad, and Allahabad. Soon a commitment to native leadership emerged. In 1843 two Indian ministry candidates, Golok Nath and Gopeenath Nundy, were licensed by their presbyteries. By 1845 the congregations and presbyteries had organized themselves further and the first meeting of the Synod of North India was held at Futtehgurh. Soon new mission stations were formed at Agra, Jalandar, Ambala and Lahore. Mr. Forman planted a small school in Lahore which grew to become one of the most influential schools of higher education in India, Forman Christian College.[30] By 1852 the total number of church members reported at the meeting of the Synod of North India[31] was 231. Writing in 1853, John Lowrie concludes his report on *Missions in North India* with a hopeful note, "The work of the missions continued to be carried forward with fidelity and zeal."

29. In 1836: the Rev. and Mrs. James R. Campbell, the Rev. and Mrs. James McEwen, Mrs. Jesse M. Jamieson, Mr. and Mrs. William S. Rogers and Mr. and Mrs. Joseph Porter. In 1838: the Rev. and Mrs. Henry R. Wilson Jr., the Rev. and Mrs. John H. Morrison, the Rev. and Mrs. Joseph Caldwell, Mr. James Craig, teacher, with his wife and Mr. Reese Morris, printer, with his wife. In 1839: the Rev. and Mrs. Joseph Warren, Mr. and Mrs. John E. Freeman, Mr. and Mrs. James L. Scott. (See Rev. Joseph Warren, DD, *A Glance Backward at Fifteen Years of Missionary Life in North India*, 1856). In 1840: the Rev. and Mrs. John C. Rankin, the Rev. and Mrs. William H. McAuley, the Rev. Joseph Owen and Miss Jane Vanderveer, teacher. In 1842: the Rev. and Mrs. Levi Janvier, the Rev. and Mrs. John Wray. In 1847: the Rev. and Mrs. Augustus H. Seeley, the Rev. and Mrs. David Irving and Mr. Robert M. Munnis, "licentiate preacher." In January 1848: the Rev. and Mrs. A. Alexander Hodge, the Rev. Charles W. Forman. In 1850: the Rev. and Mrs. James H. Orbison, the Rev. and Mrs. David E. Campbell; the Rev. and Mrs. Roberts S. Fullerton, the Rev. and Mrs. Lawrence G. Hay, Mr. and Mrs. Horatio W. Shaw. In 1852: the Rev. and Mrs. Robert E. Williams.

30. See Forman Christian College at www.fccollege.edu.pk.

31. For the successor denomination, see the Church of North India at www.cni-synod.org.

Mission in Siam[32]

As was common in the era in which John Lowrie was writing his *Manual of Missions*, there was a systematic understanding throughout the Protestant churches of the superiority of Christianity and the utter falseness of other religions. This theology of mission motivated the push for foreign missions. The understanding that the people living in heathen lands would benefit in countless ways from the Christian message was a sacrosanct and unquestioned dimension of Protestant Christianity in the middle of the nineteenth century. Thus Lowrie's description of the religion of the Siamese rings with this tone theological supremacy: "The religion of the Siamese is Buddhism, which may be characterized as a kind of atheistical idolatry."[33] A deep, theological compassion for the people living with what was considered a false and destructive religion motivated our foreign missions. "It is one of the reasons for regarding Siam with special interest as a missionary field, that it is the head-quarters of this widely-spread system of false religion, so far as this bad preeminence can be assigned to any country."[34]

The work of the Board of Foreign Missions in Siam was small and difficult. The Rev. and Mrs. William P. Buell arrived in Bangkok in August 1840 but were compelled by poor health to return home in 1844. The Rev. and Mrs. Stephen Mattoon arrived in March 1847 and were joined by Dr. Samuel R. House, MD, licentiate preacher, and the Rev. and Mrs. Stephen Bush arrived in Bangkok in April 1849. Complicating the mission was a very antagonistic relationship with the king, who ruled Siam with dictatorial power. The missionaries could not find housing because the king was against any foreign teachers and none of the common people would rent or share their property out of fear of retribution from the king. Several missionaries were temporarily imprisoned. In 1851 the king died and his successor was friendly to the missionaries and housing for the missionaries was acquired. The work of the small missionary team continued. Lowrie wrote a hopeful conclusion: "With the single exception of the embarrassment growing out of their small number, the missionaries have reason to be much encouraged in their work and its prospects. They are permitted to preach the gospel in stated services and by the way-side; and the Word has not been preached in vain. Besides the testimony thereby held forth for

---

32. Today Siam is named Thailand.
33. Lowrie, *Manual of Missions*, 46.
34. Ibid., 47.

God and against idols, and the secret convictions and impressions of many hearers, which may yet result in the open confession of Christ before men, two hopeful converts have been admitted to the church."[35]

Missions in China

As John Lowrie was writing his *Manual for Missions* the mission field in China was just beginning to open up. "The largest field of modern missions is China; and unlike India, China is a country in which nearly the whole work of evangelization is yet to be performed." Lowrie in complimenting the refined Chinese civilization makes a subtle distinction between a barbarous race and a heathen race. The Chinese, given the sophisticated development of their civilization were not a barbarous people. But because they did not yet have the gospel of Jesus Christ they remained a heathen people. These fine distinctions informed the theology of mission undergirding the Board of Foreign Missions.

> The Chinese may take a high rank as a civilized people. They have a government, a literature, many social usages, numerous industrial occupations, cities, roads, bridges, canals, boats—all indicating a state of society far removed from that of a barbarous race. Their silk fabrics, their ivory and wood carving, the beautiful works of their potteries, their being the first to discover and to use the art of printing, the compass, and gunpowder, entitle them to a place among the cultivated nations. The last example just cited, and the theatrical exhibitions which are held in high esteem among them, show that their civilization is that of our fallen nature, not of a race harmless and pure. The civilization of the Chinese wants altogether the great element of Christianity.[36]

Like the Protestant mission work in India, the missionaries to China followed the British military presence. The Protestant missionaries, at first, were included in the general suspicion the Chinese government held for the British. Thus initially no mission sites were permitted on the mainland. In 1838 the first Presbyterian missionaries, the Rev. and Mrs. Robert W. Orr and the Rev. and Mrs. John A. Mitchell, under the Board of Foreign

---

35. Ibid., 48. The Church of Christ in Thailand is the largest Protestant denomination in Thailand today. This denomination traces its history back to the first American Presbyterian missionaries.

36. Ibid., 51.

Missions' strategy for China, could only establish an initial presence on Singapore. Here the Chinese teacher whom Rev. Orr had employed to begin his immersion in their language was baptized in 1839, the first Presbyterian convert among the Chinese. After the first Opium War between the British and Chinese ended with the Treaty of Nanking in 1842, the Chinese coastal cities were opened. The board determined to establish three mission sites: Canton, Amoy, and Ningpo.[37] Soon Presbyterian missionaries started arriving with an emphasis on evangelism and medical care.[38]

A vital aspect of the Protestant mission effort into China was the desire of the missionaries to learn the many dialects, translate the Scriptures into those dialects, and provide Bibles. The Presbyterian Church was solidly behind this objective and significantly contributed to the task of translation and printing. This was challenging, difficult work complicated by the structure of the Chinese language which is composed of an estimated thirty thousand characters. The Chinese had a sophisticated and ancient system of printing using woodblocks. Although meticulous and beautiful, this system was not suited to the mass production of large texts like the Bible. An ordinary printing press of the day working in the English language only needed fifty-six individual metallic types. It would be an impossible task to render an individual metallic type for each Chinese character. Working with a remarkable degree of harmony and cooperation among themselves, the Protestant missionaries discovered a solution within the Chinese language itself. Lowrie described this discovery: "It turns on the distinction between formatives and primitives in the Chinese language, and between the divisible and the indivisible characters. The divisible are reduced to their simplest elements, and being struck off as types, can be re-composed in different characters, so that a comparatively small number of types will

---

37. Today the city name is spelled Ningbo.

38. In 1838: the Rev. and Mrs. Robert W. Orr and the Rev. John A. Mitchell. In 1840: the Rev. and Mrs. Thomas L. McBryde. In 1841 Dr. and Mrs. James C. Hepburn, MD. In 1842: Rev. Walter M. Lowrie. In 1844 Dr. D. B. McCartee, MD, Mr. Richard Cole, a printer, and his wife, the Rev. and Mrs. Richard Q. Way, the Rev. and Mrs. M. Simpson Culbertson, the Rev. and Mrs. Augustus W. Loomis. In 1845: the Rev. Hugh A. Brown. In 1846: the Rev. and Mrs. William Speer, Mr. John B. French, Rev. John W. Quarterman. In 1848: the Rev. and Mrs. Joseph K. Wight, the Rev. and Mrs. Henry V. Rankin. In1849: Mr. and Mrs. Moses S. Coulter, "having been appointed to take charge of the press at Ningpo." In 1850: the Rev. and Mrs. Samuel N. Martin, the Rev. and Mrs. William P. Martin. In 1852: the Rev. and Mrs. John Byers, Miss. Juana M. Knight, to a "female boarding school in Ningpo." In 1853: the Rev. and Mrs. John Nevius, the Rev. and Mrs. Charles F. Preston, Dr. and Mrs. J. G. Kerr, MD. In 1854: the Rev. and Mrs. Reuben Lowrie.

serve to express most the characters in common use." With this discovery of the way to reduce the Chinese characters to a manageable number of types, the Board of Foreign Missions had the forms made in Paris, at a cost of five thousand dollars, which could be used to create the types. With these types available, large print jobs using "stereotype plates on improved presses" were possible. The Board of Foreign Missions established a printing house at the Ningpo mission site; by 1845 "upwards of 3,500,000 pages were printed."[39] Providing the Bible in the native Chinese language may be the most significant and transformative contribution of the Protestant missionaries.

In May 1865, Walter Lowrie submitted his resignation as the corresponding secretary of the Presbyterian Board of Foreign Missions. At over eighty years old, Lowrie pleaded that he could no longer make the journeys which the office required and did not have the stamina for the demanding office work. The Executive Board adopted a gracious resolution appreciating and thanking Lowrie for his thirty-two years of service. The full General Assembly of the Presbyterian Church made a similar resolution at its meeting in 1865:

> Resolved, That we take great pleasure in recording our high appreciation of the invaluable services of the retiring Secretary, the Hon. Walter Lowrie, and we tender to him our heartfelt thanks and sympathy, praying that the Gospel he has striven for so many years to make known to the perishing may be his all-sufficient consolation in his declining years; and that, in God's own good time, he may have an abundant entrance ministered to him into the everlasting kingdom of our Lord and Saviour Jesus Christ.[40]

Future directions for discussion, study and prayer:
- Because of the great missionary movement, we know that Christian faith has now spread around the world. The church exists in every country in the world. How does the reality that Christianity is now

---

39. Lowrie, *Manual of Missions*, 54. The commitment to study and print the Chinese language was directly motivated by Walter Lowrie, the corresponding secretary of the Board of Foreign Missions. Walter Lowrie had himself studied Chinese and acquired fluency enough to translate simple Chinese texts. Moreover, he understood the challenge which the Chinese language presented to translation. He encouraged the innovative and expensive task of creating movable metallic types in Chinese. His leadership significantly contributed to the success of printing the Bible in Chinese. See ibid., 25.

40. Lowrie, *Memoirs*, 169.

a truly global faith influence your discipleship and service in Jesus Christ?

- Do you feel yourself connected to a truly global Christianity?
- In what ways does your local congregation witness to and participate in a global Christianity?
- What do you believe is the legacy of the long litany of missionaries who served during the great era of the missionary movement?

CHAPTER 7

Robert Speer

ROBERT ELLIOTT SPEER (1867–1947) grew up in a devout Presbyterian family in Huntingdon, Pennsylvania. Much later in his career he discovered that he shared this geographical heritage with the Lowrie clan. The Lowrie family, immigrants from Scotland, settled near Huntingdon for a time before moving further west to Butler, Pennsylvania. In the twilight of his long career, when he reflected on Walter Lowrie and then John Lowrie and then his own service as secretary, he felt historical connection and referred to the "apostolic succession" of their positions with the Board of Foreign Missions.[1]

Robert Speer

---

1. Piper, *Robert E. Speer*, chap. 1, "Roots: Blest Be the Tie That Binds," 3–31.

With a strong family background, with a father who led a reputable career as a lawyer in Huntingdon and was elected to the House of Representatives from Pennsylvania's Seventeenth Congressional District in 1870, with a formal education at Phillips Academy, with success at Princeton including excelling on the debate team, it would have been ordinary for Robert Speer to follow his dad's leading into a law career. But a different calling came. While at Princeton he attended a chapel service being led by Robert Wilder and John Forman who were itinerating for the fledging Student Volunteer Movement. In response, his diary tells the story of conversion and calling: "Am beginning to think more seriously on Missions." And the next day, "I decide. I shall go as a Missionary to preach and to teach." And the next day, "I am so gloriously relieved. All burden gone." He signed a Student Volunteer Movement Pledge: "I am willing and desirous, God permitting, to become a foreign missionary."[2] Many years later, speaking to the 150th General Assembly of the Presbyterian Church in 1938 Speer remembered that Robert Wilder and John Forman, "both sons of our missions in India, were the apostles who carried the appeal of the Movement to the colleges and universities of Canada and the United States. It was through them that my own doctrine of missions came. In truth I owe them my soul."[3] In pursuit of that calling, Speer enrolled at Princeton Theological Seminary. But he never finished; during his second year a different invitation came. Frank Ellinwood, one of the assistant secretaries of the Board of Foreign Missions, persuaded him to serve God as a foreign missionary through administrative work with the Presbyterian Board.[4] Speer served with the Presbyterian Board of Foreign Missions from 1891 to 1937. John Piper, who has provided a magisterial biography of Robert Speer, considered him an "outstanding missionary statesman," a description that nicely captures a remarkable career.[5]

Robert Speer arrived at the right time with some remarkably relevant personal experiences to bring together in his own mind and for the benefit of American mainline Protestantism two "distinct contexts for foreign missions."[6] With a personal history through his upbringing and with his short, but incomplete, education at Princeton Theological Seminary, Speer

2. Piper, "Development," 261.
3. Piper, *Robert E. Speer*, 34–38.
4. Piper, "Development," 262.
5. Ibid., 261.
6. Ibid., 262.

was immersed in the culture and ethos of the Presbyterian Church. His professional vocation was with the Presbyterian Board of Foreign Missions; he may be considered one of the most influential church leaders within all of mainline Protestantism, but certainly within Presbyterianism, in the twentieth century. Speer helped to bring the whole, growing, and vital heritage of Presbyterian foreign mission work forward into the twentieth century.

Speer began his stellar career with the Presbyterian Board as huge international momentum was gathering around the work of foreign missions in all the mainline denominations specifically and also for doing this work together with an ecumenical vision.[7] The Student Volunteer Movement (SVM) was a driving force behind a more shared, cooperative and ecumenical vision of foreign missions. Speer was involved throughout his career in support of the Student Volunteer Movement and from that base branched out in countless other ecumenical efforts. "A few other leaders of ecumenical foreign missions led denominational foreign missions boards, but no other denominational foreign missions board leader also shared leadership in as many and as varied ecumenical foreign missions ventures."[8]

The Student Volunteer Movement (SVM) vitalized the concept of ecumenical mission. With charismatic and enduring leadership from Methodist John Mott, a close friend and lifelong professional colleague of Robert Speer, the Student Volunteer Movement inspired a generation of college students with a passion for foreign mission.[9] Rallied by their famous watchword, "The evangelization of the world in this generation,"[10] the movement was primarily a recruiting forum which challenged young people with the importance of Christian commitment and recruited them for foreign mission service. For his work with the Student Volunteer Movement and the Young Men's Christian Association, John Mott was awarded the 1946 Nobel Peace Prize.

A vital, early, strategic decision of the Student Volunteer Movement was to focus on a strong Christian message and recruitment for mission service; SVM was never a sending agency for foreign missions. All recruits

---

7. "By 1900 the sixteen American missionary societies of the 1860s had swelled to about ninety." Hutchison, *Errand to the World*, 91.

8. Piper, *Robert E. Speer*, 111.

9. See Mott, *Decisive Hour*; see also Speer, *Non-Christian Religions*; and *Wikipedia*, s.v. "Student Volunteer Movement" and "John Mott."

10. See Robert, "Origin of the Student Volunteer Watchword"; see also Speer, "Evangelization of the World."

would be referred to the established denominational mission boards for training and sending forth.[11] Speer left a formal staff position with the SVM after only one year when he joined the Presbyterian Board of Foreign Missions in 1891. But he remained very involved with SVM as a volunteer for his whole career which fit hand-in-glove with his official board leadership with the Presbyterian Church. Speer was poised on both sides of the missionary recruitment process; as a volunteer leader with SVM he was involved with the recruitment of missionaries and as secretary of the Presbyterian Board he was involved with sending out Presbyterian missionaries. Because Speer was involved with SVM from its very first days he was often included in their important strategic decisions and questions. Given his penchant for large strategic thinking and conceptualization, Speer was an important part of the organizational development of SVM although he was not officially employed there and was not serving on their board. He served within a network of close ecumenical colleagues, including John Mott, as a consultant and advisor. Speer also was a recruiter and cheerleader for SVM. From his work with the Presbyterian Board, Speer knew the specific mission sites—their history, challenges and opportunities—all around the world. Moreover from his days with the Princeton debate team, Speer was an inspiring public speaker. Thus Speer was constantly sought as a presenter, preacher, Bible study leader, and lecturer at SVM gatherings. And Speer was prolific in this role. From the beginning, Speer spoke at every quadrennial meeting of the Student Volunteer Movement until 1936. In addition to this public role, he made himself accessible to individuals who were discerning a call to mission service.[12] At the dawn of the twentieth century, with remarkable leaders like Robert Speer, Arthur Judson Brown, and Frank Ellinwood, the Presbyterian foreign mission effort was emerging as a powerful global force.

In addition to his volunteer work on behalf of the Student Volunteer Movement, Robert Speer was a leading voice in pulling all the disparate denominational mission efforts into common conversation and strategic alignment. His work in support of the emerging Protestant ecumenical movement touched most every aspect, conversation and conference. There was a huge shifting, gathering, and winnowing of all the denominational

11. The peak recruitment year was reached in 1920 when the Student Volunteer Movement recruited 1,731 missionaries.

12. Piper, *Robert E. Speer*, 116. See also Wikipedia, s.v. "Student Volunteer Movement." In 1959, the Student Volunteer Movement was absorbed into the National Council of Churches.

foreign mission work in this era. As early as 1893, Speer was a founding member of the Interdenominational Conference of Foreign Missionary Boards and Societies in the United States and Canada. This work morphed into the Foreign Missions Conference of North America. In the international context which was mostly confined to the Protestant mission agencies of North America and Europe, Speer was one of the organizers of the Ecumenical Missionary Conference in New York in 1900, a speaker and leader at the World Missionary Conference in Edinburgh in 1910, involved with the International Missionary Council in 1921 and the Jerusalem Conference of the International Missionary Council in 1928. As the Presbyterian Board was beginning a push into Central and South America, Speer helped to conceive and create the Committee on Cooperation in Latin America.[13]

His many contributions as an administrator, an organizer and an orator in support of foreign missions were valuable, but Robert Speer was also a gifted systematic theologian of missions. Indeed, one of his most significant contributions was to push forward a concern "to develop more fully the theory of foreign missions" or what Speer named "the science of missions."[14] Speer was pondering a systematic science of missions very early in his career as he discerned the enormous energy that was emerging in all the Protestant churches in support of foreign missions. His objective was to pull the pieces together and allow all the various church foreign mission efforts to be coordinated with a common aim, principles and methods. Some of Speer's initial thoughts on a science of missions were publicly shared at the Ecumenical Missionary Conference 1900, which he had helped organize and plan.[15]

The Ecumenical Missionary Conference was a huge event in New York City, and offers of glimpse at the kind of energy and enthusiasm there was in the society at large for foreign missions in this era. More than two hundred thousand people sought to participate; thus many of the

---

13. Piper, "Development," 262. All of these different pieces of Protestant ecumenical conversation would gather, after World War II, into the World Council of Churches.

14. "The phrase, Science of Missions, was not his but belonged to the German missionary thinker Gustav Warneck of Halle University in Germany. Speer argued that a science of missions was possible because God had created one world full of souls needing redemption, despite 'distinct national peculiarities,' and because, as his journeys had revealed, mission problems were pretty much the same in every land. Such a science was needed if the missionary movement, after one hundred years of experience, was going to move forward and evangelize the world." Piper, "Development," 275.

15. See Ecumenical Missionary Conference, *Report of the Ecumenical Conference*.

venues—Carnegie Hall and neighboring church buildings—were filled to capacity for their scheduled events. An important indication of the vitality surrounding the foreign mission effort in America was the participation of President William McKinley and New York Governor Teddy Roosevelt, who both brought greetings to the opening session of the Conference meeting in Carnegie Hall. The official report of the conference describes the scene of this "National Welcome":

> In the evening Carnegie Hall was again crowded; spacious as is the auditorium, it was not large enough to accommodate half of the people who sought admittance. Within ten minutes of the opening of the doors there was not a vacant seat anywhere in the hall, and so completely filled did the standing spaces become that fully half an hour before the beginning of the exercises it was found necessary to close the entrances. Punctually at eight o'clock an outburst of cheering at the rear of the stage beckoned the approach of President McKinley.[16]

The president expressed his foreign policy in terms of missionary work, a tone many in America at that time would have found attractive. McKinley led the nation through a confrontation with Spain and ultimately victory in the Spanish-American War in 1898. In speaking to a group of Methodist church leaders, McKinley expressed his conviction that the American occupation of the Philippines was a missionary cause: "There was nothing left for us to do but to take them all, and to educate the Filipinos, and uplift and civilize and Christianize them, and by God's grace do the very best we could by them, as our fellow-men for whom Christ died."[17]

In his greetings to the Ecumenical Missionary Conference, President McKinley again strikes a tone of deep affinity with the foreign missions effort:

> I am glad of the opportunity to offer without stint my tribute of praise and respect to the missionary effort which has wrought such wonderful triumphs for civilization. The story of the Christian missions is one of thrilling interest and marvelous results. The services and the sacrifices of the missionaries for their fellow-men constitute one of the most glorious pages of the world's history. The missionary, of whatever church or ecclesiastical body, who devotes his life to the service of the Master and of men, carrying

---

16. Ecumenical Missionary Conference, *Report of the Ecumenical Conference*, 38.
17. The McKinley quote is in Noll, *History of Christianity*, 292.

the torch of truth and enlightenment, deserves the gratitude, the support, and the homage of mankind. The noble, self-effacing, willing ministers of peace and good-will should be classed with the world's heroes.[18]

As a leading spokesman for foreign missions, and representing one of the strongest denominational foreign mission agencies, Robert Speer understood the profound challenge of trying to separate the task of missionary work from everything else that was caught up with it. Thus a primary and sustained topic which Speer developed in his public speaking and writing was what he called the "aim" of foreign missions. This is a topic to which he returned repeatedly. John Piper sees the focus on the "aim" as one of the three dominant principles with which Speer was concerned in his teaching, writing and public speaking. Along with this focus on the aim of foreign missions, Speer emphasized also the superiority of the Christian religion in relation to the other religions of the world and the unity of the Christian church.[19] These three themes together form the powerful framework from which Speer's full understanding of the missionary enterprise was built. These three themes are developed and repeated numerous times in his published works. They are his bedrock principles.

For Robert Speer the work of foreign missions was not an expression of the foreign policy of the United States, or an effort to spread western civilization, or any desire to transform the social customs or practices of foreign cultures. The challenge, as Speer understood it, was to focus precisely on the aim of foreign missions. Everything else, including the results that may be hugely beneficial like public education and medical care, were extraneous and auxiliary. This challenge was enormous. In the era from the end of the Civil War to World War I, the prime years of Speer's career, the foreign mission effort of American Protestantism blossomed in remarkable expressions all around the world. But this was the same era as the mighty push of Western imperial expansion all around the world. For example, McKinley's Spanish American War resulted in the huge expansion of American influence in the Pacific region. While it was common to see the push of Protestant foreign missions and Western political imperialism as cut from the same cloth, Speer was adamant in teasing them apart. Thus he sought to clearly articulate the aim of foreign missions in and of itself.

---

18. Ecumenical Missionary Conference, *Report of the Ecumenical Conference*, 39.

19. Piper, *Robert E. Speer*, 235.

Thus when Robert Speer had an opportunity to speak at one of the largest gatherings ever assembled for a foreign missions conference, in the epic milieu of Carnegie Hall in New York City, from the same dais that was used by President McKinley, his address was titled "The Supreme and Determining Aim." Speer offered a powerful statement:

> It will help us in defining it to remind ourselves, for one thing, that we must not confuse the aim of foreign missions with the results of foreign missions . . . I read in a missionary paper a little while ago that the foreign mission that was to accomplish results of permanent value must aim at the total reorganization of the whole social fabric. This is a mischievous doctrine. We learn nothing from human history, from the experience of the Christian Church, from the example of our Lord and His apostles to justify it. They did not aim directly at such an end. They were content to aim at implanting the life of Christ in the hearts of men, and were willing to leave the consequences to the care of God. It is a dangerous thing to charge ourselves openly before the world with the aim of reorganizing States and reconstructing society . . . Missions are powerful to transform the face of society, because they ignore the face of society and deal with it at its heart. They yield powerful political and social results because they do not concern themselves with them . . . Having cleared the ground so far, what is the aim of foreign missions? For one thing, it is a religious aim. We cannot state too strongly in an age when the thought of men is full of things, and the body has crept up on the throne of the soul, that our work is not immediately and in itself a philanthropic work, a political work, a secular work of any sort whatsoever; it is a spiritual and a religious work. Of course, religion must express itself in life, but religion is spiritual life . . . The aim of foreign missions is to make Jesus Christ known to the world . . . Has not the time now come at last, for action, for great action, for a serious attempt by the whole Church to attain our aim?[20]

The paper Robert Speer presented at the Ecumenical Missionary Conference was the starting point for a much larger, theological project on mission theory which was published in 1902 as *Missionary Principles and Practice*. This is a massive work articulating Speer's science of missions laid out systematically in "Part I: General Principles Stated" and "Part II:

---

20. Speer, "Supreme and Determining Aim," in Ecumenical Missionary Conference, *Report of the Ecumenical Conference*, 74. Speer's paper was presented in Carnegie Hall, the largest and most popular of the public venues during the conference.

General Principles Applied." Within part 1, Speer included as chapter 5 "The Aim of Christian Missions," the paper he presented at the Ecumenical Missionary Conference. He develops upon this foundational "Aim" with his "Science of Missions" in the next chapter. He intended his science of missions to flow from the aim of foreign missions.

As the secretary of the Board of Foreign Missions, Speer was in constant correspondence with Presbyterian missionaries all around the globe; he knew their contexts, challenges and the character of their work. Building on an expectation that Walter Lowrie initiated as the board secretary, Speer traveled extensively to visit the missionaries under his care. He had visited missionaries in a trip around the world in 1896–97, in South America in 1909, in Asia in 1915, in Latin America in 1916, in India, Persia and China in 1921–22, to South America again in 1925, and in China, Japan and Korea in 1926. He also had extensive interaction with missionaries while traveling to ecumenical conferences in Keswick, England, Edinburgh, and Jerusalem.[21] Thus Speer's science of missions sought to constantly be in response to the situation of the missionaries in the field. Indeed, Speer notes in his preface to *Christianity and Nations*, which is the book version of the Duff Lectures, that they were "written on steamships while skirting the coasts of South America on a visit to the mission work in South American lands."[22] One of the important facts he learned during his world travels was the success of the mission effort in planting new churches.

When Robert Speer was invited to present the prestigious Duff Lectures in Edinburgh, Scotland, in 1910 we see a clear development and growth in his thinking about the aim of foreign missions. The Duff Lectures were created in commemoration of Alexander Duff, the first Church of Scotland missionary to India, who landed in Calcutta after a perilous journey that included two shipwrecks, in 1830.[23] The hype surrounding Speer's Duff lectures was particularly high given their organizational connection with the World Missionary Conference in Edinburgh in 1910.[24]

---

21. On Speer's travels as the secretary of the Board of Foreign Missions, see Piper, *Robert E. Speer*, 167–73.

22. Speer, *Christianity and the Nations*, 6.

23. See Duff, *India, and India Missions*; see also Duff, *Missions*.

24. The World Missionary Conference in Edinburgh was planned to be the largest and most inclusive missionary conference ever, including representatives from new, native churches emerging in the mission fields. Robert Speer had a prominent role at the Conference including an opening address immediately after the Archbishop of Canterbury. See Stanley, *World Missionary Conference, Edinburgh 1910*.

The organizers sought to connect these two events given the significant and expensive travel necessary for many people to attend the Conference. Thus the Duff lectures were scheduled for the January and February of 1910 prior to the start of the World Missionary Conference in June. The lectureship traditionally was given at the Universities in Edinburgh, Aberdeen and Glasgow. But given Speer's prominence, in addition to those venues more lectures were scheduled as well as events with smaller groups associated with the Student Volunteer Movement in Scotland, in which Speer had a famous reputation.[25]

Once again in the Duff Lectures the question of "missionary aim" is a priority concern. Although his explication of the missionary aim continues the precise definition he articulated at the Ecumenical Missionary Conference in New York in 1900, and published as *Missionary Principles and Practice*, there is an important addition in the Duff Lectures:

> What, then is the supreme and determining aim of foreign missions? It is something religious, and it is something as near the vital and living core of religion as can possibly be. It must include that and as little beside that as is possible. It is to make Christ known to the world with a view to real results, for time, as well as for eternity, and to the incorporation of these results in living national character. In other words, the aim of missions includes three things—first, the proclamation of Christ; second, the salvation of men, and third, the naturalization of Christianity.[26]

Speer knew firsthand the success of the missionary movement around the world planting new, indigenous churches. Thus his explication of the missionary aim in the Duff lectures expanded to include the planting of native Christian churches. The planting and emergence of native churches is referred to as "naturalization." "Its aim is not to impose our Western systems of theology or our Western forms of Church government upon the converts who may be gathered upon the mission field. It is to make Christ known to these peoples, to bring together those who accept him, and to establish them in indigenous organizations which will take their own forms and come to their own statements of the truth of Christianity, as wrought out in their own study of the Bible and their own Christian experience."[27]

---

25. Piper, *Robert E. Speer*, 203.
26. Speer, *Christianity and the Nations*, 60.
27. Ibid., 66.

Speer's Duff lectures adamantly pressed home the importance of encouraging the native churches to find their own way. He describes in great detail the challenge of this approach with specific examples from mission sites all around the world. The challenges in one context were very different from those in another. The articulation of universal principles for mission work seemed daunting given the scope of this global effort. But Speer pressed. He gave name, in a very public forum and with all the status of his position, to a method of missionary work that seemed easy to express in theory but was nagged with difficult realities on the ground at the actual mission sites. Speer worked to articulate the challenge of this approach to his audience in Scotland and throughout his career. How can the missionaries plant the Christian church without then controlling its form, function and style? When does support for a fledgling new church include an unbearable cultural expectation of the way things must be? How is the gospel proclaimed and shared without the accompanying cultural accoutrements of the missionary? How quickly should the native Christians take responsibility for their own spiritual life in Christ and the work of their churches? Once a native church is established how shall the missionary relate to it? Speer insisted that his audience understand the full complexity of these issues. He pushed his point rhetorically: "Should foreign money be used for the employment of native agents? Should pastors be given to churches unable to support them in whole or in part? Should men be employed whom the native Church, if it were in charge, would not employ, or for salaries which the native Church would not pay, or for work which it would not do? Should church buildings be erected for the people?"[28]

As early as 1882 John Livingston Nevius and his wife, Presbyterian missionaries in China, had struggled with these same issues and named the same goals which Speer would later adopt. Nevius articulated a "new system." "The interest which has been taken in our work in central Shantung by missionaries in other provinces is due no doubt to the fact that we have to some extent adopted new principles and methods," Nevius wrote at the start of his book explaining his new system.[29] Nevius knew the challenge in an intimate, daily way over many years in mission service planting a native church in China. In a long letter back to the Board of Foreign Missions he reflected, "I could easily supply from my stations an equally large number of men, and use private means to support them; and such a course would

28. Ibid., 137.
29. Nevius, *Planting and Development*, 7.

no doubt give an impulse to my work; but I do doubt the desirableness of such a course that I do not dare adopt it. I intend, trusting God's help and guidance, to try to work on the principles of self-support and self-propagation, which has thus far more than answered my expectations."[30] The Nevius Plan emerged out of the context of their work in China in response to a long pattern of mission work. Thus the results of this new system were ambiguous within the Chinese context since different mission stations were at different places concerning the ability to change patterns and models. But when the Presbyterian initiated a mission effort into Korea the Nevius Plan was incorporated from the start as the strategy for church planting. The historical record is clear that the Presbyterian Church in the Korean context thrived.

The method Speer was highlighting as a vital aspect of the aim of missions had been lived and breathed long before by Nevius and others. The aim was the formation of self-supporting, self-propagating and self-governing Christian churches. This became the goal, and Speer explored every nuance and challenge, every possible objection and criticism, as he pushed the missionary movement to understand clearly this aim. In the Duff Lectures this challenge is directed at both the missionary movement and the native churches:

> The missionary movement would fain see far less of imitation and far more inward acceptance of the real principle of a new life. Our lament is not that the Eastern Churches are thinking for themselves, but that they are not thinking for themselves, that they are not working out fresh theological statements on the basis of an adequate critical study of the growth of Christian doctrine, a new search of the Scriptures, and their own new experience of God in Christ. The missionary movement is left to bear too great a burden. Its aim is to be rid of this burden, to build up native Churches which will themselves carry this burden, which will deal with their own apologetic problems, work out their own institutions, support their own activities, and evangelise their own lands; in one word, to establish independent, national Churches.[31]

This aim of missions had to be distinct and separate from whatever movements Western political imperialism was making all around the globe in the same era. The brilliance of Robert Speer was his ability not only to

---

30. Nevius, *Life of John Livingston Nevius*, 404.
31. Speer, *Christianity and the Nations*, 73.

create tremendous enthusiasm and support for the work of foreign missions but, more importantly, to help the cheering people in his churches to understand the full complexity and sophistication of this work. He helped the Christians at home mature and grow by teaching that we must treat the new native churches with reverence and respect.

For the first two decades of the twentieth century the Protestant foreign mission effort thrived globally and the Presbyterian Board of Foreign Missions, under the leadership of Robert Speer, was a leader. The Board of Foreign Missions published a comprehensive annual report each year. We may arbitrarily study the report from 1920 to understand the depth and breadth that this mission work has achieved. The board's report highlighted these particular mission efforts:

1) The steadfastness of the native Christians in China during the year of political and industrial unrest . . .
2) We express our unmingled sympathy with the Korean Christians under the persecutions and restrictions to they have been subjected . . .
3) We note with satisfaction the substantial progress in the enlarged opportunities of our work in Japan . . .
4) We note with grateful praise and appreciation the work and progress of our Missions in Africa and in India . . .
5) We respectfully commend the faith and heroic sacrifice of our missionaries in Persia and Syria . . .
6) We note the continued progress in Siam and in our South American fields . . . and the native Christians in Mexico.
7) We note with interest the continuing development of the natives of the Philippines. . .

We would report that the foreign missionaries of the Presbyterian Church now number 1,428 and 6,856 native workers, that 4,534 congregations with 178,229 communicants and 417,529 adherents have been gathered and that 78,733 young men and women have been trained for Christian life and service in the 2,034 school, colleges and universities of the Board, that nine printing presses issued last year 100,669,579 pages of Christian literature and the Word of God, that 175 hospitals and dispensaries treated 693,498 patients, and set before them by work and by life the message of the Gospel.[32]

32. *Eighty-Third Annual Report*, 5.

Despite the remarkable growth of the Presbyterian mission enterprise under the leadership of Robert Speer, storms of controversy soon arose.

Future directions for discussion, study and prayer:

In his Duff Lectures in Scotland, Robert Speer reiterated his conviction that the aim of Christian missions was to make Christ known, to bring together those who accept him, and to encourage indigenous organizations of the new Christians.

- How does your experience with or participation in world mission work today compare with Speer's aim?
- What do you believe should be the aim and purpose of the church's world mission work today?

CHAPTER 8

Robert Speer versus William Hocking

IN THE 1930S WILLIAM Hocking and John D. Rockefeller Jr. joined forces and together swung the trajectory of the foreign mission movement toward a more liberal, modernist stance. Professor William Hocking (1873–1966), an active Christian in the Congregationalist Church, started his teaching career at Andover Theological Seminary. He had written his Ph.D. at Harvard and he returned there in 1914 as the Alford Professor of Natural Religion, Moral Philosophy and Civil Polity. He spent the remainder of this professional career at Harvard. His youthful vocational interests were in the direction of engineering which indicates the practical bent of his mind. His eminent career as a philosopher followed in the empirical school of William James with its emphasis on personal experience and practice.

William Hocking

Robert Speer versus William Hocking

Hocking's book *The Meaning of God in Human Experience* was a "minor classic in the liberal Protestant tradition."[1] Initially published in 1912, the book went through fourteen printings until a new edition, with a new foreword and preface by the author, was published by Yale University Press in 1962; a fifty-year run for a book of philosophy. We can see clearly in the first paragraph of Hocking's book how far away it is from the doctrines of Presbyterian fundamentalists:

> We are proposing to reach some definite conclusion about the nature and worth of religion—what it consists of in the way of experience, belief, and action; what comes of it in the way of support, outlook, and actual productiveness. As to the nature of religion, we are proposing especially to enquire how much it is concerned with theoretical propositions to be believed, metaphysical assertions, doctrines about unseen things and things past and to come—in short, how far the intellect is involved; how far, on the other hand, religion appeals to something in us deeper than intellect—to faith, to feeling, to the subconscious, to the instinctive, to the essential will.[2]

When a book of this genre is brought into conversation with Presbyterians of a more fundamentalist inclination a clash is inevitable. Hocking was interested in creating theology out of reflection on human experience. This is a worthy project in the pragmatist tradition of American philosophy, with William James as the archetype. But for Christian fundamentalists who were proclaiming the unique and eternal revelation of God in Jesus Christ, Hocking's full pragmatist direction is anathema. We are thus introduced to the challenge which the Presbyterian foreign missions effort faced and which Robert Speer was required to adjudicate. In the 1930s a liberal and pragmatic direction, led by people like Hocking and Rockefeller, was pulling the movement one way. On the other side a strong fundamentalist conviction was pulling the foreign missions movement the other way. This Presbyterian fundamentalism, led by biblical scholars like Gresham Machen, was convulsing through the whole church creating firestorms at the General Assembly and at Princeton Theological Seminary. The story of the irreconcilable conflict between Machen and Speer will be told in chapter 10.

The clash of William Hocking's philosophy of religion and Gresham Machen's fundamentalism forced Robert Speer to be the representative

---

1. Hutchinson, *Errand to the World*, 159.
2. Hocking, *Meaning of God in Human Experience*, 3.

"man in the middle."³ This clash may never have happened except for the abundant wealth of John D. Rockefeller. Rockefeller was known for his generous financial support of liberal Protestant causes; but he was also a bright theologian with a passionate vision of what the Christian church should become. His viewpoint was expressed clearly in an article published in the *Saturday Evening Post*, February 9, 1918, in the midst of the World War I. With the violence of world war shattering the innocence of Western optimism, Rockefeller names something that appealed to many people. He called for a focus on human suffering and rebuilding the common bonds of society through Christian generosity, self-sacrifice and service. He imagined a "re-born" Church that "would be called the Church of the Living God. Its terms of admission would be love for God, as He is revealed in Christ and His living spirit, and the vital translation of this love into a Christ-like life . . . It would pronounce ordinance, ritual, creed, all non-essential for admission into the Kingdom of God or His Church. A life, not a creed, would be its test; what a man does, not what he professes; what he is, not what he has."⁴ Given Rockefeller's stature the article caused a stir among the Protestant churches. Clearly, his perspective veered toward a liberal theological viewpoint.

John D. Rockefeller

3. Hutchinson, *Errand to the World*, 147.

4. Rockefeller, *Christian Church*, reprinted from *Saturday Evening Post*, February 9, 1918, 11. See University of Colorado System, digital library, World War I collection, at libcudl.colorado.edu/wwi/pdf.

In 1930 Rockefeller gathered a group of devoted laymen from his own Baptist denomination to explore the viability of creating a comprehensive, independent review and evaluation of the whole Protestant foreign missions effort. The group, at Rockefeller's recommendation, invited William Hocking as the chairperson of their whole effort, and proceeded to recruit the participation of the leading Protestant denominations involved in foreign missions. "As a result, seven denominations, each unofficially represented by a group of five men and women, joined to constitute the thirty-five Directors of the Laymen's Foreign Missions Inquiry."[5] The Laymen's Inquiry decided to limit their research to India, Burma, China and Japan and with Rockefeller's funding sent a large study team to mission sites throughout these nations. The team gathered data including interviews with missionaries and native church leaders. The Inquiry sought "an impartial and scientifically directed accumulation of data so that the judgment reached should be based on pertinent and accurately stated facts." Second, the inquiry analyzed, summarized and wrote a comprehensive report of their findings, which was, with Rockefeller's funding, widely distributed.[6] Finally a massive, seven-volume report was created. But the one final summary volume authored principally by Chairmen William Hocking immediately provoked enormous discussion and controversy within the foreign missions establishment. The report, published by Harper & Brothers in 1932 as *Re-Thinking Missions: A Laymen's Inquiry after One Hundred Years*, colloquially became known as the Hocking Report.

For the Presbyterian Church the Hocking report incited riotous controversy given the fact that it dropped right into the midst of a huge, multifaceted conflict between moderates and fundamentalists that had been agitating throughout the whole church for a decade.[7] Moreover, Robert

---

5. Hocking, *Re-Thinking Missions*, ix. The denominations represented on the Laymen's Foreign Missions Inquiry included Baptist, Congregational, Dutch Reformed, Episcopal, Methodist Episcopal, Presbyterian, United Presbyterian. Each of these had a comprehensive foreign missions program. The Presbyterian Committee included James M. Speers, Chairman, Ralph W. Harbison, Mrs. John H. Finley, George H. Richards, and Holmes Forsyth. Chairman James Speers was the president of James McCutcheon & Co., linen merchants. Speers had also been elected chairman of the International Committee of the Young Men's Christian Association and had served as vice-president of the Presbyterian Board of Foreign Missions.

6. Ibid., x.

7. It is common to date the start of the Fundamentalist and Modernist Controversy in the Presbyterian Church with the preaching of Baptist Harry Emerson Fosdick's sermon, "Shall the Fundamentalists Win?" at First Presbyterian Church in New York City

Speer was forced to significantly backpedal away from some of the report's findings which was a difficult challenge since the Board of Foreign Missions had participated in the Inquiry from the start. Speer had to communicate a delicate message that the Board of Foreign Missions was fully involved and participated in the inquiry but that the final report from the inquiry did not *in toto* represent the views of the Board.

Before seeking to dismantle and revise the whole effort of foreign missions from the ground up, the report responds to an *a priori* question: Should the work of foreign mission continue? The sort of nuanced dismissal of this question hints at the kind of philosophical depth for which the whole report reaches.

> Should the mission continue? ... We may confess that this formidable question has not proved to be highly significant. It is somewhat like asking whether good-will should continue or cease to express itself ... there is always valid impulse of love to men: one offers one's faith simply because that is the best one has to offer. It is always reasonable to ask whether this good-will might take quite different shape: but to ask whether it should cease to operate would seem to suppose that the very substance of friendship among men and races might somehow be mistaken.[8]

In the foreword introducing the report the theological diversity of the members of the Inquiry was emphasized.

> Such differences are not unimportant ... To some of our members the enduring motive of Christian mission can only adequately expressed as loyalty to Jesus Christ regarded as the perfect revelation of God and the only Way by which men can reach a satisfying experience of Him. To others, this motive would best be called the spirit of altruistic service, the desire to share with all mankind the benefits and the ideals of a Christian community. To still others, it would best be named the desire for a deeper knowledge and love of God, seeking with men everywhere a more adequate fulfillment of the divine possibilities of personal and social life.[9]

This bold statement that theological diversity was an objective for the membership of the inquiry from the start would itself be a stunning

---

on May 21, 1922. John D. Rockefeller was behind the scenes there also since he paid to have Fosdick's sermon printed and distributed to Protestant clergy all across the nation.

8. Hocking, *Re-Thinking Missions*, 4.
9. Ibid., xiv.

concept for many Protestants, in what was an era of hyper-denominationalism. But this was clearly a sign of times to come. Despite their diversity, the members of the Hocking team all assented to the conclusions that were offered in the final report. This is a remarkable accomplishment which indicates the moderate to liberal sway of the whole Inquiry. There is no clear and bold proclamation of Jesus Christ as the aim or motive of foreign missions. The Inquiry reaches for much more nuanced language which reflected Hocking's philosophical background. Thus the foreword to the report concluded that all the members of the inquiry were "welded by the common purpose and experience, the result is a significant body of agreement, which we trust may afford a firm basis for reinterpreting and redirecting one of the noblest expressions of the undying hope of the soul, the spiritual unity of mankind."[10] This language of the "spiritual unity of mankind" goes too far even for Robert Speer who criticizes the report for its lack of theological commitment to Jesus Christ. Speer's criticism is mild next to fundamentalists who denigrate the report as an attack on the very foundations of Christianity.

The Hocking Report articulated perceptions about the sweeping changes which unquestionably altered the theological and social landscape for foreign missions. These include, first, an altered theological outlook: "Western Christianity has in the main shifted its stress from the negative to the affirmative side of its message; it is less a religion of fear and more a religion of beneficence."[11] There is, second, the emergence of a new world culture which includes "a simpler, more universal, less contentious and less expressive religion coming into human consciousness which might be called the religion of the modern man, the religious aspect of the coming world-culture."[12] Third, there is a strong, aggressive new nationalism in the East: "Under these circumstances, the connection of Christianity with western life, formerly a matter of prestige, now has its disadvantages. For the sake of securing for Christianity a fair hearing it is necessary to separate it, as far as possible, from our history and our promoting agencies and to present it in its universal capacity."[13] The conclusion of these sweeping changes must be the revision of foreign mission. The report advocates for a change from traditional "temporary" style of foreign mission which was

10. Ibid., xv.
11. Ibid., 19.
12. Ibid., 21.
13. Ibid., 23.

primarily concerned with church planting to a "permanent" function, "for there is a permanent function of promoting world understanding on the spiritual level."[14]

This all required a complete change in the role of missionaries. They will not be required to preach the gospel and plant new churches. The report advocates for a missionary role as an ambassador.

> In the coming era, which might be pictured as an era of foreign service or ambassadorship, it will be natural, rather, to maintain in foreign lands a relatively few highly equipped persons, acceptable to those lands as representing the Christian way of thought and life, holding themselves ready to give advice and counsel whether to the local church or to other leaders of religion and thought; sympathetically concerned with the problems of changing local culture, and trying to minimize the strains of an abrupt breach with tradition.[15]

Thus the Hocking Report included this chart showing the transition from the old "church planting" model to the proposed "ambassadorship":[16]

Temporary Functions Church Planting	*Permanent Functions* Foreign Service, Ambassadorship
1. Sending many persons of various equipment to preach widely so that the message shall have been heard.	1. Maintaining a relatively few highly equipped persons, representing the Christian way of thought and life, acceptable or invited by the foreign land.
2. Aggressively promoting the local church through efforts actuated from home churches.	2. Standing at the service of the local church for advice and counsel, as well as of other leaders of thought and religion.
3. Expounding single-mindedly the Christianity and culture of the West; and tending to sever converts from old contexts in order to establish a distinctive body of local Christians.	3. Studying sympathetically the problems of the changing culture; trying to preserve what is valuable in the past of the people, and to minimize the dangers of abrupt break with tradition.

14. Ibid., 25.
15. Ibid.
16. Ibid., 28.

4. Carrying on educational and medical work primarily as a means of evangelizing and building up the Christian community.	4. Carrying on pioneer and experimental work in education, medicine, rural development and other social applications of the Christian view of life, primarily in view of the emerging needs of the foreign land.
5. Training nationals as leaders who will in time replace the missionaries.	5. Maintaining institutions for the study and interpretation of Christian civilization, of philosophy, theology, comparative religion, both for the higher training of qualified Christians, and as places of liaison with scholarly inquirers and interpreters of the Orient.
	6. Seeking through such intercourse a deeper grasp of the meaning of Christianity; promoting world unity through the spread of the universal elements of religion; enlivening the churches at home and abroad through rapport with each other.

Robert Speer's answer to the Hocking Report, published as *Re-Thinking Missions Examined* in 1932, was not an official response from the Board of Foreign Missions but was generally perceived as such. There were some pragmatic issues of organization concerning the work of the sending agencies and the particular work of missionaries which Speer appreciated and took under advice.[17] Nonetheless, Speer was deeply critical of the theology of the report. He criticized the report for being too much a work of philosophy, and thus was not well grounded theologically to contribute to the church. For example, the report does not consider the potential supernatural power of the gospel working through prayer and the devotional life of the missionaries. Most of all, Speer is critical that the report jettisoned the traditional claims of the Christian faith about the deity of Jesus Christ, the central importance of the incarnation, crucifixion and resurrection of

---

17. In some ways Speer was ahead of the Hocking Report concerning the necessity of organizational change. Speer had worked closely with the Special Committee on the Reorganization and Consolidation of Boards and Agencies in 1920 to reorganize the General Assembly. Because of his influence, the Board of Foreign Missions was strengthened and enlarged. See Reifsnyder, "Managing the Mission," 55–58.

Jesus and the continuing atoning power of Jesus through the present work of the Holy Spirit.[18]

The Hocking Report did not revolutionize the work of Protestant foreign missions immediately or drastically. But it did offer a vocabulary and clearly articulated a direction that was fresh and new. The report highlighted the importance of the up-building of society in work like education and medical missions as legitimate in and of themselves, not simply as subservient to the overarching goal of preaching the gospel. This theme, which parallels the tenor of the Social Gospel movement in the Protestant churches during the same era, was soon woven into the fabric of these churches. From Social Gospel to social justice to a call for social and racial reconciliation in the 1960s, to a robust peacemaking program in the 1970s this theme of social ministry became embedded in the Protestant ethos, and also became a source for bitter controversy. By the 1990s, Coalter, Mulder and Weeks could name "social service programs" as one of the vital signs in the church. "Social service programs are stirring within the new ecosystem of mainstream Protestant congregations, and this impulse can be nurtured and strengthened."[19] Within foreign missions this was exactly a point highlighted by William Hocking so many decades before.

The Hocking Report also noted, in the context of its own research team, a comfort with theological diversity which became a crucial value within the organizational structure of mainline Protestantism over future decades. This comfort with theological diversity within the church also became a feature which was constantly attacked by fundamentalists. From a long term viewpoint the Hocking report named many issues which, over decades, were fully integrated into the culture of the Presbyterian Church generally. Thus Fitzmier and Balmer conclude, "American Presbyterians had come to embrace the attitudes and strategies of the report, especially its ecumenicity, its toleration of other traditions, and its directive to fashion a missions strategy that took into account the nuances of an increasingly complex world."[20] These changes were leaven in the loaf, taking many decades to grow and develop.

In the short run, under the leadership of Robert Speer, these changes were slow and subtle. Speer with a clear vision of the *Finality of Jesus Christ*, the title of his Stone Lectures at Princeton Theological Seminary in 1933,

18. See Fitzmier and Balmer, "Poultice for the Bite of the Cobra," 123n13.
19. Coalter et al., *Vital Signs*, 116.
20. Fitzmier and Balmer, "Poultice for the Bite of the Cobra," 123n13.

held onto the proclamation of Jesus Christ as the aim of Presbyterian foreign missions until the end of his career. But, as Mark Noll concluded, "Speer's promotion of missions as the unified effort of an American Protestant phalanx did not survive long in the new century."[21] The Hocking Report offered a nuance to Speer's direction but did not significantly change it. Interestingly, the Hocking Report received publicized, celebrity praise from Pearl Buck, which exasperated the conflict surrounding the report and brings a fascinating new chapter. And before long Robert Speer was fending off a direct and at times personal attack from fundamentalist leader Gresham Machen. Machen's fundamentalists would be completely loped off and they moved on to establish their own institutions, which is also an important chapter in this story.

Future directions for discussion, study and prayer:

Along with the Social Gospel movement at home, the Hocking Report lifted up the church's responsibility for improving society in the foreign mission fields. This perspective planted an important seed in the culture of mainline Protestantism which came to full bloom in the 1960s when these churches adopted aggressive and controversial stances in support of social justice:

- What is the relationship between social ministry in support of justice and foreign missions?
- What is the relationship between social issues—poverty, education, medical care, housing—and the proclamation of Jesus Christ as Lord and Savior?
- Can these different purposes and perspectives be reconciled in the church's world mission work?

21. Noll, *History of Christianity*, 292.

CHAPTER 9

Robert Speer and Pearl Buck

THE OPENING PARAGRAPH OF Pearl Buck's (1892–1973) novel *The Good Earth* is beguiling, quickly drawing one into her story:

> It was Wang Lung's marriage day. At first, opening his eyes in the blackness of the curtains about his bed, he could not think why the dawn seemed different from any other. The house was still except for the faint, gasping cough of his old father, whose room was opposite to his own across the middle room. Every morning the old man's cough was the first sound to be heard. Wang Lung usually lay listening to it and moved only when he heard it approaching nearer and when he heard the door of his father's room squeak upon its wooden hinges.[1]

By charming historical coincidence, Pearl Buck's celebrity was washing over American society the same year as the Hocking Report was published; she also happened to be home on furlough and available to the media. Her novel *The Good Earth* was the best-selling novel in America in the years 1932 and 1933, winning the Pulitzer Prize in 1932. Pearl Buck was awarded the Nobel Prize for literature in 1938. Everyone seemed fascinated by this woman who had grown up in China the daughter of Presbyterian missionaries, who was married to a Presbyterian missionary serving in China and who had written an exquisite, bestselling novel that gave American readers a glimpse of an ordinary, poor, Chinese family. Never shy about bringing attention to China and never shy about standing in the glare of celebrity's

---

1. Buck, *Good Earth*, chap. 1.

spotlight, Buck was quick to comment on the Hocking Report. She lavished praise on it.

Pearl Buck in 1932   **Pearl Buck in 1972**

Pearl Buck was intimately familiar with the Hocking Inquiry. She had married John Lossing Buck in 1917; he was a Presbyterian missionary sponsored by the Board of Foreign Missions. Technically, Pearl herself, unlike her husband, was not a missionary and was not on the payroll of the Board of Foreign Missions; this was an important detail as the conflict around her escalated. The Bucks served in Suzhou, Anhui Province, on the Huai River; and this is the context for her popular novels *The Good Earth* and *Sons*. In 1920, the Bucks moved to the campus of the University of Nanking, where both had teaching positions. Pearl taught English literature, a position that was not formally a missionary.[2] The Bucks were in China when the research team from William Hocking's Inquiry traveled through gathering their data.

Buck was commissioned by the *Christian Century* to write a review of the Hocking Report, which was revised and published in *Harper's*, a popular national magazine at that time. Buck also made a formal presentation

2. *Wikipedia*, s.v. "Pearl S. Buck."

on the Hocking Report to a large group of Presbyterian women meeting in the Astor Hotel in New York City.[3] In a sentence that was a barely veiled barb directed at the literalism of Christian fundamentalists, Buck wrote in her essay that the Hocking Report was "the only book I ever read which seems to me to me literally true in its every observation and right it its every conclusion."[4] Thus Buck provided ample evidence for the fundamentalists growing attack on the Hocking Report and all of the foreign mission effort. Even more, Buck's strident opinion criticized the moderate, mainline Protestants who so fervently held onto the importance of direct evangelism as the primary responsibility of all missionaries. Buck gave a full-throated acknowledgement that missionary service should redirect toward a more social service orientation. "I am weary to death with this incessant preaching . . . Let us cease our talk for a time, and cut off our talkers, and try to express our religion in terms of living service."[5] These, of course, were fighting words in the midst of a great and growing debate about foreign missions. In a more thoughtful reflection, Buck agreed with the Hocking Report's analysis that the large mission agencies were obsessed with quantitative results in the field. The missionaries were under enormous pressure to produce results, to show the number of converts and new churches. This pressure, Buck argued, contradicted and undermined the more pressing need to learn the culture, history and language of the local people. Rather than quick converts, Buck and the Hocking Report advocated for building deep, authentic, lasting relationships with the local people. Pearl Buck was a child of China with an obvious deep affection for the Chinese people and their customs; she spoke their language and understood their culture; at home in the United States she was an outspoken, articulate woman in an era when this was still rare; she was a successful author in an era when the written word dominated social media; she was a celebrity. Thus everything she said contributed to and, at times, escalated the raucous debate that surrounded the work of foreign missions and the Hocking Report.

Again, Robert Speer was the man in the middle. John Piper discovered the anxiety that Speer was feeling expressed in Speer's personal letter to his friend, Reginald Wheeler, a board-sponsored missionary in China: "I may say to you frankly that I cannot remember a time of as much anxiety and trouble as this year has been—with the report of the Appraisal Committee,

---

3. Hutchison, *Errand to the World*, 167.
4. Ibid.
5. Quoted in ibid.

and Mrs. Buck and Dr. Machen. The Laymen's Report and Mrs. Buck have just played into the hands of the extremists of both wings and there have been many *injudicious* things said and done."[6]

Edwin Rian has written a history of this controversy, *The Presbyterian Conflict*, from a stance of support and appreciation for Gresham Machen.[7] Thus Rian expresses an important viewpoint representing Machen's end of the theological spectrum. In Rian's view, the Pearl Buck affair pushed Dr. Machen into his drastic action against Speer. Rian insinuates here that Robert Speer tacitly permitted Pearl Buck's viewpoint and statements, although Buck was formally outside the purview of the Presbyterian Board of Foreign Missions. But in the heat of bitter conflict such subtlety was lost. Rian concluded that the Pearl Buck affair did contribute to the escalation of the conflict:

> In fact, it was the issuance of this book [i.e., the Hocking Report] as well as the presence of Pearl S. Buck on the foreign missionary roster of the Presbyterian Church in the USA, which crystallized the thoughts of Dr. Machen on foreign missions as they were related to the Presbyterian Church in the USA. This Pearl S. Buck was no obscure missionary in a forgotten part of the world, but one of the most prominent and successful novelists of the day who lived in China and was associated with Nanking University. What makes the situation more reprehensible from the standpoint of the Board of Foreign Missions of the Presbyterian Church in the USA is the fact that Dr. Robert E. Speer, senior secretary of the board, was president of the board of founders of Nanking University. In fact, Dr. Speer's attitude was a source of amazement to Christian leaders. The manifest indifference of the board toward Pearl Buck's unbelief and the compromising attitude of the board toward *Re-Thinking Mission* produced the conviction that the time to take drastic action had come. Dr. Machen felt compelled to make public his opinion to the New Brunswick Presbytery of which he was a member.[8]

We turn to the public and irreconcilable conflict between Robert Speer and Gresham Machen.

---

6. Piper, *Robert E. Speer*, 391.

7. This book is available at the website of the Orthodox Presbyterian Church, which is the denomination that now represents the theological heritage of Gresham Machen.

8. Rian, *Presbyterian Conflict*, chap. 6, "Independent Board," at the website of the Orthodox Presbyterian Church, opc.org.

Future directions for discussion, study and prayer:

What would you say if you had been responsible for helping the Presbyterian Board of Foreign Missions craft a response to the comments of Pearl Buck and all the publicity surrounding her?

CHAPTER 10

Robert Speer versus Gresham Machen

IN 1933 GRESHAM MACHEN reached for his last, possible option in his effort to reform the Presbyterian Church toward the doctrinal purity he espoused. In his proposed overture to the General Assembly, Machen unleashed a salvo aimed directly at Robert Speer and the whole operation of the Presbyterian Board of Foreign Missions, which Speer led. This was a turning point for the work of Presbyterian foreign missions. The Board could not continue to operate if the proposed overture passed the General Assembly.

In many ways Machen's proposed overture to the General Assembly in 1933 was his last ditch effort to transform the Presbyterian Church. He viewed the church as careening wildly off course toward a moderate theology and ecumenical cooperation. Machen had been insisting on the clear, universal and unequivocal adoption of the five fundamentals—the inerrancy of Scripture, the virgin birth of Jesus, a substitutionary view of the atonement, the bodily resurrection of Jesus and the historicity of Jesus' miracles—as the essential doctrinal basis for the Presbyterian Church since early in the 1920s. This fundamentalist agenda had been brought to the General Assembly in order to be legislated as the required doctrinal basis of the church. This was never approved and provoked a significant, although unofficial, response in the Auburn Affirmation. Moreover, an official response and an expressed commitment to the principle of tolerance was lifted up by the General Assembly's Special Commission of 1925.

This was widely received and appreciated in the church; Robert Speer had served on the special commission. Many hoped this compromising resolution would put an end to a season of conflict. But Machen simply shifted his aim toward Princeton Theological Seminary specifically, demanding a clear expression of doctrine by all the faculty.

Gresham Machen taught at Princeton Seminary as an assistant professor of New Testament. Machen's criticism and proposed restructuring incited a difficult and lengthy conflict. This was significantly complicated because the General Assembly maintained a close jurisdiction over the seminary and all the internal issues at the school were played out on the national stage of the church. The end result was that Machen's proposal was rejected and cast out; Machen was dismissed from his faculty position; the General Assembly mandated a complete reorganization at Princeton to streamline administrative procedures. Machen moved forward with his incendiary plans to create the Westminster Theological Seminary in Philadelphia to carry on the teaching of the Christian faith in a manner which, in his mind, Princeton had abandoned. Thus on two fronts Machen had lost in his battle to make the Presbyterian Church and its leading seminary conform to a single, precise understanding of Christian doctrine as expressed in the five fundamentals. Now his ire was directed at the Board of Foreign Missions which was the last avenue for his proposed reformation of the Presbyterian Church along the lines of his fundamentalist perspective.

Gresham Machen

Gresham Machen's tenacious, unrelenting, uncompromising battling for the full and complete ascendancy of his theological viewpoint reflects a personality and attitude rooted in his Southern heritage. Machen was raised among the wealthy elite of the old South, passionately committed to their Old School Presbyterian heritage and Southern culture, even as his family settled in Baltimore. Bradley Longfield reflected on Machen's Southern roots and concludes: "The North and the South had been divided on a question of principle. Having lost on the field of battle, Southerners were determined to maintain true civilization, true religion, and a true love of liberty against the secularizing trends of Yankee culture. Late nineteenth-century Baltimore, the home of the Machens, proved to be a perfect environment for the cultivation of both Southern Presbyterian orthodoxy and the cult of the Lost Cause."[1]

Now the battle was brought to the Board of Foreign Missions. Machen needed the presbytery to approve his overture so it could be forwarded to the General Assembly. The overture itself was strident and direct:

> The Presbytery of New Brunswick respectfully overtures the General Assembly of 1933.
>
> 1) To take care to elect to positions on the Board of Foreign Missions only persons who are fully aware of the danger in which the Church stands and who are determined to insist upon such verities as the full truthfulness of Scriptures, the virgin birth of our Lord, His substitutionary death as a sacrifice to satisfy Divine justice, His bodily resurrection and His miracles, as being essential to the Word of God and our Standards and as being necessary to the message which every missionary under our Church shall proclaim.
>
> 2) To instruct the Board of Foreign Missions that no one who denies the absolute necessity of acceptance of such verities by every candidate for the ministry can possibly be regarded as competent to occupy the position of Candidate Secretary.
>
> 3) To instruct the Board of Foreign Missions to take care lest, by the wording of the application blanks for information from candidates and from those who are asked to express opinions about them, or in any other way, the impression be produced that tolerance of opposing views or ability to progress in spiritual truth or the like, is more important than an unswerving faithfulness in the proclamation of the gospel as it is contained

---

1. Longfield, *Presbyterian Controversy*, 38.

in the Word of God and an utter unwillingness to make common cause with any other gospel whether it goes under the name of Christ or not.

4) To warn the Board of the great danger that lurks in union enterprises at home as well as abroad, in view of the widespread error in our day.[2]

The debate of this overture at the presbytery meeting was carefully scripted. Both Gresham Machen and Robert Speer were given an hour to offer their comments on the proposal. At the end their presentations, a motion was quickly offered to move the previous question. Thus there was no debate on the floor of the presbytery, and no opportunity for rebuttal or response from either Machen or Speer. The Presbytery of New Brunswick defeated the overture; it would not be referred to the General Assembly. But the issue was not dead. A member of the Presbytery of Philadelphia brought the identical overture there, and it passed and thus was forwarded to the General Assembly.

At the 1933 General Assembly the Standing Committee on Foreign Missions first had to act on the Machen Overture. Only Machen and two others presented themselves to speak on behalf of the overture; the committee sent a majority and a minority report to the whole assembly. The majority report, approved by forty-three members of the standing committee, recommended defeating the overture and suggested full support for the Board of Foreign Missions. The minority report in favor of the overture was forwarded to the whole assembly over the signature of one committee member. The whole assembly overwhelmingly approved the majority report thus defeating Machen's overture. Even more, in direct response to the first point of the proposed overture, and in direct repudiation of Machen, the assembly expressed "its thorough confidence in the members of the Board of Foreign Missions and its belief that they have steadfastly endeavored and are endeavoring, by every means within their power, to support the secretaries and the missionaries of the Board in the Gospel enterprise." After this action, which decisively refuted Gresham Machen, it was Robert Speer's responsibility to present the board's annual report to the General Assembly. As Speer came forward he was greeted with a standing ovation and the General Assembly adopted a personal tribute thanking him for his

---

2. Quoted in "Primary Sources: Machen-Speer Debate on Modernism (1933)," at Primary Sources for the Presbyterian Masses, continuing.wordpress.com/2009/06/05/239. This was excerpted from *Christianity Today*, mid-April 1933, 19–23.

service. For Robert Speer this victory was bittersweet. He lived by a calling higher than winning and losing; he knew that reconciliation would never be possible between himself and Gresham Machen.[3]

Gresham Machen and his colleagues organized the Independent Board of Foreign Missions in an effort to run a parallel organization next to the Board of Foreign Missions. This was not action the General Assembly could tolerate. The full weight of ecclesiastical disciplinary action came down on Machen by official action of the 1934 General Assembly. "The commissioners voted by a majority so large that no division was called for that the Independent Board should cease to function within the Presbyterian Church, those ministers and laymen who were related to it should sever their relationship with it, and presbyteries should begin legal action against any ministers who did not conform to this decision."[4] Machen withdrew completely into his own Presbyterian microcosm which created the Orthodox Presbyterian Church as a new denomination,[5] taught his Reformed theology at the Westminster Theological Seminary[6] and used his new Independent Board as its foreign mission agency.[7] In 1935 New Brunswick Presbytery dismissed Machen from ministry in the Presbyterian Church in the USA. In 1935 Machen's Independent Board of Foreign Mission sponsored twelve missionaries worldwide.

Future directions for study, discussion and prayer:
- What do you believe motivated Gresham Machen?
- If you were a commissioner at the meeting of the Presbytery of New Brunswick when Machen presented his overture, how would you have voted? Why?

---

3. See Piper, *Robert E. Speer*, 384–98.
4. Ibid., 398.
5. See the website for the Orthodox Presbyterian Church at opc.org.
6. See the website for Westminster Theological Seminary at wts.edu.
7. See the website for the Independent Board of Foreign Missions at praysendgo.com.

CHAPTER 11

John Coventry Smith

IN 1934 THE GENERAL Assembly of the Presbyterian Church in the U.S.A. responded decisively to Gresham Machen, bringing to an end the decade-long Fundamentalist and Modernist Controversy and tacking into the future on a moderate and ecumenically minded bearing. Robert Speer retired from the Presbyterian Board of Foreign Missions in 1937, after a remarkable forty-four years of service. Larger transformative events were taking place in the nation. On March 4, 1933, Franklin D. Roosevelt was sworn in as the president of the United States, replacing Herbert Hoover. FDR promised to respond boldly to the devastation being wrought by the Great Depression, famously proclaiming in his inaugural address, "The only thing we have to fear is fear itself." Only weeks later the president assumed an almost pastoral role with his weekly "fireside chats" with the American people. More aggressively, FDR's New Deal with the American people was rolled out during the first one hundred days of his administration. History will never be able to conclusively decide whether or not the New Deal would have fully overpowered the pervasive Great Depression. Instead, the United States was instantly transformed and every American family touched on November 7, 1941, when Pearl Harbor was attacked. World War II was a supreme American effort. Victory in Europe came after the surrender of Berlin and Hitler's suicide in May 1945. Victory in Japan came with atomic bombs and surrender in August 1945. The United States sat at the top of a shattered world with military supremacy, industrial power, economic clout and political influence. The Protestant mainline churches in America faced a very new day.

What happened then? Through the years of the Great Depression and obviously throughout the years of World War II, because of severe travel restrictions, the foreign missions effort waned. It is not possible to exactly define a particular event or date that initiated this decline. But it is possible to quantify the decline in terms of the number of missionaries sent out. Specifically considering the northern Presbyterian Church in which Speer was the mission leader we may see the remarkable growth of this program during his career. When Speer started with the Board of Foreign Missions in 1891 they were sponsoring 598 missionaries. The high water mark of the number of missionaries sent by the Presbyterian Board was reached in 1927 when 1,606 missionaries were deployed. Although careful management allowed the board to delay the impact of the Great Depression, the difficult financial constraints finally caught up with the board and by the time of Speer's retirement in 1937 the number of missionaries had dwindled to 1,356.[1] Taking a longer time frame, the number of missionaries sent out by both the northern Presbyterian Church and the southern Presbyterian Church declined every year from 1930 to 1970.[2] In 2013, Presbyterian World Mission of the Presbyterian Church (U.S.A.) has deployed about 230 mission co-workers.

On July 1, 1948, John Coventry Smith began his service as one of the secretaries of the Presbyterian Board of Foreign Missions with responsibility for Japan, Korea, Thailand and the Philippines. Coventry Smith grew up within the loving care of the United Presbyterian Church of North America[3]

---

1. Anderson, "American Protestants," *International Bulletin of Missionary Research* 12 (1988) 101. All *International Bulletin of Missionary Research* articles are available online at internationalbulletin.org.

2. Fitzmier and Balmer, "Poultice for the Bite of the Cobra," 124–25. Although their chart only tracks until 1970 when there were 904 missionaries from the northern PCUSA and 504 from the southern PCUS; the decline has continued every year since.

3. The United Presbyterian Church of North America (UPCNA) was an ethnic Scottish denomination predominately located in western Pennsylvania. It was formed in 1858 from the merger of two smaller Scottish denominations, the Associate Reformed Presbyterian Church and the Associate Presbyterian Church. In 1958, on the occasion of its centennial, the UPCNA merged with the much larger Presbyterian Church in the U.S.A. to form the United Presbyterian Church in the United States of America (UPCUSA). The UPCUSA and the southern Presbyterian Church in the United States (PCUS) healed their Civil War split in 1983 to form the current Presbyterian Church (U.S.A.). The UPCNA always had a robust foreign mission program which was particularly strong in Egypt, Sudan and Pakistan. The mission boards of the UPCNA and the PCUSA always closely cooperated on the foreign mission field. See the "Family Tree of Presbyterian Denominations," at the website of the Presbyterian Historical Society, www.history.pcusa.org/history/denominations.cfm.

in which his father served as a pastor.[4] He has vivid memory of being examined by the session, at the age of nine years old, as part of the process of joining the church in East Mansfield, Ohio. On behalf of the session, his father asked all the questions. Both of John's parents were graduates of Grove City College in western Pennsylvania. His father was a graduate of Xenia Theological Seminary, one of the predecessor institutions of Pittsburgh Theological Seminary. Coventry Smith's parents wanted to be missionaries together but were disappointed to learn that the Board of Foreign Missions did not appoint missionaries over the age of thirty. In recollection of their desire to be missionaries, they adopted the name of their college classmate, William Coventry who served as a Presbyterian missionary in Egypt, for the middle name of their oldest son. John Coventry Smith continued his parents' commitment to Presbyterian higher education by attending Muskingum College and Pittsburgh Theological Seminary. At seminary he was very involved with the Student Volunteer Movement, attending a quadrennial conference in Detroit. Upon graduation in 1928 John married Floy Bauder; together they wanted to serve as missionaries. They were both accepted into mission service with the Board of Foreign Missions of the United Presbyterian Church of North America for positions in Egypt. But a funding shortfall delayed their departure for more than a year. Impatient while serving as the pastor of two small Presbyterian congregations in western Pennsylvania, they also applied to the Board of Foreign Missions of the Presbyterian Church in the U.S.A. They were soon on their way to Japan. John remembers his mother's comment which reflected her Presbyterianism, "After we were appointed and before we left, my mother told me for the first time that she and father had prayed before I was born that I would be a missionary."[5] John Coventry and Floy Smith landed in Yokohama, Japan, on November 1, 1929.

---

4. Biographical details from chap. 1, "Personal Beginning," in Coventry Smith, *From Colonialism to World Community*.

5. Coventry Smith, *From Colonialism to World Community*, 15.

Floy and John Coventry Smith

The mission work of the Presbyterian Board of Missions in Japan was well established before the Smiths arrived. Many of the mainline Protestant churches in the United States had mission sites in Japan by 1900; there was by the 1920s a thriving national church. Dr. James Curtis Hepburn (1815–1911) and his wife arrived in Japan in October 1859; the earliest Protestant missionaries to Japan sponsored by the Presbyterian Board of Foreign Missions.[6] Hepburn had experience in China from 1841 to 1845 working both on Hong Kong and Amoy Island. He assisted with the translation of the New Testament into Chinese and started his study of Japanese. When they arrived in Japan, living in the Jobutsu Temple in Kanagawa, he sought to create a medical clinic but was ordered to close it. He devoted his time to studying the language focusing on creating a Japanese-English dictionary. By moving to Yokahama the Hepburns were able to open a medical clinic and Mrs. Morrison started a small academy. After more than eight years of work, Hepburn published a Japanese and English dictionary in 1867. He soon published a New Testament and working with a translating committee finished a translation of the whole Bible in 1874. Before the mission station had a printing press in Japan, the actual printing work was done at the American Presbyterian Printing Press in Shanghai.

When John and Floy Coventry Smith arrived in Japan they faced a "bad psychological situation" between the native Japanese Church and the

6. On Dr. James Curtis Hepburn, see the *Biographical Dictionary of Chinese Christianity* at www.bdcconline.net.

work of the American missionaries. This experience was formative in his career. Coventry Smith later worked to help transform Presbyterian foreign mission work into ecumenical relations. Working with the Nevius model that was very successful in Korea, the Presbyterian missionaries in Japan were committed to a vision of planting self-governing, self-supporting and self-propagating native churches. The church planted in Japan was working with a Presbyterian polity and had relationships with a host of American denominations including the northern and southern Presbyterian churches, the Dutch Reformed, the Evangelical Reformed and the Reformed Churches. Missionaries from all of these western denominations connected to the Japanese church as members but did not serve as officers. The Japanese Christians were responsible for the work of their church. But this was complicated since the American missionaries were still responsible for the educational and medical mission work as well as direct evangelistic work throughout Japan. Coventry Smith reflected on this complexity:

> But the organized Mission still continued. It had once been all-powerful and it tended to retain all the power that was not specifically given to the national church. Each American denomination had its own Mission, which not only handled personal problems of missionary support but made assignments of all missionaries, produced annual reports, granted funds for budgets, and was the channel for all correspondence with the denomination's American Board, even when it concerned the churches. For the missionaries, the Mission was their power center. Very rarely did any Japanese attend Mission meetings. The Mission met annually and had an Executive Committee of six with a chairman and a secretary. Missionaries in separate geographical areas of the Mission were organized into Stations which met once a month and on call.[7]

During the years of John Coventry Smith's service, the Board of Foreign Missions had sponsored sixty-five different missionaries in Japan. The Church of Christ in Japan (Nihon Kuristo Kyokai) had about sixty-five thousand members and was the largest Protestant church in the 1930s.[8]

7. Coventry Smith, *From Colonialism to World Community*, 18.

8. In 1941 the Japanese wartime government forcibly brought together more than thirty diverse Protestant denominations to form the United Church of Christ in Japan (Nihon Kirisuto Kyodan). After World War II religious freedom was re-established by the Allied Occupation and many denominations left the United Church to reconstitute their distinctive churches. The United Church of Christ in Japan is the largest Protestant church in Japan today, a member of the World Council of Churches and a partner church with the PC(USA). See the United Church of Christ in Japan (English language) at www.uccj-e.org.

The mission had also established medical facilities and schools all around the country.

The challenge for the American missionaries was how to share the power. The American mission effort had successfully planted a national church, schools, and hospitals all over Japan. Obviously, the large contingent of American missionaries continued to feel responsibility for the work of these institutions most of which had a heritage going back to previous generations of American missionaries. Thus the Smiths and their colleagues also felt a deep responsibility to their forbearers in mission in Japan. Moreover the American missionaries were faced with the constantly shifting dynamic of the native Japanese leaders; when were the Japanese able to absorb more responsibility for the mission effort in Japan? At what point did they have the expertise necessary to sustain and grow the various institutions which the Americans had helped to plant? These shifting power dynamics were a profound challenge. A team of first-term missionaries in Japan, including the Smiths, created a bold proposal to both "to change the psychological situation," change the practice of ministry on the ground and shift the relationship between the Japanese and American Christians. "We therefore proposed that the Japanese Presbyterian Mission offer to the Nihon Kuristo Kyokai the services of all its evangelistic missionaries, together with their budgets, now to be administered as a fully integrated part of the total evangelistic work of the Japanese church."[9] With approval of their various mission boards this bold experiment was initiated. The trial was a stellar success; this innovation in Japan planted a vision of ecumenical cooperation in the mind of John Coventry Smith that bore significant fruit much later in the full transformation of the Presbyterian mission enterprise.

At the national level the Japanese church approved the proposal and created a committee of both Japanese and American leaders to implement it. Naniwa Presbytery, the largest in the Japanese church, was selected to put the plan into operation. American missionaries became members of the presbytery with one vote rotated among the five missionaries. This was the same proportional voting that was used for Japanese members who were not pastors of self-supporting congregations. The American pastors remained under the jurisdiction of their American presbyteries; Naniwa Presbytery had the authority to request new missionaries and to dismiss missionaries. A committee of six members—three Japanese and three Americans—administered all the evangelistic programs of the presbytery.

9. Coventry Smith, *From Colonialism to World Community*, 26.

Reflecting on this work Coventry Smith wrote, "We trusted each other. It was one of the richest experiences of our lives. The plan had provided the structure but the plan would not have worked without the trust that under girded our attitude in the meetings."[10] This experience taught John Coventry Smith a lesson that he carried forward into all his work in the emerging ecumenical movement. What was the very first requirement of a new missionary? "It was the attitude of the missionary toward persons of another color and culture, the willingness to work under their direction and to make contributions to the whole. This need was especially true for Westerners who had unconsciously absorbed attitudes of superiority toward less economically developed countries. We would need all the grace that God could give if we were to effectively change this."[11]

On January 31, 1941, the mothers and the young children of the American Presbyterian missionaries, including Floy Smith and their two youngsters, departed Yokohama for San Francisco. War hysteria created enormous stress in the lives of the American missionaries in Japan throughout 1941 as they tried to maintain some normalcy in their mission work and personal routines; leading Japanese Christians were supportive and protective of their American colleagues. But normalcy was impossible given the escalation of the Japanese military incursions throughout the Pacific region. In September 1941 the Japanese national church sent a memo to all its congregations encouraging the celebration of World Communion Sunday on the first Sunday in October. The memo said in part: "It is most important when hate is on the march and war is rampant in our world, that Christians everywhere should maintain an unbroken fellowship. This fellowship in Christ will stand out in contrast to our broken and disorganized world. It will bear witness to a fellowship which can cross frontiers of race, break through barriers of human prejudice, and rise above the clash and conflict of warring nations."[12]

On December 2, 1941, John Coventry Smith, all the Presbyterian missionaries and many other Americans boarded the *Tatsuta Maru* in Yokohama which was scheduled to arrive in Los Angeles on December 14. For the United States, December 7, 1941, was proclaimed by President Roosevelt as the "a date which will live in infamy"; the Japanese military had attacked Pearl Harbor, Hawaii, and escalated military aggression throughout

---

10. Ibid., 36.
11. Ibid.
12. Ibid., 71.

the Pacific region. For the missionaries on board the *Tatsuta Maru* there were actually two December 7s; one on either side of the International Date Line. Before noon on December 7, on the American side of the line, the ship turned around and headed back to Japan. The missionaries were imprisoned in Japan. They were treated fairly, guarded by regular police not the Japanese military. They were given adequate accommodations, good provisions, regular visits and support from leaders of the Japanese Church, and careful monitoring from the Swiss Embassy. On July 23, 1942, all of the American missionaries were ushered aboard the Japanese transport ship, *Asama*, stopped in Hong Kong to pick up American missionaries from Korea, and stopped in Thailand to pick up more American missionaries from Thailand, Burma and India. They sailed for five weeks across the Indian Ocean and finally landed in the Portuguese port of Lourenco Marques, Mozambique. The Americans were exchanged for almost fifteen hundred Japanese nationals who had been living in the United States. The missionaries sailed for another five weeks onboard the Swedish ship *Gripsholm* to New York City.[13]

World War II convulsed the nations of the world; after 1945 the peace ushered in a profound new era of international relations all around the world. The United States, with a new status as a military and economic superpower, massively contributed to the rebuilding of the nations of Europe and Japan. The USSR pushed back against the spread of American-style democracy with its own socialist empire thus sparking a tense Cold War which lasted another generation. The nation of Israel, after the horrors of the Holocaust, was carved into the volatile Middle East. The colonial powers of Europe which for a century had divided up Africa and many parts of Asia withdrew, creating a new birth of freedom and political chaos in a huge swath of the globe stretching from Nigeria to India. Importantly, the devastation of war and the promise of peace inspired the formation of the United Nations and correspondingly for global Christianity, the World Council of Churches.

Within the story of Protestant foreign mission work, World War II also marks a profound "paradigm shift." The phrase "paradigm shift" has become associated with the "monumental, magisterial work" by David Bosch, *Transforming Mission: Paradigm Shifts in Theology of Mission*. As Professor Gerald Anderson wrote in describing *Transforming Mission*,

---

13. See chap. 4, "Same Tax of Suffering," in Coventry Smith, *From Colonialism to World Community*.

"David Bosch's magnum opus has become his enduring legacy to all who seek to understand, to serve, and to spread the cause of Christ in the world."[14] Bosch wrote in his introduction to *Transforming Mission*, "It is, in fact, the thesis of this book that the events we have been experiencing at least since World War II and the consequent crisis in Christian mission are not to be understood as merely incidental and reversible. Rather, what has unfolded in theological and missionary circles during the last decades is the result of a fundamental paradigm shift, not only in mission or theology, but in the experience and thinking of the whole world."[15]

Now at home in the United States, John Coventry Smith was a leading advocate for the paradigm shift in the Presbyterian Church's foreign mission enterprise. After the war, on July 1, 1948, Coventry Smith began service as a secretary with the Board of Foreign Missions with responsibility for Japan, Korea, Thailand, and the Philippines. Immediately upon starting this position, Coventry Smith's task was to help distribute the proceeds of the Restoration Fund. During the war the General Assembly had created the War-Time Service Commission as an avenue by which Presbyterian congregations could support the war effort. This effort focused on supporting the families of military chaplains, direct support for military personnel on the front lines typically channeled through the Red Cross, and support for the Selective Service's conscientious objector camps. After the war, in 1946, the War-Time Service Commission was transformed into the Restoration Fund Commission. Of the 8,523 congregations in the Presbyterian Church in the U.S.A., all but 397 contributed to the Restoration Fund. After three years of active nationwide promotion, the Restoration Fund Commission reported that $25,101,432 had been raised, "the largest amount ever raised by the Presbyterian Church, or by any denomination of similar size, for a specific project in the history of the Church."[16] Coventry Smith began a whirlwind tour of all the mission stations in all the nations under his care; traveling now by airplane as much as possible. The national churches in collaboration with the missionaries were identifying programs and building projects for support from the Restoration Fund. A large portion of the Restoration Fund was earmarked for Japan and Korea, in part because of

---

14. Anderson, "In Memoriam," in Bosch, *Transforming Mission*, xii.

15. Bosch, *Transforming Mission*, 4.

16. "Report of the Restoration Fund Commission," in Presbyterian Church in the United States of America, General Assembly, *Minutes*, 1948, 1:68.

the strong Presbyterian mission presence in these nations before the war and the existence of strong national churches.

The Restoration Fund is a specifically Presbyterian example of the transformation in the way individual congregations related to foreign mission work. After World War II the immediate need of the communities and whole nations that had been devastated by the war was a constant and vivid image directly communicated, primarily by newspapers and radio, into the homes of ordinary Americans. The overwhelming magnitude of the most basic human needs motivated a massive response that quickly became part of the spiritual ethos of all types of American churches. Generally, the effort to alleviate basic human suffering replaced the preaching of the gospel as the purpose and aim of the church's foreign mission. This was not a strategic calculation at the Board of Foreign Missions. This was a change inspired in the hearts of ordinary church members. This was inspired by the overwhelming devastation of the war and the basic Christian conviction of the importance of providing food, shelter, clothing and a measure of basic human dignity to ordinary people, in Europe and Japan particularly, where the essential infrastructure of society was wiped out.

This powerful Christian motivation to respond to basic human needs also inspired the emergence of parachurch Christian organizations devoted single-mindedly to this task.[17] These organizations are now part of the culture of Christianity in America and have been instrumental in an important aspect of the paradigm shift in mission work after World War II. Individual Christians and particular congregations have sought to make direct, personal and generous commitments to respond to human suffering, locally and globally, as an expression of their understanding of mission. An early example are the "seagoing cowboys" who began shepherding donated livestock on former troop transport ships from the heartland of America to Germany and Japan. Thousands of dairy cows were shipped to Japan; thousands of dairy cows, beef cows, chickens and goats were shipped to refugee resettlement centers in Germany. This is the antecedent ministry of Christian compassion that grew into Heifer Project International. In 2013 the Heifer Project website reported that the organization works through independently managed field offices in thirty countries around the world.[18] In a parallel fashion the organization World Vision started in 1947 when founder Bob Pierce, deeply moved by the poverty he saw on Amoy Island,

---

17. See *Wikipedia*, s.v. "List of Parachurch Organizations."
18. On Heifer Project International, see heifer.org.

China, traveled around the United States raising awareness and support. World Vision reports on their website in 2013: "With 44,000 staff members worldwide, we bring sponsors and donors alongside children and communities in nearly 100 countries . . . integrating lasting solutions to the root causes of poverty and sharing God's hope for a brighter future."[19] Also the organization Compassion International has grown from an initial response of Christian compassion in South Korea. Their website reports: "Compassion's work has grown from modest beginnings in South Korea in 1952 when American evangelist Rev. Everett Swanson felt compelled to help 35 children orphaned by the Korean conflict. Our founder was inspired by Matthew 15:32 where Jesus says, 'I have compassion for these people . . . I do not want to send them away hungry' (NIV)."[20] A crucial aspect of the shifting work of foreign missions after World War II was the overwhelming desire and commitment of American Christians to respond to basic human suffering. This has become an important dimension of the ministry of individual congregations and an important expression of mainline Protestantism's foreign mission enterprise. Within the Presbyterian Board of Foreign Missions, John Coventry Smith highlighted the new "task of helping to rebuild Christian communities and their churches in Europe after the war." He concluded, "I'm sure no one understood at that time that this would lead to a new kind of relationship which would become worldwide. But it did."[21] Moreover, massive, sophisticated and global parachurch organizations grew up alongside of the churches to respond to this need also.

A different and equally sweeping aspect of the transformation of the work of foreign missions after World War II was our changed relationship with the national churches, many of which were planted by our mission efforts in previous generations. The new, national churches which were supported by missionaries before the war did not suddenly collapse and disappear when the missionaries left. This reality changed the basic assumptions of the Board of Foreign Missions. John Coventry Smith reflected on the church in the Pacific Rim with whom he was acquainted; but the Board quickly learned that this was true worldwide.

> For four of five years American missionaries had not been present and at work in Japan, Korea, Thailand, and the Philippines. That ought to be long enough for everything to come apart if it

---

19. On World Vision, see worldvision.org.
20. On Compassion International, see compassion.org.
21. Coventry Smith, *From Colonialism to World Community*, 151.

was dependent on the missionary. But the churches and their institutions had survived under their own leadership, as we had been confident they would. In Japan, catastrophe had struck in many areas, and 500 churches were destroyed, but the Christian community was still there. The people worshipped in homes when churches were burned, and there was no mistaking the fact that courage and hope were present. The Holy Spirit was at work. This ought to make us humble and teach us that we were working with a Force that is beyond our planning and our own strength. There was still another fact we recognized. This period of separation offered us a God-given opportunity to change our relationships and start over again.[22]

The Board of Foreign Missions quickly realized that what happened in the Asian countries was happening in similar ways around the world. The native churches in Africa, for example, were thriving in a new context of national freedom as the institutions of European colonialism had been wiped out by the war. The Board was wrestling with a new kind of question as it created mission strategy for a new day. At what point does an independent, self-supporting national church in Japan, Korea, India, Brazil or Ghana achieve the status as an equal in the eyes of the world Christian community? Moreover in places like Cameroon and Egypt this question was more complicated since the strong, national churches were created as part of Presbyterian Church in the United States. The churches were organizationally intertwined. Should the overlapping structures be teased apart to permit the new national church its full independence? These would become driving questions in the organizing conversations for the budding World Council of Churches. Indeed, many of the new, national churches around the world did not wait for permission from the mainline Protestant establishments in Europe and America. The new churches claimed their voice and their independence. The same kind of deep cultural changes were emerging within the United States itself after the war. Thoughtful Christians were beginning to question the complete segregation of white and black churches and the deep racial divisions in American society. It is commendable that the Presbyterian Board of Foreign Missions, with thoughtful leaders like John Coventry Smith, was able to recognize this changed situation and, in response, completely alter the work and administration of mission. This reflects an important degree of institutional flexibility and

---

22. Ibid., 143.

responsiveness. "All this points to the fact that the modern foreign mission movement had come to an end of an era."[23]

Vocabulary is vital. The Board of Foreign Missions soon realized that the questions they were tackling influenced the basic vocabulary of their work. Changes were made at this elementary level. The phrase, "foreign missions" was problematic in the new era. First of all the "s" was dropped from "missions." This reflected a theological vision that there is only one, universal church. There is only one mission of the one church. This is an important theological statement that offers a vision countering the sad reality of fractured denominationalism. The word "foreign" was clearly outdated and obsolete. Who was "foreign" clearly depended on your perspective, on where you were standing. Theologically, there are no foreigners in the universal community of believers. "Any world organization is nowhere foreign."[24] There was also discussion of the classic word "missionary." This word also seems to imply patterns and relationships that were obsolete. The board introduced the term "fraternal worker" as a substitute for "missionary" but this was not widely accepted or used.[25] Thus language and labels that had been in place since before the General Assembly officially created a Board of Foreign Missions in 1837 were cleared away, indicative of the depth of change that was occurring. In the foreword to his book *From Colonialism to World Community*, John Coventry Smith clearly expressed his view of this paradigm shift:

> The mission now belongs to this world community; and we must be aware of that fact as we profit from working together at a common and universal task . . . I also believe that the new era can be as rewarding as the era that is passing, if only the church can enlarge its vision and find its place in the common task of the world

---

23. "The postwar years were to be filled with various plans for carrying on together. We were to speak of this in various ways. It was 'Partnership in Mission,' it was 'A New Day in Mission,' it was 'Ecumenical Mission.' In these latter days a missiologist has called it 'The Decolonization of Mission,' and a perceptive psychologist has said, 'It was meeting each other at eye level.'" Coventry Smith, *From Colonialism to World Community*, 143.

24. Ibid., 154.

25. Ibid., 155. Theodore Gill wrote, "In the rebuilding of Europe, North Americans found themselves involved in mission to societies racially and culturally like their own; in some cases, American Presbyterians found themselves as 'sending churched' providing service and supplies to their own historic 'parent churches' in Europe. It was in this context that the PCUSA began referring to its missionary personnel as 'fraternal workers.'" Gill, "American Presbyterians," 133. Today Presbyterian World Mission of the PC(USA) refers to their international staff as "mission co-workers."

Christian community, a place that God is preparing for us as we face the future.²⁶

It was Coventry Smith's responsibility to report on behalf of the Board of Foreign Missions to the annual meeting of the General Assembly. He symbolized the changes that were happening when, at the 1954 General Assembly in Detroit, he held up a printed copy of the Board of Foreign Missions report and said, "This may be the last report of the Board of Foreign Missions. Next year we may come with a recommendation for a new name."²⁷

In the 1950s there were serious negotiations about the reunion of the three largest Presbyterian denominations. A plan to heal the Civil War division of the northern Presbyterian Church in the United States of America (PCUSA) and the southern Presbyterian Church in the United States (PCUS) was brought before both their General Assemblies in 1954. The smaller United Presbyterian Church in North America (UPCNA) fully participated in these negotiations and also considered the Plan of Union at its General Assembly. The UPCNA was an ethnic Scottish denomination geographically centered in western Pennsylvania and had a mature and robust foreign mission program particularly in Egypt, Sudan, Pakistan and India. The General Assembly of the southern PCUS approved the Plan of Union by a vote of 283 to 169 but the proposal did not pass the presbyteries who voted forty-two in favor and forty-three against it.

Erskine Clarke speculated that the defeat of the plan in the south, which had been worked out after many years of negotiations, may have ironically been set back by action in the larger culture only weeks earlier. On May 17, 1954, the United States Supreme Court unanimously ruled in Brown vs. Board of Education that "separate educational facilities are inherently unequal." This was an incendiary ruling for many. This may have swayed the presbytery votes, as many southerners were appalled at what they considered the Supreme Court's meddling in their local concerns and customs.²⁸ Nonetheless, the Presbyterian Church in the United States of America (PCUSA) and the United Presbyterian Church in North America (UPCNA) approved and worked forward their full reunion in 1958 and the

---

26. Coventry Smith, *From Colonialism to World Community*, 10.

27. Ibid., 155.

28. Clarke, "Presbyterian Ecumenical Activity," 161. The reunion of the northern PCUSA and the southern PCUS would wait until 1983 when the current Presbyterian Church (U.S.A.) was formed.

new name, the United Presbyterian Church in the United States of America (UPCUSA), was introduced.[29] This reunion was a personal delight for John and Floy Coventry Smith. John had been theologically educated, ordained and served congregations in the UPCNA. Their mission service in Japan and John's administrative leadership was with the Board of the Foreign Missions of the PCUSA. Thus the reunion, as he wrote, "put two halves of our lives together."[30] But the reunion of these two historic Presbyterian denominations was a challenge to those involved with their respective foreign missions. Both denominations had vigorous Boards of Foreign Missions with a healthy complement of missionaries serving around the world; these efforts needed to merge in the one, new denomination.

In 1956, in preparation for merger with the UPCNA, the PCUSA Board of Foreign Missions sponsored a two-week mission conference at a beautiful resort in Lake Mohonk, New York. Understanding the changes that were taking place in the work of mission, the board determined that this would be a very different type of conference. Rather than simply a strategic planning session for the administrative staff of the board, plans were made to include representatives from the overseas churches with whom the American Presbyterians were working in close relationship. This was the first time that the Board of Foreign Missions sponsored an event in which the majority of the participants were from overseas, national churches. Indeed, this was the first time many of these church leaders had an opportunity to meet and share with church leaders from other national churches. In addition, particularly with an eye toward the pending reunion, mission leaders from the UPCNA were included in the conference. Leaders from the PCUS and several other National Council of Churches member denominations were also included.[31] The first week of the conference was devoted to hearing reports from each of the national churches.[32] In the second week,

---

29. In 1958 the new denomination, the United Presbyterian Church in the United States of America, reported a membership of 3,159,562, with 11,801 clergy and 9,454 congregations. See Smylie, *Brief History*, 124.

30. Coventry Smith, *From Colonialism to World Community*, 172.

31. Brown and Black, "Structures for a Changing Church," 325n23.

32. International church representatives at the Lake Mohonk conference included Ah Jan Leck, stated clerk from Thailand, Ibrahim Dager from Beirut, Lebanon, Dr. Muto, the moderator the United Church of Japan, Kyung Chik Han, the pastor of the Yung Nak Church in Seoul, Korea, Bishop Sobrepena from the Philippines and chairperson of the Asia Council on Ecumenical Mission, Dr. Moreno of Mexico, Dr. Jose Borges of Brazil, and church members from Cameroon and Colombia. See Coventry Smith, *From Colonialism to World Community*, 168.

extensive discussions were held around the new concept of ecumenical mission. Particularly in Asia where there were no missionaries during the war years, how should relationships be reestablished with a new emphasis on mutuality and partnership? How should new, ecumenical relationships be created with the established churches of Europe who had experienced such devastation? How should American Presbyterians be involved with and relate to the new ecumenical organizations that were emerging around the world, for example, the Asia Council on Ecumenical Mission and the Latin America Council of Churches? The idea of missionaries to the United States, a completely new concept, was also introduced. In fact, the Board of Foreign Missions has already brought onto its New York staff Christians from national churches in India, Philippines and Japan.

Together the participants at the Lake Mohonk conference wrote a purpose statement for Christian mission: "The supreme and controlling aim of the Christian mission to the world is to make the Lord Jesus Christ known to all men as their Divine and only Savior, and to persuade them to become His disciples and responsible members of His Church in which Christians of all lands share in evangelizing the world and permeating all of life with the spirit and truth of Christ."[33] John Coventry Smith considered the Lake Mohonk conference to be "the decisive factor in the restructuring of foreign mission in our denomination."[34]

The Lake Mohonk conference offered a new theology of mission that was soon embedded in the new denomination, the United Presbyterian Church in the United States of America (UPCUSA). The committee working out the details of the reunion of the United Presbyterian Church in North America (UPCNA) and the Presbyterian Church in the United States of America (PCUSA) recommended a sweeping, comprehensive proposal concerning the foreign mission work of these two, antecedent denominations.[35] The proposal recommended fully merging the two Boards of Foreign Missions from the predecessor churches and the Permanent Committee on Interchurch Relations from the PCUSA into one large Com-

33. Ibid., 169.
34. Ibid., 170.
35. The committee responsible for creating the plan of union included Don Black, Sam Weir, Sam Shane, and Theophilus Taylor from the UPCNA, and Ralph Lloyd, Charlie Leber, John Mackay, Eugene Blake, and Glenn Moore from the PCUSA. Theophilus Taylor was elected the first moderator of the reunited church and then served as the first chairman of COEMAR. See Coventry Smith, *From Colonialism to World Community*, 170.

mission on Ecumenical Mission and Relations, soon thereafter known by the unwieldy acronym, COEMAR. The proposal for the new commission included responsibilities greater than the work that was traditionally the purview of a Board of Missions. The new commission would also include all the relationships with established churches in nations around the world where there were not missionaries; in addition the new commission included relations with all the various ecumenical organizations like the World Council of Churches, the National Council of Churches, and the regional councils of churches that were emerging. Consistent with the dominant conversation at the Lake Mohonk conference, COEMAR intended to do mission *with* Christians the world over and no longer understood mission as simply American churches sending missionaries *to* other nations. COEMAR "reflected a shift in mission philosophy from a sending receiving perspective to a partnership with the now independent Christian communities throughout the world. There was one mission on six continents, as the popular slogan put it, and the structure sought to reflect that change in strategy."[36] On May 28, 1958, in Pittsburgh the merger of the two denominations was enthusiastically approved as well as the creation of the new COEMAR.[37]

Creating the new commission at the national, denominational level was challenging; communicating the changed understanding of mission to the folks in Presbyterian pews presented a very different test. It was hoped that the new, changed theology of mission would permeate the whole church, seeping into the heart and soul of the local congregations. Staff members of COEMAR and any missionaries, now titled fraternal workers, who were available in the States, were asked to join this education and interpretation effort. COEMAR organized one day consultations with church leaders all around the nation in order to interpret and explain the new theology of mission and the work of COEMAR. John Coventry Smith summarized his interpretation in *From Colonialism to World Community*: There is not a distinct theology of mission. There is Christian theology. Christian theology

---

36. Reifsnyder, "Managing the Mission," 63.

37. The administrative staff of COEMAR would include mission leaders from both denominations: Charles Leber as general secretary was from the PCUSA Board of Foreign Missions, Donald Black as associate general secretary for administration was from the UPCNA board, Margaret Shannon as associate general secretary for ecumenical relations, John Coventry Smith as associate general secretary for ecumenical mission, and Don Pattison as treasurer. See Coventry Smith, *From Colonialism to World Community*, 171.

proclaims that everyone who is in Christ is, by definition, a witness. The Great Commission of Jesus is clear that this witness must go to the ends of the earth. This is why the earliest American Presbyterians resisted the idea of mission work being delegated to separate agencies or boards outside the church. The church is responsible for mission. The whole church is a mission agency for Christ, with each member a missionary. The success of the foreign mission movement has resulted in the Christian Church being planted in most every nation in the world. Many of these churches are vital, self-supporting and independent; many of these churches may still need support. "They are not now our children. They are our sister churches in Christ and join us in being witnesses to the whole world." But the foreign mission movement, although motivated by Christian faith, was often "unduly influenced by colonialism." The association of the mission work with colonialism was an "unplanned image." We must change "attitudes and habits" in the American church. This is no longer "our mission." We must reach out to the new Christians and the new churches with the same kind of generosity and friendship as motivated the missionary movement from the start. But the attitudes and habits of colonialism must change. This means that the structures of mission in the church which convey our attitudes and habits must also change.

> Thus the church may finally appear as a worldwide community of Christians of various races and denominations. In our kind of world this can break down the barrier where Christianity has been labeled as a tool of colonialism and imperialism. The Holy Spirit is creating a new instrument for the proclamation of the gospel to the whole world in our time. This can succeed if we all really are part of the missionary community and are joined as partners with other missionary communities around the world.[38]

Charles Leber, the first general secretary of COEMAR, died suddenly of a heart attack in 1959 while participating in a conference of the Presbyterian Alliance in Brazil. Leber had been a close colleague with John Coventry Smith for many years. Leber was the secretary of the Board of Foreign Missions in the PCUSA and with Coventry Smith helped prepare the way both for a changed understanding of mission and the creation of COEMAR. Leber was a driving intellectual and organizational force behind COEMAR and served as its first General Secretary with Coventry Smith serving as an Associate Secretary. With Leber's sudden death, John

38. Ibid., 183–84.

Coventry Smith was asked to serve as General Secretary of COEMAR and served until his retirement in 1970. John Coventry Smith's long service to the Presbyterian Church was honored in 1968 when he was elected moderator of the General Assembly; his long service to the global church was also recognized in 1968 when he was elected as one of the six presidents of the World Council of Churches.

Future directions for discussion, study and prayer:
Large institutions are perceived to be difficult to change and adapt. Yet, with the leadership of John Coventry Smith and others, the Presbyterian world mission enterprise completely transformed itself in the post-World War II era. The Board of Foreign Missions was dismantled and reconstructed as COEMAR.

- What does this say about that particular era in our church's history?
- What motivates a large institution to initiate such a massive, internal reconfiguration?
- Today, an era when we need the institutional church to change and adapt, what can we learn from the transformation of the Presbyterian mission enterprise at home and the formation of COEMAR?
- What massive, institutional paradigm shifts do we need in the Presbyterian Church (U.S.A.) and all of mainline Protestantism today?

CHAPTER 12

Clifton Kirkpatrick and Donald McGavran

IN THE YEARS IMMEDIATELY following World War II there was a burst of energy to build a grand and global organization for church cooperation; the World Council of Churches was born.[1] At the same time as the formation of the World Council of Churches brought together different pieces of Protestant cooperation and a desire to collaborate in mission; deep theological division and animosities also were permanently established. The Presbyterian Church in the United States of America had provided impressive leadership in ecumenical conversations and collaborations from the very start. Thus unquestionably the PCUSA and also the new UPCUSA, after the merger in 1958, continued to provide strong leadership and generous financial support for the World Council of Churches.[2] But this inevitable direction also separated the ecumenically minded Presbyterian leaders from a huge swath of people within their own churches, and a

1. There was a similar burst of political energy which created the United Nations after the war. This similarity is evidenced by the creation of the institutional homes of both the World Council and the United Nations in Geneva, Switzerland.

2. The financial generosity of the Presbyterian Church in the United States of America toward the postwar ecumenical movement is also seen in the establishment of the John Knox Centre in Geneva. The Knox Centre is a student hostel and conference center established in 1953 with financial support from the Presbyterian Board of Foreign Missions. Continuing today as an independent organization, the John Knox Centre is a popular conference center, retreat and hostel for visitors to the World Council of Churches, the United Nations and the International Red Cross in Geneva. See www.johnknox.ch.

huge constituency of other styles of Protestant churches that would never participate in an effort like the World Council. There is sad irony in the fact that at the same time as many Presbyterians were committed deeply to ecumenical cooperation there was also a permanent break with many other Christians who would not and could not follow the ecumenical path. It is not overly simplistic to see a deep and permanent division of American Protestantism into ecumenicals and evangelicals.[3] The ecumenical versus evangelical divide separated denominations from each other and created very different patterns of theological reflection about mission. Even more, this divide created an undercurrent of animosity and division within many denominations which has burdened every aspect of the life of these churches. The American mainline Protestant churches have carried a heavy yoke of nagging, insidious polarization. The Presbyterians have been a textbook example of such repeating and destructive conflict.

The Presbyterians were guided down the path of high ecumenical cooperation from the very start by strong leaders which often provoked either a backlash or a withdrawal from evangelicals. Robert Speer was intimately involved in the budding ecumenical movement and led the Presbyterian Church in this same path. He was an organizer and leader at the Edinburgh Conference in 1910 which is marked as the starting point for Protestant ecumenism in the twentieth century. Given the tone and influence of Speer's long leadership with the Presbyterian Board of Foreign Missions, the way of ecumenical cooperation was straightforward for Presbyterians. John MacKay, who started service as the president of Princeton Seminary in 1936, immediately after the nadir was reached with the ouster of Gresham Machen, was another authoritative voice and leader in the ecumenical movement. As president and professor of ecumenics, Mackay helped to develop Princeton's global reach.[4] In his ministry Mackay was a personal example of ecumenical commitment: he served on the provisional committee which helped organize the World Council of Churches in 1946 and then on the WCC's Central Committee; he served as chair of the International Missionary Council and thus created important links with the World Council which encouraged their merger in 1961; he served on the executive committee of the World Alliance of Reformed Churches. The Presbyterian Church (U.S.A.) applauded his ecumenical leadership by

---

3. Naming this division "ecumenicals" versus "evangelicals" is taken from Hutchinson, *Errand to the World*, 178.

4. See Mackay, *Ecumenics: The Science of the Church Universal.*

electing him as moderator of the General Assembly in 1953. John Foster Dulles was an influential Presbyterian elder who garnered huge respect as a powerful advocate behind the formation of the World Council of Churches as well as Federal Council of Churches in America, which later became the National Council of Churches. As a diplomat with the American State Department, Dulles participated in San Francisco Conference which drafted the Charter for the United Nations, and then served as a delegate to the United Nations. Later Dulles served as the secretary of state under President Dwight Eisenhower. Thus Dulles was a national, political figure whose influence within the Presbyterian Church called for high ecumenical cooperation. John Coventry Smith, an original leader within the Presbyterian Commission on Ecumenical Mission and Relations (COEMAR), also brought clout and influence which guided the Presbyterian Church into participation within the ecumenical movement. In addition to his leadership with COEMAR, Coventry Smith served as one of the presidents of the World Council of Churches. In the 1960s the Stated Clerk of the newly formed United Presbyterian Church in the USA, Eugene Carson Blake, brought the church into confrontation with the difficult social issues of the day, especially civil rights, and also advocated for a strong ecumenical involvement.[5] After his service as the Presbyterian Stated Clerk, Blake also served as general secretary of the World Council of Churches from 1966 to 1974. Clifton Kirkpatrick followed smoothly in this long tradition of ecumenical leadership. Kirkpatrick served as director of the Worldwide Ministries Division of the Presbyterian Church (U.S.A.) and then was elected and served as stated clerk from 1996 to 2008. His tenure was marked by strong ecumenical commitments. He served on the executive committees of both the National Council of Churches and the World Council of Churches; he served as president of the World Alliance of Reformed Churches and was a driving force behind the merger in 2010 which formed the World Communion of Reformed Churches.[6]

---

5. Eugene Carson Blake served as stated clerk of the PCUSA from 1951 to 1958 and continued as stated clerk after the merger with the United Presbyterian Church in North America formed the United Presbyterian Church in the USA from 1958 to 1966.

6. On the World Communion of Reformed Churches, see wcrc.ch.

Clifton Kirkpatrick

Thus strong ecumenical commitments and participation have been woven into the fabric of the Presbyterian Church by the personal witness and leadership of some of the most prominent Presbyterian leaders. Clifton Kirkpatrick summarizes these Presbyterian ecumenical associations:

> With a historic commitment to Christian unity, it is no wonder that Presbyterians helped establish and were charter members of:
>
> 1) the World Alliance of Reformed Churches (the 1970 union of the 1875 World Presbyterian Alliance and the 1891 International Congregational Council);
>
> 2) the Federal Council of Churches in 1908; and its successor,
>
> 3) the National Council of Churches of Christ in the U.S.A. (NCC) in 1950; and
>
> 4) the World Council of Church, organized in 1948. From their founding the Federal, then National and the World Councils have had exemplary leadership from Presbyterians.[7]

The path of ecumenical participation seemed inevitable, important and necessary for Presbyterians. But this path never truly encouraged a more evangelical voice within the church or in the larger Protestant culture to be heard. William Hutchison saw a dire separation between the two

7. Kirkpatrick and Hopper, *What Unites Presbyterians*, 63.

sides: "Ecumenical enthusiasm and self-confidence, which easily became a new triumphalism, not only gave offense to those who felt shunted aside; it also helped ensure that most of those nurtured in the ecumenical version of recent history would find dissent hard to deal with."[8] Kirkpatrick, who served as stated clerk through some seasons of harsh conflict, understands the dilemma of deep polarization although he uses different labels, referring to both sides as "ecumenical groupings":

> It may seem odd that there can be two kinds of calls for ecumenical cooperation in mission, and those kinds of ecumenical groupings remain separate from each other. More conservative Christians have felt their more liberal sisters and brothers in the faith placed too much emphasis in their unity on social justice kinds of issues, and they did not give sufficient attention to evangelism. Thus, when the Billy Graham organization sponsored an International Congress of World Evangelization in Lausanne, Switzerland, in 1974, neither the PCUS nor the UPCUSA participated officially in this event, but many individual Presbyterians did attend.[9]

There are a plethora of intertwining issues that have provoked the nagging tension and polarization in the Presbyterian Church. By whatever labels—fundamentalists versus modernists, ecumenicals versus evangelicals or liberals versus conservatives—there is a deep divide running through American mainline Protestantism and specifically the Presbyterian Church. A key issue in this polarization are different understandings and approaches to world mission. How did that happen?

The changing definition and focus of world mission within the World Council of Churches is illustrative. These changes exactly parallel the ways the world mission conversation developed in the Presbyterian Church; this is easy to understand given the key Presbyterian participation in the World Council in its early, formative years. The World Council of Churches is a global, ecumenical collaboration which brought together several different themes and conversations into one organization. "Predecessor bodies that have been incorporated in the Council over the decades included international conferences on 'faith and order' (theology, sacraments, ordinances) and 'life and work' (social ministries, international affairs, relief services), the International Missionary Council (IMC), a world alliance of churches for global peace as well as a council descended from the nineteenth century

---

8. Hutchinson, *Errand to the World*, 179.
9. Kirkpatrick and Hopper, *What Unites Presbyterians*, 65–66.

Sunday school movement."[10] Several of the different themes of this ecumenical conversation, particularly "faith and order," "life and work" and the IMC were all inspired by the Edinburgh Missionary Conference in 1910.

It was the International Missionary Council (IMC) which most explicitly brought forward the conversation about foreign missions after the Edinburgh Conference.[11] There was enormous energy to gather conversation and seek cooperation around the many expressions of evangelistic, educational and medical mission that had grown up during the great missionary movement in the last half of the 1800s. World War I interrupted all of these plans. After that war the International Missionary Council officially formed in 1921 as a council of mission agencies, not churches; this is a vital distinction. The IMC linked fourteen different, interdenominational mission societies from around the world including, for example, the National Council of India. But the Presbyterian Board of Foreign Missions, for example, was not a member of the IMC since it was a church board; although Robert Speer and other Presbyterian leaders were quite engaged with the IMC. The Council functioned out of an office in London, a second office opened in New York in 1924 and later a Far Eastern Office was added. The IMC sponsored a number of major, international mission conferences each with a particular focus: Jerusalem in 1928 on the relation to secularism; Tambaram, India, in 1939 on the Christian message in a non-Christian world; Whitby, Ontario, in 1947 considered mission work after World War II; Willingen, Germany, in 1952 on the question of church unity; Ghana in 1958 established a Theological Education Fund.[12]

The 1939 mission conference on the campus of Madras Christian College in Tambaram, India, was particularly influential. The gathering in Tambaram was unique both because it took place in a developing nation and, more important, half of the delegates were from new, national churches. The IMC sought to express its conviction that "the indigenous churches

---

10. See "History," at the World Council of Churches website, www.oikoumeme.org.

11. Scherer, writing in the *Encyclopedia of Christianity* (s.v., "International Missionary Council," 728), considered the International Missionary Council "the most significant and effective planning organization for international, Protestant missionary cooperation of the 20th century."

12. Although the formation of the International Missionary Council was delayed until 1921 because of World War I, the earlier planning conversations launched the journal *International Review of Missions* in 1912 which, after the merger with the World Council of Churches in 1961, continues to this day as the WCC's *International Review of Mission*.

of Asia, Africa and Latin America, rather than Western mission societies were the responsible agents for mission in their respective areas."[13] The theological tone at Tambaram was prepared by Hendrik Kraemer's important work *The Christian Message in a Non-Christian World*, which was written in advance of the conference at the request of John Mott. Hendrik Kraemer (1888–1965) was educated in Rotterdam and served with the Netherlands Bible Society in Indonesia. While there he worked to support the Indonesian Christians in growing beyond missionary support toward being a full, independent church. The *Christian Message* was a powerful and unapologetic Christocentric message. Kraemer's message, in a world now chastened by the destruction of World War I, rejected the idealism of the earlier missionary movement which presumed the inevitable and easy progress of Christianity worldwide. Kraemer called the church back to an essential theological foundation in Jesus Christ.

> The Church is emphatically reminded that it, alone of all human institutions in the world, is founded on divine commission. It is called upon to reflect on its position and situation. This, however, can only be effectively done when the Church becomes conscious in a new way of its mission in the "Christian" and the non-Christian world, because of its being founded on a divine commission. The essential nature of the Church is that it is an apostolic body.[14]

Thus the International Missionary Council took an important step beyond the naive expectation that the Christianity would inevitably convert the world. Kraemer's tone set the stage at Tambaram; the "*Christian Message* played a singular role in ending the optimism of the missionary movement of the nineteenth century and early twentieth century that one day the whole human community would embrace Jesus as its Master and Messiah, and the entire world would become Christian. In the period between the two world wars, *Christian Message* called the missionary movement back to reality."[15] This strong, focused Christocentric message coming out of the IMC's Tambaram Conference also explicitly criticized the theology of mission that William Hocking had introduced in his report in the United States.

In its first decades the IMC sought to remain an autonomous organization separate from the ecumenical conversations of the churches that were

13. Scherer, "International Missionary Council," 726.
14. Kraemer, *Christian Message*, 1–2.
15. Jongeneel, "Hendrik Kraemer's *Christian Message*," 203.

beginning to gather into the concept of the World Council of Churches. Although there was a joint committee of the IMC and the incipient WCC. This independence was important in order to continue the IMC's focus on mission.[16] The world missionary movement in the eighteenth century had been inspired by agencies and boards separate from the churches. These included the London Missionary Society, the Church Missionary Society, the Berlin Missionary Society and in the American Board of Commissioners for Foreign Missions. Although these agencies were led by devout church leaders they were not church bodies. This was an important issue for the American Presbyterians when the General Assembly intentionally created the Board of Foreign Missions in 1837 as a church board, thus breaking ties with the "voluntary society," the American Board of Commissioners for Foreign Missions. Early leaders within the IMC were cautious that a merger with the budding World Council of Churches conversation would dilute a focus on mission. Nonetheless there was a close cooperation between the IMC and the provisional committee charged with organizing the WCC.

Within the International Missionary Council, from its earliest days, there were difficult debates about the theology of mission and the methods of mission work. As early as the 1920s serious discussion questioned the American emphasis on "humanistic activism and an intellectual and religious syncretism" in mission work.[17] This debate was heating up in the international conversations at the IMC at the same time as Robert Speer's Presbyterian Board of Foreign Missions was fending off challenges from Gresham Machen and the Hocking Report at home. The ecumenical conversation was struggling with ways to include the new national churches that were emerging around the world alongside the established European and American churches which had originally sparked the great missionary movement. Foundationally these conversations were all embedded in larger questions about ecumenical relationships particularly between established and new churches, the importance and different methods of evangelism and the proper organizational structures to promote these conversations and collaborations. And, of course, all of this stimulating conversation and debate was interrupted by the ravages of World War II.

After the Second World War, the International Missionary Council continued a parallel track alongside of but separate from the fledging World Council of Churches. The IMC gathered for their mission conference in

---

16. Coventry Smith, *From Colonialism to World Community*, 180.
17. Hutchinson, *Errand to the World*, 172.

1947 in Whitby, Ontario, under theme of "Partnership in Obedience." This IMC meeting introduced a theme that would become the hallmark of world mission work: "partnership." From the start the IMC had intentionally included new Christians from new national churches all around the world in its deliberations. Thus it was encouraging to see that many of the newer churches in Asia, Africa and Oceania had developed and matured without missionary support during the during the years of the Second World War. At Whitby delegates from six continents rejoiced at the tenacity and strength that churches had shown in their own contexts despite the war. Now a new energy emerged, as the Whitby Report declared, with "an even deeper vision of the reality and fullness of the universal church." Now churches everywhere could break older models and join as partners wherein "all churches alike are called to the total evangelistic task."[18] Although the Whitby conference highlighted the important theme of partnership there remained a central vision of evangelism as the work of mission. Partnership was the framework within which evangelism was accomplished. For the IMC evangelism remained the primary work of mission. Importantly, the church stood at the center of this theoretical structure. The church was the engine that provided the work. Basically, the IMC's understanding of mission was churches working in partnership doing evangelism.

The First Assembly of the World Council of Churches gathered in Amsterdam in 1948 around the theme of "Man's Disorder and God's Design"; a theme which sought to promote theological reflection on the way forward after the devastation of the world war. Although predominantly a Protestant conversation, 147 churches from many different nations were represented. As these conversations moved into the 1950s a subtle but decisive shift was introduced. The optimism of the great missionary movement which expected the Christian conversion of the world was now chastened. Challenges on a global scale now confronted any theology of mission. The Soviet Union was expanding and claiming a huge territory with its atheistic philosophy. A tense Cold War dominated the political worldview. The nation of Israel was carved into the Middle East creating permanent conflict in that region. The tremendous missionary push into China was challenged and cast out; an anti-Christian regime had assumed power. Nationalistic tendencies erupted worldwide as nation after nation in the developing world stretched their independence seeking to cast off all manner of dependency on the West. Reading the signs of the times the International Missionary

---

18. Scherer, "International Missionary Council," 727.

Council gathered in Willingen, Germany, in 1952 seeking to strengthen the church's mission. The thinking of Johannes Hoekendijk (1912–1975) was influential at Willingen. Hoekendijk, who was raised by missionary parents in Indonesia, was himself educated and trained for mission service in the Netherlands. But his call to mission service was interrupted by World War II and then his time in Indonesia, following his parents, was cut short by his poor health. Hoekendijk served for a time with the Netherlands Missionary Council, served with the World Council of Churches office of evangelism in its early years, returned to his home and a teaching position at the State University of Utrecht in 1953, and in 1965 for the final years of his career accepted a call as chair of World Christianity at Union Theological Seminary in New York. Interestingly, although Hendrik Kraemer and Hoekendijk both had roots in the Netherlands and mission experience in Indonesia, their viewpoints on mission were opposite in many ways. Hoekendijk was attuned to the political and social situation of the post-war years and had a broad international perspective both from his experience in Indonesia and his work within the ecumenical movement. He brought ideas about the church to the IMC conference in 1952 which became kernels, well beyond his influence, that grew into massive transformations in the theology of mission in the 1960s.

Essentially, Hoekendijk offered a position in his paper "The Church in Missionary Thinking" which was "his crusade against ecclesiocentrism, his desire to embrace the secular world as the arena of God's action, and his insistence on a desacralized mission in which *shalom* rather than *church* is the keyword."[19] The perennial focus on the church and its mission work was too small, given the magnitude of the world issues. What was God doing in the world? Mission work had to focus on expressing God's work. While this line of inquiry soared with a bold vision of God's work in the world, it created a basic suspicion of "churchism." Hoekendijk offered a compelling "conviction that a preoccupation with church would blind the ecumenical movement to what is really going on in the world—the vast field of humanity in need of *shalom*."[20] This theology of mission removed the church from its central, instrumental role. Mission was not the activity of the church toward the world; such thinking was small, trite and obsolete. Mission is massively, conceptually larger. Mission is God's activity in the world; the objective of mission is the fulfillment of the kingdom of God.

19. Hoedemaker, "Legacy of J. C. Hoekendijk," 166.
20. Ibid., 167.

In his *Encyclopedia of Christianity* article James Scherer summarizes this powerful change in thinking:

> The church-centered concept of mission that had marked IMC thinking at Jerusalem and Tambaram, however, was now criticized as being too narrow. Rather, a Trinitarian understanding of mission as God's own activity (*missio Dei*[21])—with the world as locus of mission, the kingdom as its goal, and the church as privileged agent and foretaste of the kingdom—began to replace the older thesis of the church as the starting point and goal of mission. The displacement of the church from its place at the center of mission activity would have far-reaching consequences, both positive and negative in years to come.[22]

Importantly, the discussion and focus on evangelism essentially dropped out; a point that would return as a source of conflict and the rallying cry for a completely different organization for mission. But the 1952 IMC gathering at Willingen introduced into mission thinking the concept of *missio Dei*, an idea that may have been "too early."[23]

Conversations about the merger of the International Missionary Council and the World Council of Churches heated up in the 1950s. At the second assembly of the World Council of Churches at Evanston, Illinois, in 1954 a joint committee was established to study the full integration of the two organizations. The influential general secretary of the World Council, Willem Visser t'Hooft, lobbied hard for full integration believing that this would bring the IMC's compelling commitment to mission into the life of the member churches of the WCC. The general secretary of the IMC, Lesslie Newbigin, was also in favor of merging the two organizations. Newbigin was convinced that the work of mission was as important as the themes of "faith and order" and "life and work" which had come together to form the WCC. Nonetheless the merger of the IMC and the WCC was strenuously debated around many of the reoccurring questions: What was the relationship of the churches and mission agencies? The WCC was a council of churches; the IMC was a council of mission agencies. Could

---

21. "According to the concept of *missio Dei*, God is the 'sending agent,' all mission is God's alone, and all churches together cooperate in carrying out this mission in obedience to God. The field is the world, the whole world 'developed' as well as underdeveloped. This was mission theory for a post colonial age." From Gill, "Historical Context for Mission," 17.

22. Scherer, "International Missionary Council," 727.

23. Hoedemaker, "Legacy of J. C. Hoekendijk," 167.

organizations with such different models merge? Within the World Council could the new, national churches emerging in the developing world express the same theology of mission as the established churches of Europe and the United States? With all the other important themes on the agenda of the World Council, would adding an emphasis on mission create an undue dilution? Nonetheless at the 1961 meeting of the World Council of Churches in New Delhi the full incorporation was approved and the World Council's Commission on World Mission and Evangelism was created to carry on the legacy of the IMC.

In the 1960s, with the full integration of the International Missionary Council, the World Council of Churches veered strongly in a political and social direction. United Presbyterian Eugene Carson Blake was elected general secretary of the World Council in 1966 and brought an energetic commitment to social action. This created enduring divisions within the mainline Protestant churches in the United States. The tone was set at the fourth General Assembly of the World Council meeting in Uppsala, Sweden, in 1968. Again the reflections of Johannes Hoekendijk were influential. Many of the basic elements of his theology of mission were included in the Uppsala report. These included

> the positive evaluation of secularization as a fruit of the Gospel; the interpretation of "world" as "history"; the reordering of the familiar sequence of God-church-world into God-world-church, with the church occupying a noncentral position; the emphasis on *shalom* as the substance of God's action in the world; the appeal to the church to join and follow this action and to forsake its "heretical structures" to this end; the effort to solicit cooperation with sociologists in the reflection of adequate structures for missions.[24]

Clearly, the World Council was seeking in Uppsala to respond to the revolutionary tone of the times; the concern was to be theologically relevant in an era of sweeping political and social turmoil. The social and political issues of the world were setting the agenda for the churches. This was Hoekendijk's thesis that the church must not be at the center of the theology of mission. Mission is God's work in and through the structures of society bringing shalom and social reordering to the world. Norman Goodall, the editor of the Uppsala Assembly's final report, wrote,

> The most obvious and widely acknowledged feature of the Assembly was its preoccupation—at the time, almost, its obsession—with

24. Hoedemaker, "Legacy of J. C. Hoekendijk," 168.

the revolutionary ferment of our time, with questions of social and international responsibility, of war and peace and economic justice, with the pressing, agonizing physical needs of men, with the plight of the underprivileged, the homeless and starving, and with the most radical contemporary rebellions against all "establishments," civil and religious.[25]

As a concrete response to this strong theological foundation, Eugene Carson Blake was instrumental, after the Uppsala Conference, in creating the WCC's Program to Combat Racism. The program, understood as an expression of mission, began to provide funds to respond to humanitarian needs in racially separatist regimes, particularly in Rhodesia and South Africa. This grew in the next decade into a concerted response from World Council affiliated churches around the world against apartheid in South Africa.

The World Council of Churches assembly at Uppsala in 1968 provoked a powerful response and soon a complete schism with many evangelicals. Almost immediately Lesslie Newbigin expressed criticism of the direction the WCC was taking in its understanding of mission. Newbigin (1909-1998) was a prolific author in the area of missiology and a leading voice in the International Missionary Council, serving as its last general secretary before the merger with the World Council of Churches.[26] Ordained in the Church of Scotland, he served as missionary for many years in India, became a member of the Church of South India and rose to the office of bishop there. His perspective was within the ecumenical movement although with a strong commitment to the centrality of Jesus Christ in the work of mission. Thus he was critical of the WCC's veering away from a commitment to evangelism and the proclamation of the gospel in mission work. Years later, in a book review published in the *International Bulletin of Missionary Research*, Newbigin was critical of the theological position of the WCC's general secretary Konrad Raiser's 1991 book *Ecumenism in Transition* and the direction of the WCC's understanding of mission since the merger with the IMC in 1961. Newbigin cites his disagreement with the World Council's shift away from a solid grounding in the gospel:

> From the beginning, I believe, there has been at the heart of the life of the WCC the challenge to accept mutual correction in the light of God's revelation of himself in Jesus Christ as witnessed in the

---

25. Quoted in Hutchison, *Errand to the World*, 183.
26. On Lesslie Newbigin, see Newbigin.net.

Scriptures. If this mutual correction gives way to the relativism of postmodern culture and dialogue is seen simply as the "sharing of life," something has gone badly wrong.[27]

Moreover, Newbigin remembered his difficult experience as a participant at the Uppsala Assembly: "For me the most painful experience of that assembly was the struggle of the section on mission to overcome the almost implacable resistance of the drafting group to include any reference whatever to the duty of the church to bring the Gospel to those who had not heard it."[28] Newbigin saw clearly that the Uppsala Assembly introduced a new model and direction for mission, "a model not explicitly referred to but tending to dominate the WCC from Uppsala onward, a model that interprets all situations in terms of the oppressor and the oppressed and that tends to interpret the struggles of the oppressed as the instrument of redemption."[29] Nonetheless, Newbigin had a long and stellar career as a missionary, scholar of mission and ecumenical leader. He remained firmly entrenched in the ecumenical camp although he often brought a penetrating critique.

In response to the Uppsala Assembly a huge constituency of more evangelical Christians parted ways with the World Council of Churches and the mainstream ecumenical movement. Donald McGavran gave voice to a perspective around which this mighty evangelical cohort soon rallied. The child of missionaries, Donald McGavran (1897–1990) was raised in India and served for more than thirty years as a missionary, church planter and researcher there.[30] While working in the mission field in India, he became obsessed with the question of church growth; when a church is growing, why is it growing? What prevents a church from growing? He researched these questions extensively in India, Mexico, the Philippines, Thailand, Jamaica, Puerto Rico, West Africa, and North America. McGavran's substantial influence on the evangelical understanding of mission resulted from his second career when he was called from semi-retirement in 1965 to be the founding dean of the School of World Mission at Fuller Theological Seminary.[31]

27. Newbigin, "Ecumenical Amnesia," 3.
28. Ibid.
29. Ibid., 5.
30. Biographical details here are from Hunter, "Legacy of Donald A. McGavran," 158–62.
31. Hunter, "Legacy of Donald A. McGavran," 159 and 159n3. Fuller adopted the

Donald McGavran

In an article written in 1986, after his retirement from Fuller Seminary, titled "My Pilgrimage in Mission," McGavran remembered the Uppsala Assembly as a turning point:

> In January 1968, however, a radical change in my thinking took place. Up until then I had not considered the insights that God had given me as in any way opposed to those being promoted by the World Council of Churches and its Division on World Mission and Evangelism. Alas, in January 1968 as I read with amazement the documents that prepared the way for the great Uppsala assembly, I saw that if Uppsala endorsed what the preparatory documents said, the World Council of Churches and all its member denominations would be turning away from mission as Christianization to mission as humanization. Instead of seeking to disciple *panta ta ethne*,[32] winning them to Christian faith, and multiplying

---

term "world mission" to connote the school's vision. "The term 'world mission' was needed because many mistook 'mission' for 'everything the Church does,' thereby blurring the focus of classical apostolic mission. McGavran and his colleagues advocated evangelism and church planting as perennial and indispensable parts of mission." The School of World Mission at Fuller Theological Seminary is today the School of Intercultural Studies. See www.fuller.edu/sis.

32. "Panta ta Ethne" is a transliteration of the Greek words in Matthew 28:19

churches among them, the effort would be to spread brotherhood, peace, and justice among all people regardless of what religion or ideology they espoused.[33]

In response to the Uppsala Assembly, McGavran's *Church Growth Bulletin* devoted an issue to critiquing what he considered the World Council's changed emphasis in mission toward social action and social justice. For McGavran, the World Council had veered wildly. The World Council had abandoned the central task of mission which, for McGavran, was evangelism. His journal asked "in big black letters across the front page 'Will Uppsala Betray the Two Billion?' The whole issue was devoted to exposing and discussing the massive error of the new definition of mission."[34]

With Fuller Seminary as the locus, McGavran and his colleagues Alan Tippert and Ralph Winter established a movement within the global mission conversation which became known as the Church Growth Movement. This movement, based in solid, empirical research from around the world, defined methods and strategies for evangelism, the proclamation of the gospel and the growth of the church. The Church Growth Movement became a powerful counterpoint to the World Council of Church's approach to global mission. McGavran and his colleagues expressed a perspective that resonated with evangelicals who desired to keep evangelism and proclamation at the center of mission work. There was a sophisticated theological basis behind this perspective that has motivated many Christians around the world which is divorced from the mainstream ecumenical movement represented by the World Council of Churches.

The world mission conversation has divided into evangelical and ecumenical streams, and seldom since the Uppsala assembly, have the two met. George Hunter clearly outlined the way McGavran and his colleagues articulated the evangelical perspective:

> McGavran's church growth school developed a distinctive and enduring approach to evangelism and mission. Consider the following distinctive themes and claims:
>
> 1. The perennial and indispensable work within total mission is apostolic work, that is, continuing the work of the earliest

---

translated in English as "all nations." The phrase has become a watchword in evangelical circles for the commitment to reach out in mission to the unreached people groups of the world. A Google search on "Panta ta Ethne" will find many examples.

33. McGavran, "My Pilgrimage in Mission," 54.
34. Ibid.

apostles and their congregations in reaching lost people and peoples.
2. The key objective in evangelism is not to "get decisions" but to "make disciples."
3. The key objective in mission is to plant an indigenous evangelizing church among every people group.
4. There is no one method for evangelizing or church planting that will fit every population, but the church growth field research approach can help leaders discover the most reproducible methods for reaching any population.
5. The pragmatic test is useful in appraising mission and evangelism strategies and methods, so churches should apply the approaches that are most effective in the given population.
6. The Christian movement can be advanced by employing the insights and research tools of the behavioral sciences, including the gathering and graphing of relevant statistical data for mission analysis, planning, control and critique.
7. The church growth movement affirms a high doctrine of the church: the church is Christ's body, all people have the inalienable right to have the opportunity to follow Christ through his body, and the living Christ has promised to build his church.
8. The supreme reason for engaging in evangelism and mission is Donald McGavran's most famous declaration: "It is God's will that his church grow, that his lost children be found."[35]

The organizational impetus for a global organization which emphasizes the centrality of evangelism in mission work was launched in 1974 when the Billy Graham Evangelistic Association organized the First Lausanne Congress which continues today as a robust international movement. The First Congress gathered under the theme "The Whole Church taking the Whole Gospel to the Whole World." Their website offers this definition: "Lausanne is a global movement that mobilizes evangelical leaders to collaborate for world evangelism. Together we seek to bear witness to Jesus Christ and all his teaching, in every part of the world—not only geographically, but in every sphere of society and in the realm of ideas."[36] At the First Lausanne Congress,

---

35. Hunter, "Legacy of Donald A. McGavran," 158–59.
36. See www.lausanne.org. The Lausanne Movement organized the Third Lausanne Congress of World Evangelization in Cape Town, South Africa, in 2010.

some 2,700 participants and guests gathered in Lausanne, Switzerland, for ten days of discussion, fellowship, worship and prayer... Speakers included some of the world's most respected Christian thinkers of the time, including Samuel Escobar, Francis Schaeffer, Carl Henry, and John Stott. Ralph Winter's plenary address in which he introduced the term "unreached people groups," was hailed as "one of the milestone events in missiology." Some were calling for a moratorium on foreign missions, but Winter argued the opposite. Thousands of groups remained without a single Christian, and with no access to Scripture in their tongue, so cross-cultural evangelization needed to be the primary task of the Church.[37]

Importantly the Lausanne Covenant was developed at the First Congress. Anglican John Stott was driving force behind this document which has been widely appreciated as a definition and rallying point for evangelicals worldwide.[38]

Neither the northern or southern Presbyterian Churches in the United States, the UPCUSA or the PCUS, officially participated in the Lausanne Congress nor did these denominations financially contribute to the Lausanne Movement. Although it is impossible to quantify there are, of course, many American Presbyterians whose personal affinity would lean toward the evangelical stance of Lausanne and who have been critical of their denominations' involvement in and support of the large ecumenical organizations like the National Council of Churches and the World Council of Churches. This criticism has been a consistent theme of the Presbyterian Lay Committee, for example. The first edition of the *Presbyterian Laymen* in 1968 expressed criticism of both the WCC and NCC. There are different ways to describe the polarization that has divided the American Presbyterians and all of mainline Protestantism. But this deep divide between evangelicals and ecumenicals around an understanding of and approach toward global mission work may be an essential feature of the Protestant landscape in the United States since the WCC Uppsala Assembly in 1968 and the Lausanne Congress in 1974; these events may have deepened the separations. The future of the Presbyterian presence in the United States, and of the mainline Protestant ethos generally, depends on some reconciliation of these different perspectives and overcoming these deep divisions. Even more, a full Christian witness must understand the vitality of both

37. See http://www.lausanne.org/en/about.html.
38. See the Lausanne Covenant at www.lausanne.org.

perspectives. The ecumenical perspective, since Uppsala, argued for the social responsibility of the church. Mission work must respond to the ills of society, calling for and working toward a more just and peaceable world. The evangelical perspective, since Lausanne, argued for the lifesaving gift of Jesus Christ which is available to every person. Mission work must emphasis the sharing and proclamation of this gospel. Are these themes not both essential aspects of Christian faith?

The influential missiologist David Bosch, in his important book *Transforming Mission*, argued that both perspectives were in fact features of Christianity, particularly in North America, since the beginning and that it is necessary to overcome these distinctions. Bosch sees the two themes showing up clearly as early as the work of Jonathan Edwards. "According to Edwards God's work of redemption has two facets. One consists in the converting, sanctifying, and glorifying of individuals; the other pertains to God's grand design in creation, history, and providence."[39] This same dichotomy is evident in the different theological perspectives offered in the Civil War era, and again in the Presbyterian fundamentalist and modernist controversy of the 1920s. After World War II these distinctions exploded into worldwide divisions particularly in the varying approaches to mission of the WCC and the Lausanne Movement. But are these not dimensions of the one, universal Christian faith? Is part of the problem the presumption that these different perspectives are, in fact, different, distinct, and separate? Thus Bosch argues:

> The moment one regards mission as consisting of two separate components one has, in principle, conceded that each of the two has a life of its own. One is then by implication saying that it is possible to have evangelism without a social dimension and Christian social involvement without an evangelistic dimension. What is more, if one suggests that one component is primary and the other secondary, one implies that the one is essential and the other optional.[40]

Indeed, there have been robust efforts to bring the pieces together. Bosch cites the gathering of several hundred delegates at the Lausanne Congress in 1974 that immediately criticized the Lausanne Covenant on this point. The group issued a statement strenuously rejecting the distinction that had split ecumenical social responsibility from evangelical

39. Bosch, *Transforming Mission*, 403.
40. Ibid., 405.

proclamation: "There is no biblical dichotomy between the word spoken and the word made visible in the lives of God's people . . . There are times when our communication may be by attitude and action only, and times when the spoken word will stand alone: but we must repudiate as demonic the attempt to drive a wedge between evangelism and social concern."[41] The same concern to bridge the gap between ecumenical and evangelical perspectives came from the other direction when the World Council of Churches itself drafted a policy paper, "Mission and Evangelism: Ecumenical Affirmation," in response, in part, to the Lausanne Congress. The Ecumenical Affirmation was written after the debate about mission at the 1975 Nairobi Assembly. The statement was initially drafted by Emilio Castro, the director of the WCC's Commission on World Mission and Evangelism. There was a concerted effort to hear, understand and respond to the evangelical stance:

> There is no evangelism without solidarity; there is no Christian solidarity that does not involve sharing the knowledge of the kingdom which is God's promise to the poor of the earth. There is here a double credibility test: a proclamation that does not hold forth the promises of the justice of the kingdom to the poor of the earth is a caricature of the gospel; but Christian participation in the struggles for justice which does not point towards the promises of the kingdom also makes a caricature of a Christian understanding of justice.[42]

In the church's global mission work, can the conversation to bring together the great themes of evangelical proclamation and ecumenical commitment to social responsibility move forward to a new day? Specifically within Presbyterian Church (U.S.A.) Clifton Kirkpatrick has been a prominent voice for exactly this. After fifteen years as the director of the Worldwide Ministries Division in the Presbyterian Church (U.S.A.), Kirkpatrick was elected stated clerk by the General Assembly in 1996. With his wealth of experience working in support of world mission and at the start of his service as the most prominent ecclesiastical officer in the denomination, Kirkpatrick published a book, *What Unites Presbyterians: Common Ground for Troubled Times*, in anticipation of the meeting of the General Assembly in 1997. This book was a rallying cry and ardent prayer for unity,

---

41. Ibid., 406.

42. "Mission and Evangelism: An Ecumenical Affirmation," 2. See also Bosch, *Transforming Mission*, 408.

written with the conviction that the Presbyterian tradition has a unique theological, historical, organizational heritage out which the unity of the church may be bolstered. Kirkpatrick rejects the idea that a single theological or missiological perspective must be adopted as normative to the rejection of others. "Obediently following Jesus' command to witness in all the world is difficult enough without adding the burden of internal squabbling, which leads nowhere but to the torpedoing of the purity of the message of the love of God. Any determination of churchwide evangelism or mission advance can be held hostage to the forces that demand a battle to the death over the correctness of one's position."[43] What is clear, and the conviction around which the church must rally, is Jesus Christ. "There is no dispute about our foundation. All Presbyterians give a ringing endorsement to the centrality of Jesus Christ, who is at the center of our faith; we start there."[44] Nonetheless, in the Presbyterian tradition there must be openness to new theological reflection. Kirkpatrick appeals to what he considers a crucial "Reformation principle" as a way forward:

> The Reformation principle that the church is always reforming has an implication that is not always accepted in fact. That implication is that the church, led by the Spirit, is always open to new revelation and to fresh expressions of old truths. In practice, the church should never fear "new theologies"; therefore, newer insights and emphases are not to be rejected out of hand, but are to be studied, pondered, and considered for possible inclusion in one's own theological formulations, as well as in the corporate theological statements of the church. The Holy Spirit is alive![45]

Given his tenure of service as an administrator of the church's world mission program, of course, Kirkpatrick celebrates the long heritage of Presbyterian mission work going back to the founding to the Board of Foreign Missions in 1837. But this heritage must lead to a continuation of mission commitment in the future at every level of the church and with deep ecumenical cooperation. Out of this rich heritage of mission work and ecumenical leadership, Kirkpatrick offers a vision of the church which must grow past old separations. There must be a new way beyond past dichotomies: "Evangelism and social justice are two sides of the same coin. We do

---

43. Kirkpatrick and William, *What Unites Presbyterians*, 6.
44. Ibid., 12.
45. Ibid., 20–21.

not present the full gospel unless and until we demonstrate both issues."[46] Writing at the same time, Presbyterian leaders Milton Coalter, John Mulder and Louis Weeks also see the unity of social service and the proclamation of the Christian message as a powerful vital sign for the church.

> Social service programs are stirring within the new ecosystem of mainstream Protestant congregations, and this impulse can be nurtured and strengthened. The church can wield tremendous power in our society by reminding people that they are not powerless; they can in fact make a difference with God's direction and power. What is critical, however, is that churches provide a specifically Christian framework to supply motivation and meaning to people's gift of time, energy, and money. Prayer, Bible study, worship and discussion should be explicit and unapologetic features of the evangelism of service.[47]

The way forward in global mission work will not come from complete theological unanimity. As the global church continues to grow and expand in remarkable new ways and places in the twenty-first century the way forward comes from a different direction. The church is moving forward with a significant commitment to the concept of partnership in mission.

Future directions for study, discussion and prayer:
- How would you describe the different perspectives of Clifton Kirkpatrick and Donald McGavran?
- Within your congregation, is there any participation in the work of either the World Council of Churches or the Lausanne Congress?
- How would you describe your congregation's commitment to ecumenical relationships?

---

46. Ibid., 100.
47. Coalter et al., *Vital Signs*, 116.

CHAPTER 13

Hunter Farrell

THE HEADLINE SCREAMS "THE World's Most Polluted Places." La Oroya, Peru, is on *Time* magazine's online list which was researched and created by the Blacksmith Institute.[1] The pollutants at La Oroya include lead, copper, zinc and sulfur dioxide which are all products of the mining industry in the area. Lead is the contaminant of most concern because of its devastating impact on the health of children. High in the Andes Mountains in the mining community of La Oroya, Peru, 99 percent of the children have bloods levels of lead well above the recommended safe limits of the World Health Organization. A toxic level of lead will remain in the soil, due to generations of mining activity, for centuries. The metal refining company called Doe Run Peru, owned by the United States–based Renco Group, was cited by the Peruvian government for environmental violations and in response shut down the smelter in 2009. Now lawsuits in the United States and Peru will determine to what extent the mining and processing can continue in an environmentally safe way and to what extent the corporation is responsible for years of toxic pollution.

A group of concerned parents, after learning of the elevated levels of lead in their children's blood, organized a grassroots group called Movement for the Health of Oroya. This grassroots organization, supported by a number of humanitarian and mission agencies including OxFam and the Presbyterian Church (U.S.A.), has been working in support of the people

---

1. See "World's Most Polluted Places," at *Time.com*, http://content.time.com/time/specials/2007/completelist/0,29569,1661031,00.html.

of Oroya.[2] In Peru the group is calling on the government to hold firm on its environmental regulations; in the United States the group is calling on the government to insure that the Renco Group is held responsible for the cleanup of the polluted town and the legacy of devastating health concerns among the people there.

With leadership from Presbyterian mission co-workers in Peru, including Ruth and Hunter Farrell, an effort to network together a number of concerned community organizations and church groups came to fruition in 2000 with the formation of Joining Hands in Peru.[3] This network of Peruvian civil and faith based organizations, including Movement for the Health of Oroya, and North American mission groups was launched to collaboratively address the root causes of poverty throughout Peru, and especially the host of concerns directly related to the mining industry. A focus of the network's concern has been in La Oroya.

The tasks of networking, collaboration and partnership among many different constituencies in different nations were a crucial part of Hunter Farrell's service as a mission co-worker in Peru. It is this deep commitment to networking and partnership that has defined Farrell's service as the Director of Presbyterian World Mission. In the press release announcing his new position with Presbyterian World Mission in 2007, Farrell stated, "I sense an urgent call to bring together the newly emerging energy, creativity, resources and commitment of thousands of congregations across the Church with our denomination's remarkable mission history . . . In my missionary work in Africa and Latin America, I have seen that our Church had developed a solid reputation as a Christ-centered, responsible church-in-mission, a partner in Christ that can be counted on. We must build on that witness."[4]

---

2. See "La Oroya, Peru: Poisoned Town," at oxfamamerica.org.

3. Currently Jed Koball is serving as a Presbyterian mission co-worker in Peru and works with the Joining Hands effort in Oroya. See the Joining Hands website at PresbyterianMission.org/ministries/joininghands/peru. On the Rev. Jed Koball, see PresbyterianMission.org/ministries/missionconnections/koball-jed.

4. Marter, Jerry Van, "Long Term missionary Hunter Farrell named head of World Mission program area," News Release published at reformed-online.net.

Hunter Farrell

Under the leadership Hunter Farrell, the mission enterprise of the Presbyterian Church (U.S.A.) is working within an overarching framework of partnership. At Presbyterian World Mission's online directory of mission personnel there is a clear proclamation of this commitment: "The Presbyterian Church (U.S.A.) works with partner churches and organizations in more than 100 countries."[5] With the leadership of Hunter Farrell both the theological foundations and the financial support for Presbyterian World Mission have been invigorated. Here we will consider the historical development of the concept of partnership in mission particularly in the Presbyterian Church. Moreover the vital importance of partnership as a central, core value for mission will be explored. Doing mission in partnership always includes significant challenges, particularly when the mission work seeks to cross significant cultural barriers. A comprehensive understanding and expression of partnership in our world mission work is necessary to guide this work into the future, particularly in relationship with the vibrant, growing and often poor churches of the global south.

The concept of partnership is not new in the Presbyterian discussions about mission work. The concept emerged with a renewed emphasis when

---

5. See www.presbyterianmission.org/ministries/global.

the Commission on Ecumenical Mission and Relations (COEMAR) was formed in 1958 to carry on the work of the Presbyterian Board of Foreign Missions. Thus in the 1960s, the theological foundations for mission work and their practical, real life expression in the actual work of our mission personnel around the world significantly shifted with COEMAR's new direction. COEMAR initiated a thoroughgoing process of study and evaluation which included our mission partners. In addition, COEMAR also was committed to the hard work of implementing this new learning in the real, institutional life of the church's mission enterprise. The massive redirection which COEMAR introduced was essentially a comprehensive commitment to partnership in all our mission work. This was not a new idea, but now it was embedded into the institutional structure of the church's mission enterprise with a thorough tenacity.

COEMAR initially organized an advisory study to consider the strategy and direction of the church's mission work given the merger of the UPCNA with the PCUSA, and given the emerging issues in the contemporary culture. But COEMAR organized a study with a unique feature; Christian leaders from churches around the world were included on the study team.[6] As Presbyterian mission work was poised to move into the chaotic 1960s, the "Advisory Study" emphasized that a new relationship must exist between the older established churches and the younger churches of the world before "there can be a genuine partnership in mission."[7] The "Advisory Study" significantly influenced the direction of COEMAR. This is evidence of the church's remarkable institutional self-reflection and flexibility. Stanley Rycroft summarized the important insight that changed the strategic direction of COEMAR's work. Moving toward a vision of genuine partnership, it was

> recognized that a younger church must achieve authentic selfhood before this can take place, and that relationships between older and younger churches go through three stages: dependence, independence, and interdependence. In order to facilitate these changes in relationships and to allow an authentic selfhood to develop among churches in the mission field, the Commission has

---

6. "The fifteen members of the committee were drawn from Brazil, Cuba, Egypt, France, India, Iran, Korea, Lebanon, Nigeria, Switzerland, Taiwan and the United States. Three were Commission members, two were United Presbyterian missionaries. Among the group were ministers, laymen, laywomen, educators, student workers, a doctor, a sociologist, and a specialist in audio-visual work." Rycroft, *Ecumenical Witness*, 230.

7. Ibid., 235.

had to disentangle itself from the inner life of these churches, so that they might be independent, and free to engage in mission as churches in their own right. Partnership in mission, therefore, did not automatically come into existence.[8]

Thus Rycroft quotes from the commission's "Advisory Study" indicating the careful balance which must be achieved in the relationship between churches seeking authentic partnership: "The Commission on Ecumenical Mission and Relations has stated that partnership in mission presupposes two or more autonomous church bodies which voluntarily limit their own independent action in missionary outreach in order to insure a mutually satisfactory and a more highly productive interdependence in missionary endeavor."[9] Thus the newly formed United Presbyterian Church in the U.S.A., working through the Commission on Ecumenical Mission and Relations, sought to pull back the international missionaries deployed in order to encourage the full independence of the younger churches around the world.[10] The relationships between younger, indigenous churches and the missionaries who were working in their midst were being recast. In some places these relationships were generation's old, reaching back to the earliest days of the missionary movement. This strategic disengagement with younger churches all around the world was a deliberate shift to pave the way for partnership and mutuality in the future. Moving forward there was an effort to create equal, church-to-church partnerships. Thus practically the responsibility for the mission personnel working in nations all around the world shifted to the host churches. This transition was challenging as host churches in different nations had different capabilities and expectations for the relationships with mission personnel working in their countries. Despite the challenges, the younger churches were encouraged to move toward self-support and sustainability where, under the traditional model, they had been dependent on the expertise of missionaries. New collegial relationships between church leaders, who now needed to work together in more intentional ways, were fostered; ecumenical and cooperative

---

8. Ibid., 235.
9. Quoted from the "Advisory Study," in ibid., 237.
10. The southern Presbyterian Church, the Presbyterian Church in the United States, reached the same conclusion at their consultation held at Montreat, North Carolina, in 1962.

relationships between church bodies were advanced.[11] Thus the relationships between churches across the globe were shifting.

While mission work around the world was shifting in response to COEMAR's work, in the 1970s and 1980s the institutional landscape for American Presbyterians was also being massively restructured. After years of planning, a major, internal restructuring within the United Presbyterian Church in the U.S.A. was approved in 1972. This included redistricting of the synods, in part, so that major, metropolitan areas would not be divided into separate synods. Concerning world mission work, this restructuring created the Program Agency which merged COEMAR, and the Boards of Christian Education and National Missions. Thus the official life of COEMAR as the home of northern Presbyterian world mission work lasted from 1958 to 1972.[12]

Even more significant, after fourteen years of negotiation and planning, the long-delayed reunion of the northern and southern Presbyterian bodies, the UPCUSA and the PCUS, was approved by the respective General Assemblies and by the appropriate number of presbyteries. For 122 years these churches had been divided by the regional, political and theological differences of the Civil War era. Reunion was close in 1958, but the southern church had barely defeated the reunion proposal which was consummated between the northern branch and the smaller United Presbyterian Church of North America. Another twenty-five years would pass before the historic reunion of the northern and southern branches of the Presbyterianism took place in June 1983 in Atlanta, Georgia, creating the Presbyterian Church (U.S.A.).[13]

Careful planning went into the reunion of these two churches. The merging of the two world mission organizations in the reunited church was intentionally delayed for five years. Thus the Mission Board of the southern church and the Program Agency of the northern church, which included COEMAR, cooperated closely but maintained their separate mission programs until 1988 when the General Assembly Council was created with

11. Brown, *Presbyterians in World Mission*, 44.

12. See Reifsnyder, "Managing the Mission," 73.

13. Importantly, all three of the large, mainline branches of Presbyterianism in the United States, the UPCUSA, the PCUSA and the PCUS, were fully engaged in the international, ecumenical conversations throughout the twentieth century including Life and Work, Faith and Order, the International Missionary Council which were united as the World Council of Churches in 1961. All three of the branches of Presbyterianism were also involved in the National Council of Churches since its formation.

various ministry units, including the Global Mission Ministry Unit. In an era of serious membership decline and diminishing financial support, another major restructuring was approved in 1993 in an effort to simplify and become more directly responsive to congregations. The Worldwide Ministries Division was thus created with Clifton Kirkpatrick as director. This division included a sweeping mandate of responsibilities including all world mission work and ecumenical relationships.[14]

With Kirkpatrick's shepherding, the Worldwide Ministries Division proposed and the 1993 General Assembly approved a comprehensive policy paper which articulated a theology of mission: "Mission in the 1990s: A Strategic Direction in the Worldwide Ministry for the Presbyterian Church (U.S.A.).[15] The new policy responds to "a time of incredible change" in the world.[16] The policy document also responds to the deep changes that were transforming the Presbyterian Church (U.S.A.). The policy was written in the early 1990s when the denomination was staggering from decades of significant membership loss and the corresponding financial loss; these, of course, had altered the influential role of Presbyterians in the larger culture. Importantly, the policy paper recognized an important power shift within the church itself; this was a result, in part, of a pervasive anti-institutional tone of the era and the deep polarization of the culture wars. "Replacing an earlier assumption, that the General Assembly and its agencies did mission for the churches, is a new understanding that the local congregation is a major agent of God's mission in both the local community and the globe."[17] Also, the new policy had to respond to the remarkable "shift in the

14. The Worldwide Ministries Division included responsibility for missionary personnel, relations with overseas churches, global and international evangelism, ecumenical relations, global education and leadership development, international health, hunger programs, disaster relief, self-development of people, refugee programs, and global awareness and involvement. See Brown, *Presbyterians in World Mission*, 45–46.

15. The policy document, a study guide "Mission: Commitment to God's Hopeful Vision," and essays by Filipino church leader Erme R. Camba and Brazilian church leader Claude E. Labrunie are published in the PCUSA journal *Church and Society*, vol. 84 (September/ October 1993).

16. The paper lists these major global events as part of the new context for world mission: "the fall of the Berlin Wall, the end of the cold war, the breakup of the Soviet Union, the freedom of Nelson Mandela and a first opening of apartheid, the specter of starvation in countries throughout Africa, a war in the Persian Gulf, a dramatic rise in racial and ethnic tensions, a growing gap between the rich and the poor throughout the world, an ecological crisis that threatens the future of our planet." See "Mission in the 1990s," 7–8.

17. Ibid., 8.

center of gravity" of global Christianity with, by the 1990s, the majority of Christians living in Africa, Asia and Latin America. Given the significantly changed context in the world and within the church itself what was called for, however, was a new "style of mission." There is here a vital distinction between the substance and the style of mission. What is advocated is a change in style, tone, attitude and stance for the work of mission. The essential, timeless substance of mission work is consistent: "The urgency for world evangelization, for ministries of compassion, for justice and peace, and for the unity of all God's people is a great as it has ever been."[18] The style of mission is the personal, spiritual attitude with which these classic, mission objectives are carried out.

> It must not be one of arrogance or domination, but one of humility and repentance. It must be one of partnership and mutuality with the worldwide body of Christ. Our submission as Presbyterians to the principalities and powers that drive our culture and dominate our world is massive. We have fallen woefully short in bringing the gospel mandate to bear in effective ways in this world. Repentance and obedience must be the beginning point for mission in the way of Christ who redeemed the world through his suffering for all humanity.[19]

A major section of the policy paper was titled "The Way We Carry Out Our Mission." This section emphasized the importance of style and attitude. The calling to work in partnership is named as the primary commitment of our mission enterprise. This has always been a strength of Presbyterian mission work which has created close relationships with churches around the world and has encouraged collaboration through the ecumenical movement. Thus the Presbyterian Church must demonstrate the "strategic effectiveness of an ecumenical and partner-church based approach to mission. We must consult and work with partners in directing our outreach to new frontiers of mission and evangelism as we seek to find new patterns of mutuality, people-to-people relations, and sharing in mission."[20]

The church's foreign mission enterprise was reiterating a theology of partnership which had been conceptualized long before. The challenge of a comprehensive commitment to partnership in mission had already been experienced much earlier when COEMAR introduced the idea in the

---

18. Ibid.
19. Ibid..
20. Ibid., 15.

1960s. At that time the difficulty of older, established churches working in partnership with newly emerging, young churches was identified. It was challenging for mission personnel who had traditionally brought expertise and a wide breadth of resources to the mission field to quickly transform to a new role as partners in mission. Their partners in the new, emerging churches were often not equipped with the same expertise and experience. Nonetheless COEMAR was conceptually committed to work toward the full independence of its new, partner churches around the world.

By the era of the 1990s it was recognized that many of the younger, emerging churches around the world had grown to become vibrant denominations in their own right. But there remained huge economic chasms between the nations of the world and thus between the different churches. In many contexts the gap between the rich and the poor had increased. How is it possible for a rich, established church like the Presbyterian Church (U.S.A.) to be in full and mutual partnership with a younger, much poorer church in the developing world? The challenge of partnership as a style and attitude for mission work is profoundly difficult in a context of vast differences in wealth. In his essay responding to the "Mission in the 1990s" policy document, Professor Claude Emmanuel Labrunie considered the New Testament basis of the relationship of rich and poor churches to be the essential challenge to doing mission in partnership.[21] He offered the provocative idea, which he considered biblical, that "the poor are Christ for the rich." He wrote out of his experience as a leader with the Presbyterian Church of Brazil, a denomination with a long history of shared mission, partnership and at times conflict with the Presbyterian Church (U.S.A.):

> There's nothing more difficult than the aid of the rich to the poor. Aid rather than humiliation will only take place with the liberating help of the Holy Spirit. This is the situation of the incarnation of Christ. "Always from the situation of the poor" means from within that situation, in a free exercise of a liberating struggle of and by the poor. It is impossible for the rich to transform the poor into free persons within this existential context of poverty. Only the poor can invent, discern, and construct their own freedom. The

---

21. Claude Emmanuel Labrunie was the president of the Presbyterian Mission of Brazil, served as moderator of the Presbytery of Victoria and as a moderator of the General Assembly of the United Presbyterian Church of Brazil from 1987–89. See Labrunie, "Poor as Christ," 94.

rich can help, yes, by extending a hand, so to speak; but it behooves the poor to decide if, and, or how this hand is accepted.[22]

The 1993 policy paper "Mission in the 1990s" set an important tone for the work of Presbyterian World Mission which has been affirmed repeatedly since then. In 2003 this conceptual foundation for the work of world mission was reiterated with the approval of "Presbyterians Do Mission in Partnership," a policy statement of the General Assembly.[23] In this new twenty-first century, although the foundational concept of partnership has remained essential for our mission work the context has shifted again in light of the enormous proliferation of short-term mission trips and thus the general fragmentation of the mission enterprise. By 2003 there was a wider and deeper need for the practice of partnership. The national bureaucracy for world mission was no longer, in an increasingly fragmented and divided church, the center of mission work. There was now, in the emphasis on partnership, an explicit understanding that this is an essential practice not only with other churches in other nations but within the Presbyterian Church (U.S.A.) itself. Thus the World Mission website declares, "The practice of partnership guides our whole connectional church. It guides us individually as members, officers and pastors. It guides us collectively as congregations, presbyteries, synods, General Assembly ministry and related institutions."[24] This is a key direction for the future of the church as it continues to finds its footing as a large, national, mainline denomination within the new religious landscape. Being a cheerleader and advocate for a solid theology of partnership at all levels of the church—local, national and global—is an important role for our national mission agencies today.

The 2003 policy paper "We Do Mission in Partnership" calls for the discipline of partnership throughout the church. This is an essential theological commitment if the church is to overcome our increasing fragmentation into a plethora of mission groups each working independently. Too often our mission enterprise is constrained by the shortsightedness of each council within the denomination—sessions, presbyteries, synods and the

---

22. Labrunie, "Poor as Christ for the Rich," 95.

23. This policy is currently hyperlinked at the Presbyterian World Mission website as one of the foundational documents for mission work in the PCUSA. See "Presbyterians Do Mission in Partnership," at www.presbyterianmission.org/ministries/global/mission-partnership.

24. Quoted from "We Do Mission in Partnership," at www.presbyterianmission.org/ministries/global/mission-partnership.

General Assembly—often focusing on their own ministry and mission. The discipline of partnership is a commitment to reach out and connect with other parts of the church as a visible expression of the call to unity. This is a sweeping, broad theology of mission that encompasses the whole life of the church, not only relationships internationally. The concept of partnership is vital today within the internal workings of the church, especially between congregations and the various councils. Thus our theology of mission, which highlights a concept of partnership, is key to the future of the whole church. The discipline of partnership is a high calling rooted in the "fundamental unity in Jesus Christ." "We understand 'Mission' to be God's work for the sake of the world God loves. We understand this work to be centered in the Lordship of Jesus Christ and made real through the active and leading power of the Holy Spirit. Recognizing our human limitations and because of our fundamental unity in Jesus Christ, we believe we are called to mission through the discipline of partnership."[25]

As a General Assembly policy statement this document, "We Do Mission in Partnership," is clearly looking in two directions; on one hand this discipline of partnership is advocated as the practice of mission with all our international partnerships. This is a difficult calling since the Presbyterian Church (U.S.A.) is one of the classic, missionary churches that had, through the generations, the power, resources, and expertise within the global mission relationships. Can the Presbyterian Church pull back from such a position of power and wealth to truly be a partner in Christ? This is a question that has reverberated through Presbyterian mission strategy since, at least, the formation of COEMAR in 1958. This long history underscores how difficult it is to create and sustain true partnership in the mission enterprise around the world.

On the other hand, the General Assembly through its statement "We Do Mission in Partnership" is looking back into the structure of the denomination itself. Can the discipline of partnership be the impetus for a new connectionalism in the Presbyterian Church (U.S.A.)? Will the congregations and the presbyteries seek to be partners in mission with the General Assembly? This is the proclamation and the hope:

> We give visible recognition of our belonging to one another as one denominational family. We give this recognition as Presbyterians through our connectional system of congregations, presbyteries, synods, General Assemblies and related institutions. The one table

25. See ibid.

around which we gather is God's table and the one mission to which we are called in God's mission . . . We believe that doing mission in partnership broadens our awareness of how interconnected God's mission is at the local, national and global levels.[26]

In a new era of world mission in which each congregation, each presbytery and each small constituency of Christians has easy access to the transportation and communication technology to reach the whole world the challenges to do mission in partnership are magnified. The discipline of partnership in mission is the antidote for the "go-it-alone" approach to mission of many Presbyterian congregations and other North American Christian groups.[27] In her recent book in support of Presbyterian World Mission, Sherron Kay George, a long-serving Presbyterian mission coworker in Brazil, offered a passionate lament against the prevalent 'go-it-alone' attitude:

> But is it either denominational agencies or local congregations doing mission? Why can't local churches, presbyteries, the national mission agency, and other mission agencies work together for the greater good? Do we need to split ourselves into opposing interest groups? Why don't the streams majoring in evangelism, compassion, and prophetic justice dialogue with one another? Who is helped when we compete and tear one another down? How can we learn from one another, support one another, and be united in our mission efforts? Can we learn to focus on the big picture of God's mission rather than on the small parts? How can we fit the pieces of this mission puzzle together into a whole? What would it look like to value those who are working on other parts? Where can we find guidance in the quest for new patterns?[28]

Thus Sherron George proposes a "missionary dialogue" as an important step toward the full expression of partnership in Presbyterian mission.

26. Ibid.

27. Sherron George wrote: "In today's global world we see broadening opportunity for direct involvement in international mission. This can bestow great blessing as involvement in mission transforms individuals, their congregations, and the mission structures of our church and of our partner churches. It also presents inherent dangers as differences of wealth, power, worldview, and cultural awareness vary widely among those who seek to do God's work. Direct congregational or personal mission efforts sometimes bypass, or miss, the guidance of the church as God has created it in other places as well as the hard-won learnings that have come out of previous mission involvement." George, *Called as Partners*, xi.

28. George, *Better Together*, xiii.

In actual practice, George wants to bring together the different focuses of mission—"people involved in ministries of evangelism, compassionate service, and social justice"—in a dialogue and thus step away from the increasingly competitive, fractured and fragmented reality of Presbyterians doing mission.[29]

Sherron George also created a study guide to support the implementation of the General Assembly's policy statement "We Do Mission in Partnership." Here George reached for a soaring, conceptual vision of partnership that is thoroughly biblical and theological. Her soaring, theological vision of partnership is inspired by the doctrine of the Trinity: "Partnership is not merely a means, method or approach to mission. Partnership is a fundamental dynamic of the triune missionary God of love who is, acts, and relates in mutual partnership in sending the Son, the Spirit and the church into the world as instruments of God's saving mission."[30] George continued in her book to create a solid biblical foundation for the understanding of partnership in mission.

In his study paper published in support of the "We Do Mission in Partnership" statement, Professor Philip Wickeri traces the history of the concept of partnership through its discussion in the ecumenical movement. Indeed, Wickeri confirms the long history of discussion about partnership in ecumenical circles. This is not a new conversation or vision. "Partnership in mission, an expression of what it means to be united in Christ in mission, was central to the emerging understanding of world mission in the twentieth century and has been the subject of ecumenical discussion for at least seventy-five years."[31] But partnership has proved to be a slippery concept, easy to discuss and difficult to implement. Significant barriers between established and new churches, differences between rich and poor churches, different understandings of the meaning and practice of mission, and different ways to organize and administer the work of mission all compromised and belittled the fullness of partnership in mission. The discussion of partnership in mission is not new. Nonetheless its full expression remains elusive and challenging. "The discussion of partnership, solidarity and transforming mission structures is needed not because partnership has been tried and found wanting, but because churches have not been willing to follow through with the radical demands of what partnership and

---

29. Ibid., 5.
30. George, *Called as Partners*, 1.
31. Wickeri, *Partnership, Solidarity, and Friendship*, 1.

working together in God's mission requires."³² With a beautiful grounding in solid Bible study, Wickeri offered a deeper, spiritually rich vision of partnership. Partnership is a high calling for all relationships among Christians: "Partnership reinterpreted as solidarity in friendship involves a recovery of this concept of sharing that is central to the biblical witness. Another way of saying this is that sharing in solidarity is an expression of the justice, courtesy, and love that partners have for one another."³³

From a different location outside of Presbyterian circles, Cathy Ross offered a compelling "Theology of Partnership" in an article in the *International Bulletin of Missionary Research*.³⁴ Her work reflects the fact that the commitment to partnership in mission is much wider than simply a Presbyterian Church (U.S.A.) conversation and may be one of the essential themes in missiology today. Ross seeks a theology of partnership that is thoroughly theological; she uses Paul Tillich's classic work *Love, Power and Justice* as the theological foundation for her reflections on partnership. From Tillich, Ross claims his deep listening as a vital, first ingredient in any partnership:

> In order to know what is just in a person-to-person encounter, love listens. It is its first task to listen. No human relation, especially no intimate one, is possible without mutual listening . . . All things and all men, so to speak, call on us with small or loud voices. They want us to listen, they want us to understand their intrinsic claims, their justice of being. They want justice from us. But we can give it to them only through love which listens . . . Listening love is the first step to justice in person-to-person encounters.³⁵

Only with a commitment to such profound person-to-person relationships does partnership have any foundation on which to build. The powerful intimacy of listening love which understands implicitly the demands of justice in the other person creates the ground upon which a partnership may be established. Only then can we move toward a theology of partnership which Ross sees involving three dimensions: "First, that partnership is an idea essential to the very nature of God. Second, that partnership speaks

---

32. Ibid., 3.

33. Ibid., 13.

34. Cathy Ross manages the Crowther Centre for Mission Education at the Church Mission Society in the United Kingdom. Previously she worked in Rwanda, Congo and Uganda with the New Zealand Church Mission Society.

35. Ross, "Theology of Partnership," 145.

of God's relationship with humanity. Third, that partnership indicates the true relationship between human beings."[36] Such relationships are idealistic and visionary. So many challenges in the everyday world of mission work interfere with our ability to nurture such relationships. Ross recognizes the multiplicity of challenges; and the one, profound challenge that continually haunts the creation of true partnership in the realm of mission work the world over: "There is one issue that distorts all the fine ideals and makes the practice of partnership difficult and demanding. This is the issue of power. It is difficult to have a truly mutual relationship when the two parties possess unequal power. But that is the reality of our world today. We know that money, resources, education, land, access to technology, ownership, and much more are unfairly and unequally distributed."[37] Thus for Cathy Ross a comprehensive theology of partnership offers an elusive, challenging goal and an inspiring vision for the church rooted in the movements of love, power and justice.

In his massive textbook, *Understanding Christian Mission*, Professor Scott Sunquist includes a full chapter on partnership.[38] Since 2012, Sunquist has served as the dean of the School of Intercultural Studies and professor of world Christianity at Fuller Theological Seminary in California. Sunquist has had extensive experience as a missionary in Asia where he was a lecturer in church history, ecumenics, and Asian Christianity at Trinity Theological College (1987–1995) and also served as pastor of Covenant Presbyterian Church in Singapore.

Sunquist understands the shift that has taken place which allows Christians from every place to do mission to every place. In response he offers three compelling reasons why a robust theology of partnership in mission is vital today. First is the practical matter of the easy availability of travel and communication technology which connects the world. "Individual churches can communicate directly with synods, presbyteries, or parishes around the world with little or no oversight or previous knowledge. Individuals or small groups can travel easily, and often decide on their own to 'help' a church in another country. Much of this help is impulsive and

---

36. Ibid., 147.
37. Ibid., 148.
38. Sunquist, *Understanding Christian Mission*; see esp. chap. 12, "Global Community: Partnership in Mission."

counterproductive—missiologically speaking—because it ignores partnership as a means of and mode for mission."[39]

Second, the massive expansion of global Christianity has also now changed the field. It seems as if every Christian group in every land is now committed to mission. There is no longer a short list of mission agencies that dominate and control all mission work.

> In the past few decades, the major players and major church councils have greatly decreased in influence and size. They have been replaced by thousands of local societies, indigenous churchs, NGOs, and non-Western churches and mission. The expansion of Christianity in the past half century has also meant the diversification of structures and organizations. Christian mission is much harder to grasp, but it is much more active from and to all the corners of the world. Moving from hierarchical Western missions to a global network of mission requires greater partnership in each place.[40]

Today the transformation from heathen to partner is complete. The era of the large, western mission agencies recruiting and sending missionaries to save the heathen in the far off, foreign lands of the world is a strategy that has become a relic. Our new global Christianity finds vital Christian groups is every place; and in every place the Bible is studied and believers are inspired to gather into Christian communities and reach out in mission. Thus for Sunquist, "Thirdly, partnership has come to the fore because of the sudden reorientation of global Christianity that has occurred in recent history. In almost any country to which a missionary might be sent, there are now local Christian gatherings or even a mature Christian church."[41]

Given the essential need to work in partnership, Sunquist develops a comprehensive, theological understanding of this concept: "Partnership, theological speaking, is grounded in four basic theological and biblical concepts: the Trinity, Jesus' high priestly prayer, the church as the body of Christ and the apostolic missions in the New Testament."[42] In addition to this strong theological foundation, he also develops an outline of practical advice for working in partnership. Thus for Sunquist,

---

39. Ibid.
40. Ibid.
41. Ibid.
42. Ibid.

not only does Christian theology point to cooperation and partnership in mission, but the size and complexity of global concerns to which the church should speak requires this partnership. No one individual church, or even national church can solve the major issues of violence and human trafficking, nor can they alone reach the mass of unreached people in the world. The *missio Dei* requires that we work together as the body of Christ, not building personal kingdoms, but looking forward in our ministry to the city built by God (Hebrews 11:10).[43]

Thus a full biblical, theological and practical concept of partnership is crucial to a robust commitment to mission work today.

The General Assembly of the Presbyterian Church (U.S.A.) officially established a solid theology with the policy statement in 1993 "Mission in the 1990s: A Strategic Direction in Worldwide Ministry for the Presbyterian Church (U.S.A.)," and also the 2003 policy statement "We Do Mission in Partnership." These are important resources for understanding the basis and direction of the Presbyterian mission enterprise today. Hunter Farrell began his service as director of Presbyterian World Mission fully committed to this direction and tone but also fully aware of the "seismic shift" that has taken place in the practice of mission. Thus throughout 2008 and 2009 the Presbyterian Mission Agency contracted with the Konterra Group, a management consulting company, to help with the development of a new strategic direction for World Mission.[44] This new strategic direction was reported as an "Action Item" to the February 24–25, 2010, meeting of the General Assembly Mission Council.[45]

Presbyterian World Mission's new strategic direction included a precise Theological Statement, Vision and Mission Statement, Core Values, and Directional Goals. The first directional goal was one of the most innovative and thoughtful features of the new plan: Community of Mission Practice. An important concept paper was attached explaining this new idea. This direction clearly shows the influence of Farrell's leadership. Given his many years of experience in the mission field, he participated in and witnessed the paradigm shift in mission work. This shift is the driving motivation for

---

43. Ibid.

44. On the Konterra Group, see www.konterragroup.net. Under the heading of "What We Do" their website explains, "We help organizations and their people develop solutions that sharpen clarity, strengthen resilience and incorporate learning."

45. Item A.103, For Action: New Strategic Direction for World Mission, General Assembly Mission Council, February 24–25, 2010.

the new strategic plan and the concept of Community of Mission Practice. The concept paper explains:

> This paradigmatic shift from the direct mode of mission to working in partnership characterized by mutuality was not an easy one. But the fruits of the last half century of mission in partnership have proven that our forbearers rightly discerned the Spirit's call . . . Today, we believe the Spirit is calling our church to a deeper understanding of partnership . . . This seismic shift in the understanding and practice of mission has opened the door to direct involvement of U.S. Presbyterians at unprecedented levels. Greatly increased involvement and giving and the opportunity for personal and congregational transformation have been some of the positive effects of the change. But our global partners note our mission efforts have become highly uncoordinated and, in some cases, less responsive to the needs as perceived by the local community . . . This shift, from one highly centralized agency to thousands of highly decentralized agencies, is a massive one and invites Presbyterian World Mission to reform its self-understanding and the focus of its work to include many U.S. Presbyterian mission constituents—congregations, middle governing bodies, validated mission support groups and other mission organizations—as partners in mission, and to continue its commitment to engaging in God's mission in a spirit of humility and mutuality.

Thus emerges the Community of Mission Practice.

A Community of Mission Practice is the overlapping space where it may all come together in and through Jesus Christ. This conceptual Community of Mission Practice includes three circles of participants which overlap and cooperate. (1) Presbyterian World Mission with its long heritage of recruiting and sending long-term, professional, mission co-workers is a vital participant. (2) In the new culture of mission work in which local groups of Presbyterians are reaching out around the world, a Community of Mission Practice must also include the often short-term mission work of other Presbyterians including congregations and presbyteries. (3) The Community of Mission Practice must include the global partners themselves. We must be intentional about reaching out in partnership to the churches and Christian groups that already exist in the contexts where we seek to serve. This includes the bold, new indigenous churches that are growing throughout the global south. A Community of Mission Practice will meet together in a common, spiritual space to be "shaped by disciplines of prayer, Bible study, reflection and worship." Such Communities of Mission Practice are a bold vision and a high calling in this new era of mission work. In recent decades tremendous, fragmented and fractured energy and commitment have flowed out from countless churches, groups and organizations into the entire world, often expressed as "go-it-alone" mission work. This energy has often clashed and collided with the long term mission work which mission agencies and denominational boards have sustained for generations. Moreover the mission work flowing from these new efforts and from the traditional mission agencies has also often been at odds with the powerful new commitment to mission which Christians in every place, including the younger churches of the global south, now claim as their calling. The insight which the concept of Community of Mission Practice offers is that this massive, new energy for mission, wherever its source, is not be denigrated or rejected but rather harnessed and coordinated. The individual congregations and presbyteries across the PC(USA) are not going to stop their direct involvement in mission now that the transformative power of this work has been experienced. On the other hand, the powerful heritage of professional mission work organized and sponsored by national, denominational mission agencies, like Presbyterian World Mission, will also continue and is highly sought by church partners around the world who need support and expertise. There is now an important role for our denominational mission agencies. In this new day, the concept of Community of Mission Practice is a space where all involved bring their energy, commitment, passion and vision together. "A community of mission practice shares an identity derived from a common passion."

A direction is set. Once upon a time Christians, including many Presbyterians, went out with a powerful conviction to convert the heathen in foreign mission fields with the proclamation of the gospel of Jesus Christ. Today Christians, including many Presbyterians, move out in mission from every place to every place with an equally powerful conviction and calling. Coming from every direction and going in every direction Christians today may easily crash into one another or simply walk past one another. Or with the whole world easily within reach, Christians today have an opportunity to find a common space where they may meet together to listen and learn, nurturing the spiritual intimacy that leads to partnership. In these common spaces new communities of mission practice may emerge which find more energy together than if each remained separate. Out of these overlapping circles where all mission-committed people with a common passion may gather, the proclamation of the gospel of Jesus Christ will continue to ring out. Thanks be to God.

Future directions for discussion, study and prayer:
- What does the concept "partnership in mission" mean to you?
- In pondering your own involvement in world mission, do you have any experiences of truly working in partnership?
- What would be the impact and consequences if our work in world mission was deeply and thoroughly committed to working in partnership?

APPENDIX I

Presbyterians Do Mission in Partnership

2003 General Assembly Policy Statement[1]

Presbyterian Church (U.S.A.)

Summary

As heirs to God's grace in Jesus Christ, and joint heirs with all who confess him Lord, we affirm our place as Presbyterians in the whole Body of Christ, the Church. We understand "Mission" to be God's work for the sake of the world God loves. We understand this work to be centered in the Lordship of Jesus Christ and made real through the active and leading power of the Holy Spirit. Recognizing our human limitations and because of our fundamental unity in Jesus Christ, we believe we are called to mission through the discipline of partnership.

The practice of partnership guides our whole connectional church. It guides us individually as members, officers and pastors. It guides us collectively as congregations, presbyteries, synods, General Assembly ministries and related institutions. In doing mission in partnership, we seek to be guided by certain principles:

1. Shared Grace and Thanksgiving.

---

1. Available at http://www.pcusa.org/resource/presbyterians-do-mission-partnership.

Appendix I

2. Mutuality and Interdependence.
3. Recognition and Respect.
4. Open Dialogue and Transparency.
5. Sharing of Resources.

Statement

As heirs to God's grace in Jesus Christ, and joint heirs with all who confess him Lord, we affirm our place as Presbyterians in the whole Body of Christ, the Church. We give visible recognition of our belonging to one another as one denominational family. We give this recognition as Presbyterians through our connectional system of congregations, presbyteries, synods, General Assemblies and related institutions. The one table around which we gather is God's table and the one mission to which we are called is God's mission.[2]

The Presbyterian Church (U.S.A.) declares that wherever one part is engaged in God's mission, all are engaged.[3] Whenever and wherever one engages in that mission, one bears witness to the saving love of God in Jesus Christ. Through this love, empowered by the Holy Spirit, all are made one. This unity is a gift of God's grace that extends across cultural, linguistic, economic and other barriers that divide us within the Body of Christ and across the human family.

Mission

As Christians, we understand "Mission" to be God's work for the sake of the world God loves. We understand this work to be centered in the Lordship of Jesus Christ and made real through the active and leading power of the Holy Spirit. The "where" and "how" and "with whom" of mission is of God's initiative, sovereign action, and redeeming grace. The message we are called to bear is the Good News of salvation through Jesus Christ. The PC(USA) claims responsibility for bearing the Good News in this way: "The Church is called to be Christ's faithful evangelist

---

2. in Latin, Missio Dei.
3. Book of Order (G-9.0103).

Presbyterians Do Mission in Partnership

1. going into the world, making disciples of all nations, baptizing them in the name of the Father and of the Son and of the Holy Spirit, teaching them to observe all he has commanded;

2. demonstrating by the love of its members for one another and by the quality of its common life the new reality in Christ; sharing in worship, fellowship, and nurture, practicing a deepened life of prayer and service under the guidance of the Holy Spirit;

3. participating in God's activity in the world through its life for others by

    - healing and reconciling and binding up wounds,
    - ministering to the needs of the poor, the sick, the lonely and the powerless,
    - engaging in the struggle to free people from sin, fear, oppression, hunger and injustice,
    - giving itself and its substance to the service of those who suffer,
    - sharing with Christ in the establishing of his just, peaceable, and loving rule in the world."[4]

Partnership

As Presbyterians, we recognize the Reformed tradition as one part of the larger Body of Christ, the Church. Other communions in the household of God have equally unique and valued places at the table of God's mission. Recognizing our human limitations and because of our fundamental unity in Jesus Christ, we believe we are called to mission in the discipline of partnership. We believe that doing mission in partnership broadens our awareness of how interconnected God's mission is at the local, national and global levels. Jesus invites us as friends to follow his commandment of love and bear fruit that will last (John 15:12–17). Like Paul and Titus, we become partners with each other and with Christ in united and mutual service (II Corinthians 8:16–24). Guided by Christ's humility, we work to empty ourselves of all pride, power, sin, and privilege so that God may be glorified (Philippians 2:5–11). Within and beyond our connectional community, doing mission in such true partnership opens us to opportunities

---

4. Book of Order (G-3.0300).

for mutual encouragement, mutual transformation, mutual service and mutual renewal.

The practice of partnership guides our whole connectional church. It guides us individually as members, officers and pastors. It guides us collectively as congregations, presbyteries, synods, General Assembly ministries and related institutions. Through prayer, humility and a mutual openness to one another, we develop a cooperative witness that exalts the Lord we serve.

The discipline of partnership assumes that mission can best be done by joining hands with those who share a common vision. Partnership in mission involves two or more organizations who agree to submit themselves to a common task or goal, mutually giving and receiving and surrounded by prayer so that God's work can be more faithfully accomplished. Theologically and biblically, partnership is based on the fundamental belief that God's love for the world is greater than any one church can possibly comprehend or realize. Knowing the breadth of God's love for the world, we affirm that there are different forms of partnership with different patterns of cooperation. We may join around a common goal with other churches, with secular organizations or with other faith communities. In any case, work for the common good extends partnership — and the service of God's mission — to all people.

Principles of Partnership

In doing mission in partnership, we seek to be guided by certain principles:

1. Shared Grace and Thanksgiving. Partnership calls all partners to confess individual and collective failings, to seek forgiveness for complicity with powers of injustice, to repent from histories of shared exploitation, to move toward common celebration of Christ's sacrifice of reconciliation, and together to give thanks and praise to God for all gifts of grace and renewal.

2. Mutuality and Interdependence. Partnership calls for interdependence in which mutual aid comes to all, where mutual accountability resides, and no partner dominates another because of affluence or "expertise."

3. Recognition and Respect. Partnership calls all partners to respect other partners in Christ, and to recognize one another's equal standing before God.
4. Open Dialogue and Transparency. Partnership calls for open dialogue where a common discernment of God's call to mission is sought, where Scripture is the base for prophetic challenge, where local initiative is respected, where differences are meditated in a Christ-like manner, and where all partners are transparent with regard to their activities and support.
5. Sharing of Resources. Partnership calls for the sharing of all types of resources: human, cultural, financial and spiritual; especially including friendly conversation and faith-transforming life experiences.

Partnership Commitments

Doing mission in partnership, we commit to be guided by these principles both individually and collectively. In the spirit of candid evaluation, we commit to asking ourselves discerning questions. For each principle, certain approaches are suggested:

Shared Grace and Thanksgiving

Is there courage to confess human sins and confront the forces which deny the abundant life God promises to all in Jesus Christ?

Is God's forgiveness mutually shared in Jesus Christ?

Does the community of partners join in thankful worship to celebrate God's gift of grace and renewal?

Mutuality and Interdependence

- Is each partner's self-reliance affirmed, with mutual giving and receiving?
- Is there space for all partners to be guided by self-determination?
- Beyond unhealthy dynamics of power and dependency, is there openness to new dynamics of mutual service and mutual renewal?

Appendix I

Recognition and Respect

- Is there recognition of the self-affirmed identities of each partner?
- Are the unique contexts of all partners recognized and respected?
- Are gifts and needs of all partners affirmed and respected?
- Are cultural differences being mediated with sincerity and in a Christ-like manner?

Open Dialogue and Transparency

- Is there local initiative in mission discernment and mission activity?
- Does God's Word shape us to lovingly confront one another's failings and prophetically challenge the world's systems of power and domination?
- Is there transparency with all partners about what is being done in mission, even if there is disagreement?

Sharing of Resources

- Do partners minister to and inspire one another, listen to and critique one another?
- Is there mutual accountability in the exchange of all resources, including human,
- cultural, financial and spiritual?
- In trusting relationship, have partners moved beyond two-way relationships into open mission networks and ever-expanding webs of mission relationships?

As heirs to God's grace in Jesus Christ and joint heirs with all who confess him Lord, we commit to wrestle with these questions. We look toward the promise of Christ. We count on the subtle power of the Holy Spirit to guide and limit us. We hope, standing firm in common praise to the Triune God, that our practice of partnership may be transformed; that our participation in the Missio Dei may more fully contribute to the abundant life that God promises all people and all creation.

APPENDIX II

Communities of Mission Practice
New Strategic Direction for World Mission
General Assembly Mission Council, February 2010

Presbyterian World Mission,

in collaboration with U.S. Presbyterians

and global partners

    inspires, equips and connects

        in order to engage communities of mission practice

            in God's mission.

Beginning in 1837 the Presbyterian Church's Board of Foreign Mission sent missionaries into the world to preach, teach and heal. Today total personnel engaged in World Mission exceed 200 serving in approximately 50 countries.

World Mission leaders have begun to work intentionally in "Communities of Mission Practice."

Appendix II

Communities of Mission Practice are

The space where...
    PC(USA) mission participants,
        global partners and
            World Mission (including mission personnel)

                Commit to interact regularly to learn and grow as a community;

                Come together to share an identity derived from a common mission passion;

                Are guided and shaped by the practices of prayer, Bible study, reflection and worship.

World Mission, in consultation with global partners, mission personnel, PC(USA) mission leaders, and other General Assembly Mission Council Ministries, has identified three "critical global issues" to focus its energy and resources:

- Strengthening the Church's capacity to survive, to thrive and to witness to the good news in Jesus Christ,
- Addressing the root causes of poverty, including the negative effects of economic globalization on the poorest and most vulnerable in every society, paying special attention to women and children, and
- Engaging in reconciliation amidst cultures of violence.

Bibliography

Anderson, Fred. *The War That Made America: A Short History of the French and Indian War*. New York: Viking, 2005. Kindle edition.

Anderson, Gerald H. "American Protestants in Pursuit of Mission: 1886–1986." *International Bulletin of Missionary Research* 12 (1988) 98–118.

Applegarth, Margaret T. *The Career of a Cobbler: The Life Story of William Carey*. New York: Revel, 1922. http://commons.ptsem.edu/id/careerofcobblerlooappl.

Bosch, David J. *Transforming Mission: Paradigm Shifts in Theology of Mission*. New York: Orbis, 2006.

Briggs, Charles Augustus. *American Presbyterianism: Its Origins and Early History*. . . . New York, 1885. http://commons.ptsem.edu/id/americanpresbyteoobrig.

Brown, G. Thompson. *Presbyterians in World Mission*. Rev. ed. Decatur, GA: CTS, 1995.

Brown, G. Thompson, and T. Donald Black. "Structures for a Changing Church." Chapter 3 in *A History of Presbyterian Missions 1944–2007*, edited by Scott W. Sunquist and Caroline N. Becker. Louisville: Geneva Press, 2008.

Buck, Pearl S. *The Good Earth*. New York: Open Road Integrated Media, 2013. Kindle edition.

Bullock, Robert H., Jr., ed. *Presbyterians Being Reformed: Reflections on What the Church Needs Today*. Louisville: Geneva Press, 2006. Kindle edition.

Carey, William. *An Enquiry into the Obligations of Christians, to Use Means for the Conversion of the Heathens*. . . . Leicester, 1792.

Clarke, Erskine. "Presbyterian Ecumenical Activity in the United States." In Coalter et al., *Diversity of Discipleship*, 149–69.

Coalter, Milton J., et al. *The Diversity of Discipleship: The Presbyterians and Twentieth-Century Christian Witness*. Louisville: Westminster John Knox, 1991.

———. *Vital Signs: The Promise of Mainstream Protestantism*. Grand Rapids: Eerdmans, 1996.

Coventry Smith, John. *From Colonialism to World Community: The Church's Pilgrimage*. Philadelphia: Geneva Press, 1982.

Duff, Alexander. *India, and India Missions, including Sketches of the Gigantic System of Hinduism*. . . . Edinburgh, 1839. http://commons.ptsem.edu/id/indiaindiamissioooduff.

———. *Missions: The Chief End of the Christian Church*. Edinburgh, 1877. http://commons.ptsem.edu/id/missionschiefendooduff.

Ecumenical Missionary Conference. *Report of the Ecumenical Conference on Foreign Mission . . . April 21 to May 1*. Vol. 1. New York: American Tract Society, 1900. http://commons.ptsem.edu/id/ecumenicalmissioo2ecumuoft.

Bibliography

Edwards, Jonathan. *The Life and Diary of David Brainerd with Notes and Reflection.* Amazon Digital, 2013. Kindle edition.

The Eighty-Third Annual Report of the Board of Foreign Missions of the Presbyterian Church in the United States of America. Presented to the General Assembly, May 1920, New York, Presbyterian Building, 156 Fifth Avenue, 1920.

Fitzmier, John R., and Randall Balmer. "A Poultice for the Bite of the Cobra: The Hocking Report and Presbyterian Missions in the Middle Decades of the Twentieth Century." Chapter 4 in Coalter et al., *Diversity of Discipleship.*

George, Sherron Kay. *Better Together: The Future of Presbyterian Mission.* Louisville: Geneva Press, 2010.

———. *Called as Partners in Christ's Service: The Practice of God's Mission.* Louisville: Worldwide Ministries Division, PC(USA), 2004.

Gill, Theodore, A., Jr. "American Presbyterians in the Global Ecumenical Movement." In Coalter et al., *Diversity of Discipleship,* 126–48.

———. "Historical Context for Mission, 1944–2007." In *A History of Presbyterian Missions 1944–2007,* edited by Scott W. Sunquist and Caroline N. Long, 13–35. Louisville: Geneva Press, 2008.

Gillett, Ezra H. *History of the Presbyterian Church in the United States of America.* Rev. ed. Vol. 1. Philadelphia, 1864. http://commons.ptsem.edu/id/historyofpresbyto1gill.

Green, Ashbel. *A Historical Sketch or Compendious View of Domestic and Foreign Missions in the Presbyterian Church of the United States of America.* Philadelphia, 1838. http://commons.ptsem.edu/id/historicalsketcoogree.

———. *The Life of Ashbel Green, V. D. M.* New York, 1849. http://commons.ptsem.edu/id/lifeofashbelgreenoogree.

Hocking, William Ernest. *The Meaning of God in Human Experience: A Philosophic Study of Religion.* New Haven: Yale University Press, 1912.

Hoedemaker, Libertus A. "The Legacy of J. C. Hoekendijk." *International Bulletin of Missionary Research* 19 (1995) 166.

Hunter, George G., III. "The Legacy of Donald A. McGavran." *International Bulletin of Missionary Research* 16 (1992) 158–62.

Hutchison, William R. *Errand to the World: American Protestant Thought and Foreign Missions.* Chicago: University of Chicago Press, 1987.

Jongeneel, Jan A. B. "Hendrik Kraemer's *Christian Message in a Non-Christian World*: A Magnum Opus after Seventy-Five Years." *International Bulletin of Missionary Research* 37 (2013) 203–6.

Judson, Edward. *The Life of Adoniram Judson.* New York, 1883. https://archive.org/stream/lifeofadoniramjuoojuds#page/n7/mode/2up. Revised 1894 edition is available at http://books.google.com/books?id=MC07AQAAMAAJ&pg=PP1#v=onepage&q&f=false. All footnote references are to the 1883 ed.

Kirk, J. Andrew. *What Is Mission? Theological Explorations.* Minneapolis: Fortress, 2000. Kindle edition.

Kirkpatrick, Clifton, and William H. Hopper Jr. *What Unites Presbyterians: Common Ground for Troubled Times.* Louisville: Geneva Press, 1997.

Kraemer, Hendrik. *The Christian Message in a Non-Christian World.* New York: Harper, 1938.

Labrunie, Claude Emmanuel. "The Poor as Christ for the Rich." *Church and Society* 84 (1993) 94–96.

Bibliography

Latourette, Kenneth Scott. *The Centuries of Advance.* Vol. 3 of *A History of the Expansion of Christianity.* Grand Rapids: Zondervan, 1970.

———. *The Great Century: Europe and the United States.* Vol. 4 of *A History of the Expansion of Christianity.* Grand Rapids: Zondervan, 1970.

Loetscher, Lefferts A. *A Brief History of the Presbyterians.* 4th ed. Philadelphia: Westminster, 1983.

Longfield, Bradley J. *The Presbyterian Controversy: Fundamentalists, Modernists and Moderates.* New York: Oxford University Press, 1991.

———. *Presbyterians and American Culture: A History.* Louisville: Westminster John Knox, 2013. Kindle edition.

Lowrie, John C. *A Manual of Missions; or, Sketches of the Foreign Missions of the Presbyterian Church.* New York, 1854. http://commons.ptsem.edu/id/manualofmissions00lowr.

———. *Two Years in Upper India.* New York, 1850. http://commons.ptsem.edu/id/twoyearsinupperi00lowr.

Lowrie, Walter. *Memoirs of the Hon. Walter Lowrie.* New York, 1896. http://commons.ptsem.edu/id/memoirsofhonwa00lowr.

Mackay, John A. *Ecumenics: The Science of the Church Universal.* Englewood Cliffs, NJ: Prentice-Hall, 1965.

McGavran, Donald. "My Pilgrimage in Mission." *International Bulletin of Missionary Research* 10 (1986) 53–58.

"Mission and Evangelism: An Ecumenical Affirmation." *International Review of Mission* 71 (1982) 427–57.

"Mission in the 1990s: A Strategic Direction in Worldwide Ministry for the Presbyterian Church (U.S.A.)." *Church and Society* 84 (1993) n.p.

Moffett, Eileen F. "Betsey Stockton: Pioneer American Missionary." *International Bulletin of Missionary Research* 19 (1995) 71–76.

Moorhead, James H. "The 'Restless Spirit of Radicalism': Old School Fears and the Schism of 1837." *Journal of Presbyterian History* 78 (2000) 19–33. www.jstor.org/stable/23335295.

Mott, John R. *The Decisive Hour of Christian Missions.* New York: Board of Foreign Missions, PC(USA), 1910. http://commons.ptsem.edu/id/decisivehourofoomott.

Myers, John Brown. *William Carey: The Shoemaker Who Became the Father and Founder of Modern Missions.* New York: 1887. http://commons.ptsem.edu/id/williamcareyshoe00myer.

Nevius, Helen Sanford Coan. *The Life of John Livingston Nevius: For Forty Years a Missionary in China.* New York, 1895. http://commons.ptsem.edu/id/lifeofjohnlivingoonevi.

Nevius, John L. *The Planting and Development of Missionary Churches.* New York, 1899. http://commons.ptsem.edu/id/plantingdevelopmoonevi.

Newbigin, Lesslie. "Ecumenical Amnesia." Review of *Ecumenism in Transition: A Paradigm Shift in the Ecumenical Movement?*, by Konrad Raiser. *International Bulletin of Missionary Research* 18 (1994) 2–5.

Noll, Mark A. *A History of Christianity in the United States and Canada.* Grand Rapids: Eerdmans, 1992.

Piper, John F., Jr. "The Development of the Missionary Ideas of Robert E. Speer." Chapter 11 in *North American Foreign Missions, 1810–1914: Theology, Theory, and Policy*, edited by Wilbert R. Shenk. Grand Rapids: Eerdmans, 2004.

———. *Robert E. Speer: Prophet of the American Church.* Louisville: Geneva Press, 2000.

Bibliography

Presbyterian Re-Union: A Memorial Volume, 1837–1871. New York, 1870. http://commons.ptsem.edu/id/presbyterianreun1870oonewy.

Reifsnyder, Richard W. "Managing the Mission: Church Restructuring in the Twentieth Century." Chapter 2 in *Organizational Revolution: Presbyterians and American Denominationalism*, edited by Milton J. Coalter et al. Louisville: Westminster John Knox, 1991.

Robert, Dana L. *Christian Mission: How Christianity Became a World Religion*. Malden, MA: Wiley-Blackwell, 2009. Kindle edition.

———. "The Origin of the Student Volunteer Watchword: 'The Evangelization of the World in This Generation.'" *International Bulletin of Missionary Research* 10 (1986) 146–49.

Rockefeller, John D., Jr. *The Christian Church: What of Its Future*. Reprinted from *Philadelphia Saturday Evening Post*, February 9, 1918.

Ross, Cathy. "The Theology of Partnership." *International Bulletin of Missionary Research* 34 (2010) 145–48.

Rycroft, Stanley W. *The Ecumenical Witness of the United Presbyterian Church in the U.S.A.* Published by the Commission on Ecumenical Mission and Relations of the United Presbyterian Church in the U.S.A., 1968.

Sanneh, Lamin. *Translating the Message: The Missionary Impact on Culture*. Rev ed. New York: Orbis, 2009.

Scherer, James A. "International Missionary Council." In *The Encyclopedia of Christianity*, edited by Erwin Fahlbusch and Geoffrey W. Bromiley, 2:726–28. Grand Rapids: Eerdmans, 2001.

Shenk, Wilbert R., ed. *North American Foreign Missions, 1810–1914: Theology, Theory, and Policy*.

Smylie, James Hutchinson. *A Brief History of the Presbyterians*. Louisville: Geneva Press, 1996.

Speer, Robert E. *Christianity and the Nations: The Duff Lectures for 1910*. New York: Revell, 1910. http://commons.ptsem.edu/id/christianitynatioospee.

———. "The Evangelization of the World in This Generation." Chapter 44 in *Missionary Principles and Practice: A Discussion of Christian Missions*. New York: Revell, 1902. http://commons.ptsem.edu/id/missionaryprinoospee.

———. *The Non-Christian Religions Inadequate to Meet the Needs of Men: An Address*. New York: Board of Foreign Missions, PC(USA), 1906. http://commons.ptsem.edu/id/nonchristianrelioospee.

———. *Some Great Leaders in the World Movement: The Cole Lectures for 1911*. New York: Revell, 1911. http://commons.ptsem.edu/id/somegreatleadeoospee.

———. *Studies of Missionary Leadership: The Smyth Lectures for 1913*. Philadelphia: Westminster, 1914. http://commons.ptsem.edu/id/studiesofmissionoospee.

Stanley, Brian. *The World Missionary Conference, Edinburgh 1910*. Grand Rapids: Eerdmans, 2009.

Sunquist, Scott W. *Understanding Christian Mission: Participation in Suffering and Glory*. Grand Rapids: Baker Academic, 2013. Kindle edition.

Webster, Rev. Richard. *A History of the Presbyterian Church in America, from Its Origin until the year 1760*. Philadelphia, 1858. http://commons.ptsem.edu/id/hispresbytoowebs.

Weeks, Louis B. *A Sustainable Presbyterian Future: What's Working and Why*. Louisville, Geneva Press, 2012. Kindle edition.

Bibliography

Wells, John D. *Hon. Walter Lowrie.* New York, 1869. http://commons.ptsem.edu/id/honwalterlowrieoowell.

Wickeri, Philip L. *Partnership, Solidarity, and Friendship: Transforming Structures in Mission; A Study Paper for the Presbyterian Church (U.S.A.).* Louisville: Worldwide Ministries Division, PC(USA), 2003. Available at www.pcusa.org/resource/partnership-solidarity-and-friendship-transforming.

Wilson, Joshua Lacy. *Four Propositions Sustained against the Claims of the American Home Missionary Society.* Philadelphia, 1831. http://commons.ptsem.edu/id/fourpropositionso9wils.

Wood, Henry. *The History of the Presbyterian Controversy: With Early Sketches of Presbyterianism.* Louisville, 1843. http://commons.ptsem.edu/id/historyofpresbytoowood.

Index of Names

Alward, Jonathan, 91
Anderson, Fred, 26
Anderson, Gerald, 141
Andrews, Jedidiah, 12
Applegarth, Margaret, 63

Barnes, Albert, 44
Bauder, Floy, 136, image on 137
Beecher, Lyman, 44
Bellamy, Joseph, 43
Blake, Eugene Carson, 155, 164, 165
Bosch, David, 141, 171
Boyd, John, 18
Brainerd, David, 3, 22–33, image on 27
Brainerd, John, 31
Briggs, Charles, 3, 12, 14, 20, 23
Brown, Arthur J., 103
Buck, John Lossing, 125
Buck, Pearl, 5, 123, 124–28, images on, 125
Buell, William, 95
Bush, Stephen, 95

Campbell, Alexander, 16
Canfield, Oren, 91
Castro, Emilio, 172
Carey, William, 5, 60–77, image on 62, 92
Clarke, Erskine, 147
Cloud, John, 91
Coalter, Milton, 174
Coventry, William, 136
Coventry Smith, John, 6, 7, 134–52, image on 137, 155

Davies, Samuel, 12
Dickinson, Jonathan, 22
Duff, Alexander, 108
Duffield, George, 44
Dulles, John Foster, 155

Edwards, Jonathan, 27, 28, 31, 35, 43, 171
Emmons, Samuel, 43
Ellinwood, Frank, 103

Farrell, Hunter, 7, 175–94, image on 177
Farrell, Ruth, 176
Finney, Charles, 44
Fletcher, Benjamin, 15
Forman, Charles, 94
Forman, John, 101
Fulton, Robert, 69

Gilbert, Eliphalet, 55
Gillett, Ezra, 11
George, Sharon Kay, 186
Graham, Billy, 157, 169
Green, Ashbel, 3, 4, 9, 23, 32, 34–52, image on 36, 53, 58
Green, Jacob, 38

Hampton, John, 12
Harrison, Edmund, 18
Hepburn, James Curtis, 137
Hocking, William, 114–23, image on 114, 125
Hoekendijk, Johannes, 162, 164
Hopkins, Samuel, 43
Horton, Azariah, 23, 24

Index of Names

Hunter, George, 168
Hutchison, William, 156
Hyde, Edward (a.k.a. Lord Cornbury), 17

Jackson, William, 17
James, William, 114, 115
Jefferson, Thomas, 15
Judson, Abigail Brown, 69
Judson, Adoniram, 60–77, image on 68
Judson, Anne, 70
Judson, Edward, 69
Judson, Elnathan, 69

Kirkpatrick, Clifton, 7, 153–74, image on 156, 181
Kraemer, Hendrik, 159, 162

Labrunie, Claude Emmanuel, 183
Laird, John, 91
Leber, Charles, 151
Loetscher, Lefferts, 10
Longfield, Bradley, 131
Lowrie, John C., 78–99, image on 81, 100
Lowrie, Reuben P., 82
Lowrie, Walter, 5, 78-, 99, image on 78, 100
Lowrie, Walter M., 81
Lung, Wang, 124

Machen, Gresham, 5, 115, 123, 129–33, image on 130, 154, 160
Maclean, John, 71
McGavran, Donald, 153–74, image on 167
Makemie, Francis, 2, 3, 9–21, image on 10, image on 13, image on 16
Marshman, Hannah, 67
Mather, Increase, 15
Mattoon, Stephen, 95
MacKay, John, 154
McKinley, William, 105, 106
McNish, George, 11
McPherrin, Amelia, 79
McPherrin, John, 79
Mills, Samuel, Jr., 70
Mitchell, John A., 96

Moffet, Eileen, 54, 58
Monroe, James, 90
Moorhead, James, 42, 45
Mott, John, 102
Mulder, John, 174

Nath, Golok, 94
Nevius, John Livingston, 110
Newbigin, Lesslie, 163, 165
Newton, John, 93
Noll, Mark, 123
Nott, Samuel, Jr., 70
Nundy, Gopeenath, 94

Orr, Robert W., 96

Pierson, John, 38
Pinney, John, 91
Piper, John, 101, 106, 126

Raiser, Konrad, 165
Reed, William, 80, 93
Rian, Edwin, 127
Richards, James, 70
Rice, Luther, 70
Robert, Dana, 47
Rockefeller, John D. Jr., 5, 114, 116, image on 116
Roosevelt, Franklin D., 134
Roosevelt, Teddy, 105
Ross, Cathy, 188
Rycroft, Stanley, 178

Sanneh, Lamin, 76
Sargent, John, 23
Scherer, James, 163
Speer, Robert, 5, 6, 65, 86, 88, 100–113, image on 100, 114–23, 124–28, 129–33, 134, 154, 160
Smith, George, 63
Smith, Henry Boynton, 46
Stewart, Charles, 56, 57
Stewart, Harriet, 56, 57
Stockton, Betsey, 52, 53–59, image on 53,
Stockton, Elizabeth, 54, 55
Stockton, Robert, 54
Sunquist, Scott, 189

Index of Names

Taylor, Nathaniel, 12
Taylor, Nathaniel William, 44
Temple, James, 91
Tennant, William, 31
Tillich, Paul, 188
Tippert, Alan, 168

Vesey, William, 15
Visser t'Hooft, Willem, 163

Weeks, Louis, 3, 174

Wells, David, 82
Whitefield, George, 35
Wheelock, James, 44
Wickeri, Philip, 187
Wilder, Robert, 101
Wilson, James, 93
Wilson, John, 12
Wilson, J. L., 50
Winter, Ralph, 168
Wood, Henry, 11, 35

www.ingramcontent.com/pod-product-compliance
Lightning Source LLC
Chambersburg PA
CBHW070318230426
43663CB00011B/2175